The Ideals Guide to

Places of the American Revolution

THE IDEALS GUIDE TO

PLACES OF THE AMERICAN REVOLUTION

BY JULIE SHIVELY

IDEALS PUBLICATIONS, A DIVISION OF GUIDEPOSTS
NASHVILLE, TENNESSEE
WWW.IDEALSPUBLICATIONS.COM

ISBN 0-8249-4181-0

Published by Ideals Publications,
a Division of Guideposts
Suite 250, 535 Metroplex Drive
Nashville, TN 37211

1 0 8 6 4 2 1 3 5 7 9

Publisher, Patricia A. Pingry
Art Director, Eve DeGrie
Designer, Travis Rader
Copy Editor, Amy Johnson
Assistant Editor, Amy Williams

Front Cover: Liberty Bell Pavilion, Philadelphia, PA. SuperStock.

Back Cover: Great Chain at Trophy Point, West Point, NY. U.S. Military Academy.

Library of Congress Cataloging-in-Publication Data

Shively, Julie, 1964–
        The Ideals guide to places of the American Revolution / by Julie Shively.
                p. cm.
        Includes index.
        ISBN 0-8249-4181-0 (alk. paper)
        1. United States–History–Revolution, 1775–1783–Battlefields–Guidebooks. 2. United
States–History–Revolution, 1775–1783–Monuments-Guidebooks. 3. United
States–History–Revolution, 1775–1783–Museums–Guidebooks. 4. Historic
sites–United States–Guidebooks. 5. United States–Guidebooks. I. Title.

        E230 .S49 2001
        917.304'929–dc21   2001016667

Color scans by Precision Color Graphics, Franklin, Wisconsin

Printed and bound by RR Donnelley & Sons

TABLE OF CONTENTS

Introduction

Those who have read or studied the events of the Revolutionary War stand in awe of the final outcome. The Patriots faced a monumental task. They had no army. They had no ships. In fact, they had no government. There were only thirteen colonies, each of which had been formed for a different reason with different motives, yet now they had to work together. The penalty for defeat would be treason.

Today, we have forgotten that from 1775 to 1783, battles were fought in Pennsylvania, South Carolina, North Carolina, New York, off the Atlantic coast, and in other cities that have never since heard the roar of cannon. We are not aware that places like Boston, New York City, Philadelphia, and Newport were under British occupation for several months or even years. We do not think about the fact that George Washington, a Virginian, was chosen as commander in chief of a Continental army that didn't exist; and that he was put in charge of a militia made up of New Englanders. And we never consider that the bulk of the people did not directly pay the taxes on tea but only wanted to live without an overseas power making the laws.

We are privileged in that many of the sites of the Revolutionary War are still preserved today. An hour spent at any one of these sites forces us to realize that the freedom we take for granted was not a certainty in 1775. A visit to the sites that are listed in the pages to follow makes us realize that we owe our way of life to those men and women who dared to dream of liberty. In the words of Daniel Boone: "Enough of honour cannot be paid."

About the Author

Julie Shively is a graduate of the United States Air Force Academy, a veteran C-141 pilot, and a former member of the Air Force's prestigious Eighty-ninth Airlift Wing. She holds a Master of Education and teaches fifth grade. The author lives with her husband and daughter in Georgia.

CHRONOLOGICAL LIST OF MAJOR BATTLES AND ENGAGEMENTS

The following list of battles is by no means comprehensive but merely provides a glimpse of the enormity of the Revolutionary War.

1773

Dec. 16 . . . . .Boston Tea Party

1774

Sept. 15-Oct. 26 . .First Continental Congress meets

1775

Apr. 18 . . . . .The "midnight ride" of Paul Revere and William Dawes to warn the colonists
              of the British
Apr. 19 . . . . .Battle of Lexington and Concord, Massachusetts
May 10 . . . . .Battle of Fort Ticonderoga, New York
June 15 . . . . .Congress appoints George Washington leader of the Continental army
June 17 . . . . .Battle of Bunker Hill, Massachusetts

1776

Feb. 27 . . . . .Battle of Moores Creek Bridge, North Carolina
July 4 . . . . .United States Declaration of Independence signed
Aug. 27-29 . . . . . . .Battle of Long Island, New York
Sept. 22 . . . . .Nathan Hale executed
Oct. 28 . . . . .Battle of White Plains, New York
Nov. 16 . . . . .Battle of Fort Washington, New York
Dec. 25-26 . . . . . . .Battle of Trenton, New Jersey

1777

Jan. 3 . . . . .Battle of Princeton, New Jersey
June 14 . . . . .Congress approves the flag of the United States with 13 stars and 13 stripes

July 7 . . . . Battle of Hubbardton, Vermont
Aug. 16 . . . . Battle of Bennington, Vermont
Sept. 9-11 . . . . Battle of Brandywine, Pennsylvania
Sept. 19 . . . . Battle of Saratoga — Freeman's Farm, New York
Oct. 7 . . . . Battle of Saratoga — Bemis Heights, New York
Nov. 10-15 . . . . Siege of Fort Mifflin, Pennsylvania

 ## 1778

June 27 . . . . Battle of Monmouth, New Jersey
Aug. 8 . . . . Siege of Newport, Rhode Island

 ## 1779

Feb. 25 . . . . Battle of Fort Sackville, Vincennes
July 15-16 . . . . Battle of Stony Point, New York
Oct. 9 . . . . Battle of Savannah, Georgia

 ## 1780

May 12 . . . . Battle of Charleston, South Carolina
Aug. 16 . . . . Battle of Camden, South Carolina
Oct. 7 . . . . Battle of Kings Mountain, South Carolina

 ## 1781

Jan. 17 . . . . Battle of Cowpens, South Carolina
Mar. 15 . . . . Battle of Guilford Courthouse, North Carolina
May 22-June 19 . . Siege of Ninety Six, South Carolina
Sept. 28 . . . . Siege of Yorktown, Virginia
Oct. 19 . . . . British surrender at Yorktown, Virginia

 ## 1783

Feb. 4 . . . . England officially declares an end to hostilities in America
Apr. 11 . . . . Congress officially declares an end to hostilities in America
June 13 . . . . Continental army begins to disband
Sept. 3 . . . . The Treaty of Paris signed by the United States and Great Britain

EXPLANATORY NOTES

A compass denotes those sites directly related to the battle described in the previous pages.

■ The green marks on the maps represent the general location of the places. Although interstates, federal highways, and some state highways are included for orientation, space limitations prevent precise directions. In some states, the state map is not complete and shows only that area of the state that contains an American Revolution place. In other states, some of the places of the American Revolution are not included on the map because of space restrictions. Please refer to the information on the site provided in each state chapter for more specific directions.

Map abbreviations:

Am. . . . . . .American	Mem. . . . . .Memorial	Plant. . . . . .Plantation
Btlfd. . . . . .Battlefield	Mil . . . . . . .Military	Pt. . . . . . . .Point
Ch. . . . . . . .Church	Mon. . . . . .Monument	Rev . . . . . . .Revolutionary
Ctr. . . . . . . .Center	Mt. . . . . . . .Mount	Soc. . . . . . .Society
Dept. . . . . .Department	Mtn. . . . . . .Mountain	St. . . . . .State
Ft. . . . . .Fort	Mus. . . . . . .Museum	Vis. Ctr. . . .Visitor's Center
Headqtrs. .Headquarters	Nat'l. . . . . .National	
Hist. . . . . . .Historic	Pk. . . . . . . .Park	

CONNECTICUT

Connecticut was settled as early as 1636 when Reverend Thomas Hooker, Reverend Samuel Stone, and landowner John Haynes, who had been elected governor of Massachusetts Bay Colony, outgrew the Bay Colony and left Cambridge to make towns of their own. They settled Hartford, Windsor, and Wethersfield. Two years later, London Puritans chose New Haven as a site for a business hub that would, they hoped, rival New York and Boston. Each group had its own governing laws; but in 1662, King Charles II combined the settlements to be known as the Colony of Connecticut.

Throughout the Revolutionary War, Connecticut became the main source of the army's supply of food. Governor Jonathan Trumbull, who was also a business man, managed to find flour and beef for the troops. He also set up a cannon foundry, a shoe shop, and a plant for repairing damaged muskets.

Connecticut had few loyalists; estimates put the figure at only eight percent of the total population. This may have been due, in part, to the colony's "Sons of Liberty" and their regular "Tory hunts," in which loyalists were forced to recant their loyalty to the crown or leave the colony.

This fierce independence is evidenced by its most famous Revolutionary War hero, and America's first spy, Nathan Hale. Twenty-one-year-old Hale volunteered to spy on the British. He was caught and hanged, but not before declaring, "I only regret that I have but one life to lose for my country."

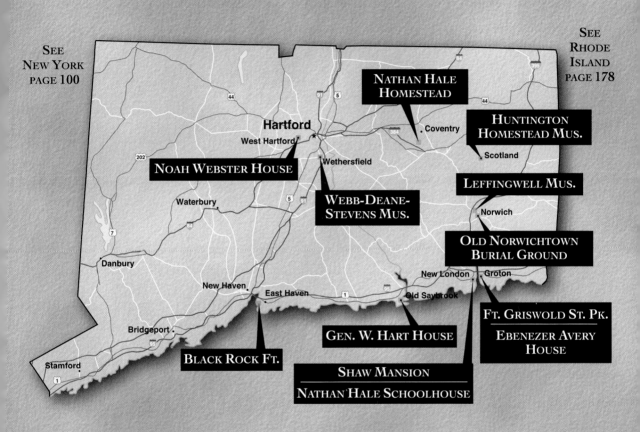

SEE MASSACHUSETTS
PAGE 52

SEE
NEW YORK
PAGE 100

SEE
RHODE
ISLAND
PAGE 178

NATHAN HALE HOMESTEAD

HUNTINGTON HOMESTEAD MUS.

Coventry

Scotland

Hartford

West Hartford

NOAH WEBSTER HOUSE

Wethersfield

LEFFINGWELL MUS.

WEBB-DEANE-STEVENS MUS.

Norwich

Waterbury

OLD NORWICHTOWN BURIAL GROUND

New London · Groton

Danbury

New Haven · East Haven · Old Saybrook

FT. GRISWOLD ST. PK.

EBENEZER AVERY HOUSE

Bridgeport

GEN. W. HART HOUSE

Stamford

BLACK ROCK FT.

SHAW MANSION

NATHAN HALE SCHOOLHOUSE

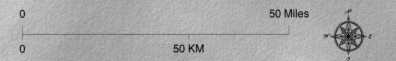

0   50 Miles

0   50 KM

NOAH WEBSTER HOUSE

227 South Main Street, West Hartford, CT 06107

PHONE: 860-521-5362

HOURS: Open Thursday to Monday from September to June and Thursday to Sunday from July to August.

ADMISSION: A fee is charged; seniors and children discounted.

The Noah Webster House was the home of the author of the first American dictionary. The home features tours of Webster's restored colonial birthplace, which offers a glimpse of how a typical family lived on the eve of the Revolution. The site features a gift shop and garden along with small exhibits on local history.

Interior of the Noah Webster House

Noah Webster House

THE WEBB-DEANE-STEVENS MUSEUM

211 Main Street, Wethersfield, CT 06109

PHONE: 860-529-0612

HOURS: Open Wednesday to Monday from May to October and Saturday and Sunday from November to April.

ADMISSION: A fee is charged; senior and student discounts available.

The Webb-Deane-Stevens Museum

The Webb-Deane-Stevens Museum is housed in three separate homes built over the period of 1752 to 1788. The Webb home was built in 1752 by Joseph Webb, a prominent merchant. As the American Revolution was nearing its end in 1781, George Washington visited there to meet with Compte de Rochambeau to plan the final battle strategy. The Webb house features the "Washington chamber," and the interior has been restored to its original period. The Silas Deane house was built next door to the Webb house in 1788. Silas Deane was a member of the Continental Congress and a participant in the first diplomat party to France. The third house in the three-house museum was the home of Isaac Stevens.

NATHAN HALE HOMESTEAD

2299 South Street, Coventry, CT 06328

PHONE: 860-742-6917

HOURS: Open Wednesday to Sunday from mid-May to mid-October.

ADMISSION: A fee is charged.

Nathan Hale was the United States's first martyr who, after being captured as a spy, stated, "I only regret that I have but one life to lose for my country." His homestead was built by his family in 1776, the same year he died. The interior has been restored and displays period pieces and exhibits that tell of his life and death.

Nathan Hale Homestead

HUNTINGTON HOMESTEAD MUSEUM

36 Huntington Road, Scotland, CT 06264

PHONE: 860-456-8381

HOURS: Open on the first and third Saturdays from May to October and by appointment.

ADMISSION: Donations accepted.

WEBSITE: www.huntingtonhomestead.org/

The Huntington House, circa 1723, is the birthplace of Samuel Huntington (1731-1796), a signer of the Declaration of Independence, two-term president of the Continental Congress, and ten-term governor of Connecticut. The house, which is on the Washington-Rochambeau Revolutionary War Route, is being restored, and the homestead will soon be the site of a major history museum.

Huntington House

THE LEFFINGWELL HOUSE MUSEUM

348 Washington Street, Norwich, CT 06360

PHONE: 860-889-4400

HOURS: Open Tuesday to Sunday from mid-May to mid-October.

ADMISSION: A fee is charged.

The Leffingwell House was originally built as a simple two-room house by Stephen Backus in 1675. Thomas Leffingwell later bought the house and converted it into an inn. His grandson, Christopher Leffingwell, served as a colonel in the Connecticut militia during the Revolutionary War. He took part in raids in Long Island and guard duty along the Connecticut seacoast. In addition, he was in charge of procuring supplies for the Continental army. Leffingwell distributed food, arms, and clothing donated by Connecticut, and his own mill provided paper for bullet cartridges. Following this, Connecticut became known as "The Provision State."

OLD NORWICHTOWN BURIAL GROUND

Town Street, Norwich, CT 06360

The Old Norwichtown Burial Ground is a traditional New England Village Green surrounded by eighteenth- and nineteenth-century homes. Nearby is the Old Burying Ground, located behind the home of Samuel Huntington, a signer of the Declaration of Independence. The cemetery's gates were built in honor of the Revolutionary War soldiers buried there. Brochures are available for self-guided tours at the Cemetery Lane entrance.

FORT GRISWOLD BATTLEFIELD STATE PARK

Monument Street, Groton, CT 06340
PHONE: 860-343-0079
HOURS: Park open daily. Museum and Groton Monument open daily from Memorial Day to Labor Day and Saturday and Sunday from Labor Day to Columbus Day.
ADMISSION: Free.

Fort Griswold Battlefield Park marks the site of the 1781 skirmish that was later known as the Battle of Groton Heights. Here British troops under the command of Benedict Arnold defeated and killed eighty-eight American soldiers. A granite obelisk monument commemorates the men who defended Fort Griswold during the Revolutionary War. The ramparts of Fort Griswold are still intact and may be toured.

EBENEZER AVERY HOUSE

Fort Street, near Fort Griswold, Groton, CT 06340
PHONE: 860-446-9257
HOURS: Open Saturday and Sunday from June to Labor Day.
ADMISSION: Free.

The Ebenezer Avery House stands on the grounds of the Fort Griswold Battlefield Park, west of the fort. It has been said that after the Battle of Groton Heights ended, the victorious British put wounded American soldiers in a wagon and rolled it down the hill. Occupants of the Avery house brought the soldiers inside and tended to their wounds. The house was moved from its original location on nearby Thames Street in 1971.

Shaw Mansion

SHAW MANSION ——

11 Blinman Street,
New London, CT 06230
PHONE: 860-443-1209
HOURS: Open Wednesday to
Saturday year-round.
ADMISSION: A fee is charged.

The Shaw Mansion was built by a wealthy merchant and sea captain, Nathaniel Shaw. General George Washington and Lafayette both stayed at the house. During the Revolution, the house was used as the naval headquarters for the state of Connecticut. Today, the mansion features antiques, paintings, and period pieces from the Shaw and Perkins families, as well as colonial-period gardens. The extensive genealogical records are open to researchers by appointment.

NATHAN HALE SCHOOLHOUSE ——

Union Plaza, New London, CT 06230
PHONE: 860-443-7949
HOURS: Open during the summer from Thursday to Sunday.
ADMISSION: Free.

In 1774, Nathan Hale was teaching in this schoolhouse until hostilities broke out in Massachusetts and he was commissioned as an officer in the Continental army. Washington was desperate for information in order to counter British undercover operations. Hale volunteered to spy on British troop movements in Long Island. He was captured, and on September 22, 1776, twenty-one-year-old Nathan Hale was hanged by the British. As was customary, he was permitted to make a statement. Hale spoke of a citizen's responsibilities, ending with the memorable words, "I only regret that I have but one life to lose for my country."

Nathan Hale Schoolhouse

GENERAL WILLIAM HART HOUSE

350 Main Street, Old Saybrook, CT 06475

PHONE: 860-388-2622

HOURS: Open on weekends from June to September; archives and library open on Wednesday and Thursday year-round or by appointment.

ADMISSION: A fee is charged for Hart House only.

General William Hart, who served in the Revolutionary War, built this Georgian home as a wedding gift for his wife Esther Buckingham in 1767. The house has been restored to its original condition and now serves as the Old Saybrook Historical Society's headquarters and museum. The house features architectural designs that include twelve over twelve windows, center hallway, and twin chimneys that serve eight corner fireplaces in the main house. The interior has wide floorboards and old wainscoting, paneling, and moldings. The property contains an authentic colonial garden with fruit trees, flowers, and herbs. The carriage house contains the society's archives and library.

General William Hart House

BLACK ROCK FORT

East side of New Haven Harbor, CT

PHONE: 203-946-6970

HOURS: Open daily from Memorial Day to Labor Day.

ADMISSION: Free.

Black Rock Fort was built in 1775. Five months after the outbreak of war at Lexington and Concord, the General Court of Connecticut ordered its militia to Black Rock in order to protect New Haven from the British. The fort was overwhelmed twice by the British. It was abandoned at the end of the Revolutionary War and fell into disrepair. However, restoration was completed in time for the bicentennial celebration in 1976. Both the Revolutionary and Civil War forts at Black Rock are undergoing renovation but can still be toured today.

DELAWARE

Called the "Three Lower Counties" of Pennsylvania, the future state of Delaware had been purchased by William Penn from the Duke of York but was overlooked in the royal charter of Pennsylvania. These three counties had their own assembly, but their governor was always the same as Pennsylvania.

Tiny Delaware sent only one regiment to the war, the Delaware Continentals, but they were called the "best uniformed and equipped in the army of 1776." Their outfits consisted of blue coats lined in red, white waistcoats, buckskin trousers, white woolen stockings, and black hats. The English muskets they carried bore bayonets and made this regiment one of the few that had bayonets. The regiment distinguished itself in battles at Germantown, White Plains, and Camden.

The only battle that occurred in Delaware was at Cooch's Bridge outside of Newark. The bridge is marked by a granite monument. In 1787, Delaware became the first colony to ratify the Constitution.

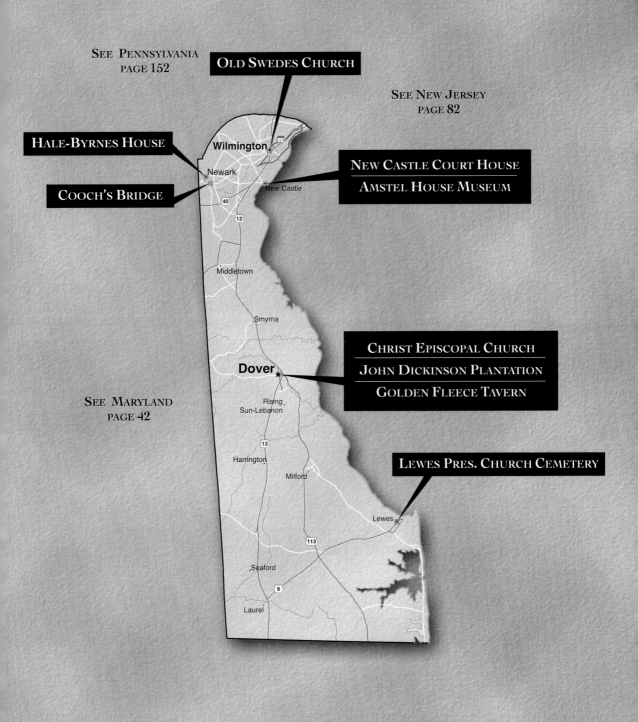

SEE PENNSYLVANIA
PAGE 152

OLD SWEDES CHURCH

SEE NEW JERSEY
PAGE 82

HALE-BYRNES HOUSE

Wilmington

Newark

NEW CASTLE COURT HOUSE

AMSTEL HOUSE MUSEUM

New Castle

COOCH'S BRIDGE

40

13

Middletown

Smyrna

CHRIST EPISCOPAL CHURCH

JOHN DICKINSON PLANTATION

GOLDEN FLEECE TAVERN

Dover

SEE MARYLAND
PAGE 42

Rising
Sun-Lebanon

13

Harrington

LEWES PRES. CHURCH CEMETERY

Milford

113

Lewes

Seaford

9

Laurel

0   50 Miles

0   50 KM

HALE-BYRNES HOUSE

606 Stanton-Christiana Road, Newark, DE 10713
PHONE: 302-998-3792
HOURS: Open first Wednesday of each month except for holidays and by appointment at other times.
ADMISSION: Free.

The Hale-Byrnes House was built in 1750. It was a meeting place of General George Washington and his staff, including General Lafayette, between the Battle of Cooch's Bridge in Delaware and the Battle of Brandywine in Pennsylvania.

Hale-Byrnes House

COOCH'S BRIDGE

State Route 4, Newark, DE

The only battle fought in Delaware during the Revolutionary War was the Battle of Cooch's Bridge on September 3, 1777. Brigadier General William Maxell's Light Infantry Brigade was sent to delay General Howe's advance toward Pennsylvania. They met at Cooch's Bridge, today marked by a granite monument. Although the delaying action failed, according to tradition the new thirteen-star flag, the Stars and Stripes, was first unfurled at this battle.

OLD SWEDES CHURCH

606 Church Street, Wilmington, DE 19801
PHONE: 302-652-5629
HOURS: Guided tours available Monday to Saturday.
ADMISSION: A fee is charged.

Old Swedes Church

The Old Swedes Church was built between 1698 and 1699. In 1777, after the Battle of Brandywine, British soldiers were quartered in the church. Small cannonballs are still embedded in the churchyard. Also on the grounds is the Hendrickson House Museum, a Swedish farmhouse circa 1690.

AMSTEL HOUSE MUSEUM

2 East 4th Street, New Castle, DE 19720
PHONE: 302-322-2794
HOURS: Open daily from March to December and by appointment throughout the year.
ADMISSION: A fee is charged.

The Amstel House Museum features a look at life in the eighteenth and nineteenth centuries and boasts a complete colonial kitchen. George Washington attended a wedding at this home.

Amstel House

NEW CASTLE COURT HOUSE MUSEUM

211 Delaware Street, New Castle, DE 19720
PHONE: 302-323-4453
HOURS: Open Tuesday to Sunday; closed state holidays.
ADMISSION: Free.

Built in 1732, the New Castle Court House served as the meeting place of the colonial and state assemblies. Delaware's signers of the Declaration of Independence were sent from this legislative body. Here, in 1776, Delaware declared its independence from Pennsylvania and Great Britain and adopted the first state constitution. The court house museum features exhibits that illustrate the creation of Delaware's unique boundaries and colonial government. Period portraits, furnishings, and artifacts are on display.

JOHN DICKINSON PLANTATION

Kitts Hummock Road, Dover, DE 19901
PHONE: 302-739-3277
HOURS: Open Tuesday to Sunday; closed Sundays in January and February and state holidays.
ADMISSION: Free.
www.destatemuseums.org

John Dickinson Plantation

John Dickinson Plantation was the boyhood home of John Dickinson, known as the "Penman of the Revolution" because of his writings in support of independence. Dickinson wrote the "Declaration of Rights and Grievances," the "Petition to the King," and the fourteen "Farmer's Letters." At first Dickinson voted against the Declaration of Independence, but when fighting began, he volunteered for military duty. After the war, he headed the congressional committee that drafted the Articles of Confederation and was a member of the Federal Constitutional Convention from Delaware, working for ratification of the Constitution. The plantation home is furnished with period antiques. Farm outbuildings and a logged dwelling have been constructed to complete the interpretation of an eighteenth-century Delaware plantation.

CHRIST EPISCOPAL CHURCH

South State and Water Streets, Dover, DE 19901
PHONE: 302-734-5731
HOURS: Open Monday to Friday.
ADMISSION: Free.

Christ Episcopal Church was built in 1734. In the graveyard is a monument to Delaware's Caesar Rodney, a signer of the Declaration of Independence.

SITE OF GOLDEN FLEECE TAVERN

The Green, South State Street, Dover, DE 19901
PHONE: 302-739-4266 (Delaware State Visitor's Center)
HOURS: None available.
ADMISSION: Free.

At the Golden Fleece Tavern, Delaware delegates ratified the Constitution in December, 1787, and made Delaware the first state. The original tavern no longer exists, but a placard marks the site where it once stood.

LEWES PRESBYTERIAN CHURCH CEMETERY

133 Kings Highway, Lewes, DE 19958
PHONE: 302-645-5345
HOURS: Open daily.
ADMISSION: Free.

The Lewes Presbyterian Church was founded in 1692, and the first meetinghouse was built on this site in 1707. The current structure is the third building on this site. In the cemetery are the graves of patriots Colonel David Hall and Reverend Matthew Wilson. Wilson was the minister of Lewes Presbyterian from 1756-90 and was an active opponent of the Tories.

GEORGIA

The Colony of Georgia was founded in 1733 by General James Charles Oglethorpe, who in 1730 obtained a charter for the Trustees of Georgia. Oglethorpe was interested in helping the poor debtors who under the laws of the period were confined indefinitely in jail. He wished to give them a fresh start in the New World. Oglethorpe himself founded Savannah in 1733, leading 114 settlers that year. Georgia did not prosper; and in 1752, it was turned over to the crown as a royal province.

Georgia did not attend the first Continental Congress in 1775 and very nearly stayed out of the Revolution. The British organized a Loyalist civil government in Georgia. Although the state was briefly under American control, by 1779 it had been recaptured and was in effect back in the British Empire.

When the colony failed to send representatives to the first Continental Congress, residents in Midway, who were some of the few Georgians who supported independence, sent two of their own as representatives. Today, the town has a museum dedicated to the Revolution.

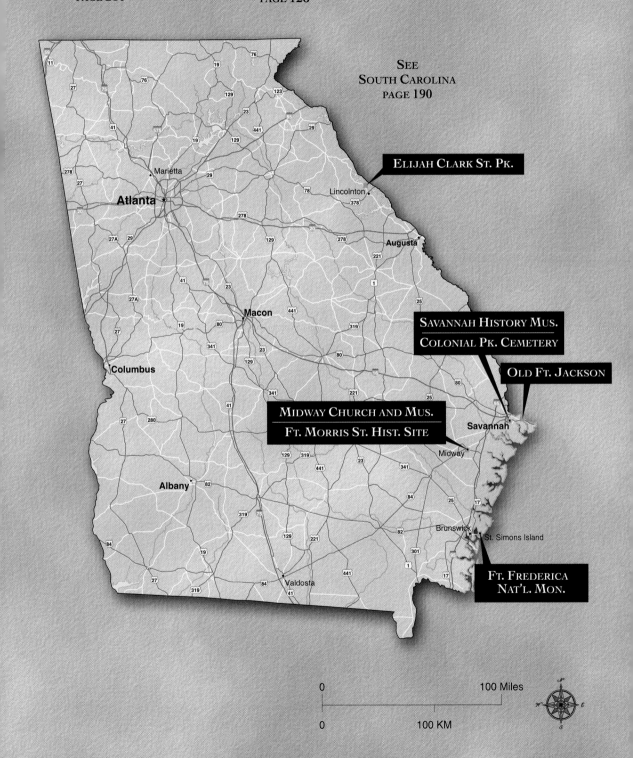

SEE TENNESSEE
PAGE 210

SEE NORTH CAROLINA
PAGE 126

SEE
SOUTH CAROLINA
PAGE 190

ELIJAH CLARK ST. PK.

Lincolnton

Marietta

Atlanta

Augusta

SAVANNAH HISTORY MUS.
COLONIAL PK. CEMETERY

OLD FT. JACKSON

Macon

Columbus

MIDWAY CHURCH AND MUS.
FT. MORRIS ST. HIST. SITE

Savannah

Midway

Albany

Brunswick

St. Simons Island

FT. FREDERICA
NAT'L. MON.

Valdosta

0   100 Miles

0   100 KM

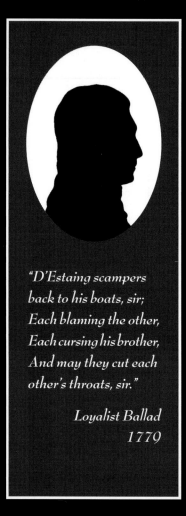

BRITISH

COMMANDER:
Gen. Augustine Prevost

STRENGTH: 3,200

CASUALTIES: 113

BATTLE OF SAVANNAH

October 9, 1779

In late 1778, much of Georgia was occupied by the British. In June of that year, British General Clinton evacuated Philadelphia and headed south toward Georgia and Florida. This was to be his base of operations from which to assault South Carolina. The Americans soon looked to reclaim the important port of Savannah while at the same time destroying British strength in Georgia. By October 1779, events turned toward Savannah.

The city stood on a bluff overlooking the Savannah River and was surrounded by ruined earthworks which were indefensible. The British set about rebuilding old defenses as well as building new ones. By the time Americans began heading to Georgia, the British had constructed earthworks, and an abatis was built from the river below to the swamps above. On the north, three redoubts were built, and on the south, two redoubts were built of heavy logs. British regular troops were stationed in the center, west of the town. Many of the 3,200 British troops were Loyalists from Georgia.

In an effort to recapture this important port, American General Benjamin Lincoln turned to French Admiral d'Estaing. On September 12, 1779, 6,000 French troops began unloading on the Georgia coast. Three days later, troops under Count Casimir Pulaski joined with the French, and d'Estaing issued a proclamation to British General Prevost to surrender. Although Prevost requested twenty-four hours in which to consider a surrender, the British were actually using this time to strengthen their position.

In the meantime, General Lincoln's army was marching from Charleston, South Carolina, with 1,350 troops. He joined d'Estaing on September 16, and the total American-French force numbered approximately 5,000 against a British force of 3,200. If d'Estaing had attacked immediately, he might have prevailed; but he delayed and allowed the British to increase their guns from twenty-three to more than a hundred.

On October 9, at one in the morning, the combined forces gathered. The French formed three columns, Americans were in two columns, and an additional 500 militia formed as a feint

Attack on Savannah, October 8, 1779

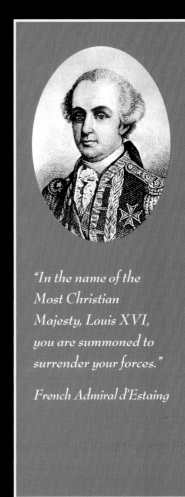

"In the name of the Most Christian Majesty, Louis XVI, you are summoned to surrender your forces."

French Admiral d'Estaing

to draw attention from the main attack. Unfortunately, Sergeant Major Curry overheard the discussion of the plan. He deserted to the British and revealed all the plan's details.

D'Estaing was to attack before daylight, but the troops did not move until past dawn. One column lost its way and came out in the open, where it received heavy fire and retreated. Pulaski's column attempted to force a passage through the abatis. Crossfire confused the men, and Pulaski was hit and killed. His men stopped fighting to carry their beloved leader from the field.

Although Lincoln wanted to continue the fight, d'Estaing took what was left of his troops back to their ships and sailed away, never to return. Lincoln marched his troops back to Charleston. The result of the Battle of Savannah led to deep mistrust of the French. The debacle at Savannah, combined with the French's defection at Newport, Rhode Island, the previous year, shook American confidence in this ally.

AMERICAN

COMMANDERS:
Gen. Benjamin Lincoln, French Adm. d'Estaing

STRENGTH:
approximately 5,000

CASUALTIES:
over 800

Elijah Clark State Park

2959 McCormick Highway, Lincolnton, GA 30817
PHONE: 706-359-3458
HOURS: Open daily.
ADMISSION: A parking fee is charged.

Elijah Clark State Park is located on the western shore of Clarks Hill Lake, the largest man-made lake east of the Mississippi River. The park is named for a frontiersman and Georgia war hero who led pioneers during the Revolutionary War. A renovated and furnished log cabin museum displays furniture, utensils, and tools circa 1780. Visitors can also view the graves of Clark and his wife, Hannah. Weekend tours of the log cabin are available.

 # Savannah History Museum

303 Martin Luther King Jr. Boulevard, Savannah, GA 31401
PHONE: 912-238-1779
HOURS: Open daily.
ADMISSION: A fee is charged.

The Savannah History Museum is housed in the old Central of Georgia railroad passenger shed. It stands on the site of the 1779 siege and battle of Savannah. Exhibits in its 20,000-square-foot exhibit area include historic costumes, uniforms, and other memorabilia interpreting Savannah's history. An annual memorial service is held to commemorate the Siege of Savannah.

Colonial Park Cemetery

201 East Oglethorpe Avenue, Savannah, GA 31401
PHONE: 912-651-6843 (City of Savannah Department of Cemeteries)
HOURS: Open daily.
ADMISSION: Free.

Colonial Park Cemetery contains grave markers that date back to the 1700s. Many of Savannah's original settlers are buried here. Button Gwinnett, the state's signer of the Declaration of Independence, is buried here, although the exact location of his grave is unknown. A monument commemorating Button Gwinnett is also located in the cemetery. Archibald Bulloch, a delegate to the Continental Congress in 1775, is also buried here, as are several Revolutionary War soldiers. Today the cemetery functions mainly as a park.

Old Fort Jackson

1 Fort Jackson Road, Savannah, GA 31404
PHONE: 912-232-3945
HOURS: Open daily.
ADMISSION: A fee is charged.

Old Fort Jackson is the oldest standing brick fort in Georgia. Original construction began as early as the 1740s on what was called "Mud Fort." The site was fortified during the Revolutionary War as an earthen battery. The site houses displays, artifacts, and a film on the military history of Savannah.

New flagpole and sentry box at Old Fort Jackson

FORT MORRIS STATE HISTORIC SITE

2559 Fort Morris Road, Midway, GA 31320
PHONE: 912-884-5999
HOURS: Open Tuesday to Sunday
ADMISSION: A fee is charged; special rates for tour groups.

Fort Morris was the last American post in Georgia to fall during the American Revolution and is one of only a handful of earthwork fortifications that still exist from the Revolutionary War. The Continental Congress ordered construction of the fort in July 1776 in order to protect the seaport town of Sunbury, Georgia, a port-of-entry. The British overtook the fort during their second attempt on January 9, 1779. The visitor's center features a short historical film, gift shop, and museum with uniforms, weapons, and other artifacts. The site features a cannon, blacksmith shop, nature trail, picnic area, and birdwatching. Special programs are held throughout the year.

Fort Morris

MIDWAY CHURCH AND MUSEUM

State Highway 17, Midway, GA 31320
PHONE: 912-884-5837
HOURS: Open Saturday and
Sunday; closed Mondays and
all holidays.
ADMISSION: A fee is charged.

The Midway Museum is dedicated to
the Revolutionary period. In 1775,
when the Continental Congress called
for representatives from each colony,
Georgia failed to respond. The town of
Midway became outraged and sent two
of its own, one of whom was Button
Gwinnett. The museum, built in the
raised cottage-style architecture that is
typical of eighteenth-century plantation homes, showcases exhibits, documents, and furnishings used in coastal
Georgia homes from colonial days until
the Civil War.

Midway Church

Midway Museum

Fort Frederica National Monument

Route 9, St. Simons Island, GA 31522

Phone: 912-638-3639

Hours: Open daily, closed Christmas Day.

Admission: A fee is charged.

Fort Frederica was a British settlement during the 1730s and 1740s that guarded the colony of Georgia against the threat of Spanish attack from Florida. Although it was intended as a permanent settlement, it survived only about twenty years before being virtually abandoned and falling into ruin. Established in 1945, the park preserves the ruins of this one-time thriving colonial town. Archeological excavations done mostly in the 1950s have uncovered the earthen walls of the fort and revealed some of the brick and tabby foundations of the houses and other buildings from the eighteenth century. The park features a twenty-five minute film entitled *This Is Frederica*, exhibits including a small-scale model of the fort and town, and walking tours of the grounds. An annual festival with food, music, and activities including living history demonstrations and children's games occurs on the first Saturday of March.

Fort Frederica

INDIANA & KENTUCKY

In 1775, Kentucky and Indiana were still mostly wilderness, part of the Ohio Valley that was inhabited by the Native Americans. Only men like Daniel Boone had penetrated the wilderness with dreams of inhabiting the land. The war, however, did intrude upon this frontier. The British armed Native Americans in the area and goaded them into attacking the settlers. George Rogers Clark, older brother of the famous William of the Lewis and Clark expedition, had an idea to strike at the British in this area. Clark and his militia subdued much of the western territories and took control of Fort Sackville at Vincennes.

In Kentucky, the last battle of the Revolutionary War was fought at Blue Licks. The British had already surrendered at Yorktown, Virginia, but the frontiersmen continued to be attacked by the Native Americans. At Blue Licks, Israel Boone, son of Daniel Boone, was killed. The words of the boy's father provide a fitting memorial for all the patriots in this war, "Enough of honour cannot be paid."

LOCUST GROVE

BLUE LICKS BTLFD. ST. PK.

GEORGE ROGERS CLARK
NAT'L. HIST. PK.

JACK JOUETT HOUSE

OLD FT. HARROD ST. PK.

SEE
VIRGINIA
PAGE 222

SEE TENNESSEE PAGE 210

Blue Licks Battlefield State Park

State Route 68, Mount Olivet, KY 41064
PHONE: 859-289-5507
HOURS: Open daily from April to October.
ADMISSION: A fee is charged.

Blue Licks Battlefield State Park commemorates the Battle of Blue Licks, which was the last battle of the Revolutionary War. Although the surrender at Yorktown was the symbolic end to the war, the war continued to be fought west of the Appalachian mountains. Many battles in these territories were between frontiersmen-turned-militia and Indians goaded on by the British. Such was the Battle of Blue Licks. On August 19, 1782, American Major Hugh McGary, against the advice of Daniel Boone to wait for reinforcements, led 200 troops in pursuit of 1,100 Indians and fifty British troops. They all met at Blue Licks, where the Kentuckians were ambushed and sixty, including Israel Boone, son of Daniel, were killed in fifteen minutes. The 241-acre park encompasses the site of the battle, and a park museum portrays pioneer relics and prehistoric artifacts, as well as displays interpreting the battle. A monument for the fallen soldiers has a quote by Daniel Boone that ends with this tribute: "Enough of honour cannot be paid."

Jack Jouett House

Craig's Creek Road, Route 33, Versailles, KY 40383
PHONE: 859-873-7902
HOURS: Open weekends from April to October.
ADMISSION: Free.

Jack Jouett House

The Jack Jouett House was built circa 1793 by Captain Jouett, who moved to Kentucky after distinguished service in the Revolutionary War in Virginia. Jouett has been called the Paul Revere of the South. On June 3, 1781, he rode forty miles through the night to Charlottesville to warn Thomas Jefferson and the Virginia legislature that the British were en route to arrest them.

Locust Grove

561 Blankenbaker Lane, Louisville, KY 40207
PHONE: 502-897-9845
HOURS: Open daily.
ADMISSION: A fee is charged; seniors and children discounted.

Locust Grove was established by William and Lucy Clark Croghan in 1790. Croghan was the brother-in-law of George Rogers Clark, founder of Louisville and Revolutionary War hero. Locust Grove was the final home of Clark, who lived with the Croghans from 1809 until his death in 1818. Clark's brother William explored the Louisiana Territory with Meriwether Lewis. Locust Grove teaches the story of Clark, early Kentucky history, and life on the frontier.

OLD FORT HARROD STATE PARK

State Route 68, Harrodsburg, KY 40330
PHONE: 859-734-3314
HOURS: Open daily.
ADMISSION: A fee is charged.

Old Fort Harrod State Park commemorates the first permanent settlement west of the Alleghenies. In March 1774, Captain James Harrod and thirty-two Pennsylvanian men set out for Kentucky to claim lands and make a settlement. On June 16, 1774, Harrod and his men laid out a town in Kentucky and named it Harrodstown. Today, Old Fort Harrod is a replica of the original and offers a living history experience with cabins and *Old Fort Harrod* blockhouses, complete with pioneer furnishings and costumed craftspeople performing tasks such as weaving, tinsmithing, woodworking, broom making, and blacksmithing.

GEORGE ROGERS CLARK NATIONAL HISTORICAL PARK

401 South Second Street, Vincennes, IN 47591
PHONE: 812-882-1776
HOURS: Open daily; closed Thanksgiving Day, Christmas Day, and New Year's Day.
ADMISSION: A fee is charged.

The George Rogers Clark National Historical Park commemorates the capture of Fort Sackville from British Lieutenant Governor Henry Hamilton and his troops by Lieutenant Colonel George

Rogers Clark and his frontiersmen on February 25, 1779. Clark and his men marched from Kaskaskia on the Mississippi River in midwinter to defeat the British. The park's twenty-six acres feature a visitor's center with an audio visual program and displays which depict the Clark campaign and the construction of the George Rogers Clark Memorial. Costumed living history interpreters also provide programs at various times during the year. Fort Sackville is believed to have been located between the present-day George Rogers Clark Memorial by the Wabash River and the Lincoln Memorial Bridge.

George Rogers Clark Memorial

MAINE

*M*aine was not a colony and didn't become a state until 1820; but in 1775, the Continental Congress attempted to annex Quebec as the fourteenth colony, and Maine was the primary road to this Canadian province. The Arnold Trail, along which Benedict Arnold took his troops to Canada, begins at Popham and is well marked up to Coburn Gore. Maine also boasts the John Paul Jones Memorial State Historic site located on the mainland, a short distance from Badger's Island, where Jones's sloop Ranger was built and launched.

The waters off the coast of Maine also saw the first naval engagement of the Revolution, which was fought off the coast of Fort O'Brien five days before the Battle of Bunker Hill.

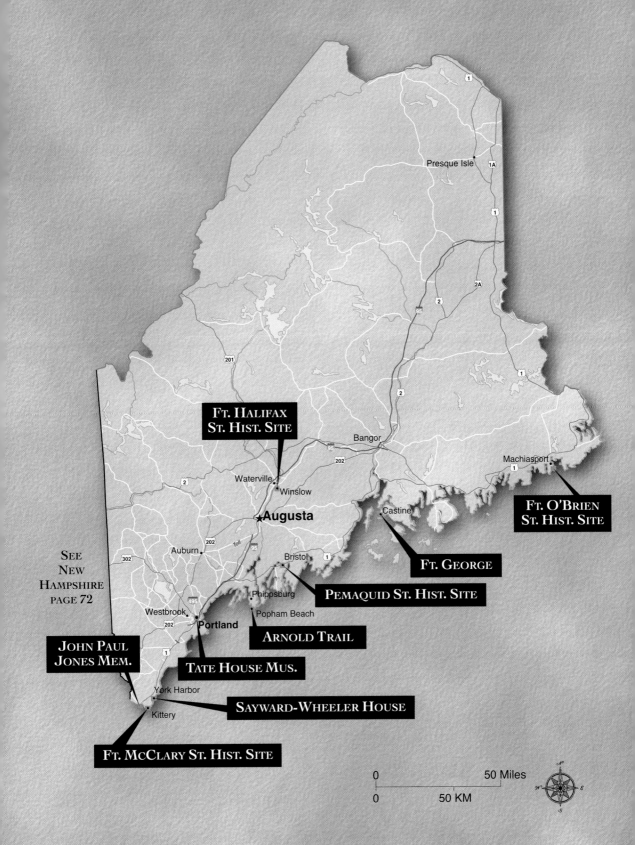

Presque Isle

Bangor

FT. HALIFAX
ST. HIST. SITE

Waterville
Winslow

★Augusta

Machiasport

FT. O'BRIEN
ST. HIST. SITE

Castine

FT. GEORGE

SEE
NEW
HAMPSHIRE
PAGE 72

Auburn

Bristol

PEMAQUID ST. HIST. SITE

Phippsburg

Popham Beach

ARNOLD TRAIL

Westbrook

Portland

JOHN PAUL
JONES MEM.

TATE HOUSE MUS.

York Harbor

SAYWARD-WHEELER HOUSE

Kittery

FT. MCCLARY ST. HIST. SITE

0   50 Miles

0   50 KM

JOHN PAUL JONES MEMORIAL STATE HISTORIC SITE

U.S. Route 1, Kittery, ME 03904
PHONE: 207-439-2845
www.state.me.us/doc/parks.htm

Although the John Paul Jones Memorial State Historic Site is named for the Revolutionary War naval hero, the imposing and beautiful granite and bronze sculpture is a memorial to Maine's soldiers and sailors who served in World War I. John Paul Jones's sloop *Ranger* was built and launched from nearby Badger's Island.

FORT MCCLARY STATE HISTORIC SITE

Kittery Point Road, Route 103, Kittery, ME 03904
PHONE: 207-439-2845
HOURS: Open daily from Memorial Day to September 30.
ADMISSION: A fee is charged.
www.state.me.us/doc/parks.htm

The first fort on this site, Fort William, protected the town and nearby shipyard from the Royal Navy. The British never attacked the fort. Fort William was replaced by Fort McClary in 1844. The buildings on the site represent several different periods of construction. The fort site remained active during the five wars from the American Revolution to World War I.

Fort McClary

ARNOLD TRAIL

From Popham to Coburn Gore, U.S. 201 and Maine 16 and 27

Arnold's 194-mile route from Popham to Coburn Gore on the Canadian border is marked intermittently as it travels from Popham through Hallowell, Skowhegan, Solon, Moscow, Stratton, and Sarampus. The Arnold Trail also includes Colburn House, the circa 1770 house of Major Reuben Colburn, who supplied batteaux to Benedict Arnold for Arnold's march to Quebec. Colburn House is located in Pittston.

Sayward-Wheeler House

70 Barrell Lane Extension, York Harbor, ME 03911
Phone: 207-384-2454
Hours: Open Saturday and Sunday from June 1 to October 15.
Admission: A fee is charged.
www.spnea.org/visit/homes/sayward.htm

The Sayward-Wheeler House was originally built about 1718 and was enlarged in the 1760s by Jonathan Sayward, a local merchant and member of the Massachusetts legislature. Sayward steadfastly supported the British, but his neighbors tolerated and respected him during the Revolution. Many original furnishings and family portraits purchased by Sayward have been preserved by six generations of the family, making this a model of a Revolutionary War home.

Sayward-Wheeler House

Tate House Museum

1270 Westbrook Street, Portland, ME 04104
Phone: 207-774-9781
Hours: Open Tuesday to Sunday from June 15 to September 30 and Friday to Sunday during October.
Admission: A fee is charged.

A large and elegant dwelling, Tate House was built in 1755 as the home of Maine Mast Agent Captain George Tate and his family. Tate was responsible for overseeing the cutting and shipping of white pine trees from Maine to England for masts. The pre-Revolutionary house museum features unique architecture, fine period furnishings, and historically-accurate gardens and grounds.

Colonial Pemaquid State Historic Site

Colonial Pemaquid Drive, Bristol, ME 04554

Phone: 207-677-2423

Hours: Open daily from Memorial Day to Labor Day.

Admission: A fee is charged.

www.state.me.us/doc/parks.htm

Colonial Pemaquid State Historic Site is located at the mouth of the Pemaquid River in Bristol. Extensive archeological excavations have unearthed fourteen foundations of seventeenth- and eighteenth-century structures as well as the officers' headquarters of Fort William Henry and Fort Frederick.

Fort William Henry

Fort William Henry

FORT HALIFAX STATE HISTORIC SITE

US Route 201, Winslow, ME 04901
PHONE: 207-941-4014
HOURS: Open daily from Memorial Day to Labor Day.
ADMISSION: Free.
www.state.me.us/doc/prkslnds/halifax.htm

Fort Halifax was built in 1754 as an outpost during the French and Indian War. It was a way station for Arnold's Expedition. The fort contained the oldest blockhouse in the United States until it was destroyed by a flood in 1987. A reconstructed blockhouse, which incorporates many timbers from the 1754 blockhouse, stands on the fort's original site at the confluence of the Kennebec and Sebasticook Rivers in Winslow.

FORT GEORGE

Wadsworth Cove Road, Castine, ME 04421
PHONE: Not available.
HOURS: Open daily from Memorial Day to Labor Day.
ADMISSION: Free.

Fort George, originally covering almost three acres, was built by the British when they reclaimed Castine in 1779. The fort was to be a base of operations against American coastal waters. The Massachusetts authorities, without consulting Congress or the Continental army, mounted the largest amphibious operation of the Revolution consisting of twenty fighting ships and another twenty vessels carrying 2,000 militia troops. The grandfather of Henry Wadsworth Longfellow commanded the militia, and Lieutenant Colonel Paul Revere was in charge of the American artillery. British naval reinforcements arrived just as the American militia debarked, and the Americans were soundly defeated. During the ensuing round of accusations for the defeat, Revere was accused of disobedience, unsoldierly conduct, and cowardice. It was two years before Paul Revere was acquitted at a court martial of all charges.

FORT O'BRIEN STATE HISTORIC SITE

Route 92, Machiasport, ME 04655
PHONE: 207-941-4014
HOURS: Open daily from Memorial Day to Labor Day.
ADMISSION: Free.
www.state.me.us/doc/prkslnds/obrien.htm

Fort O'Brien was built in 1775 and destroyed by the British in the same year. In 1777 the fort was rebuilt but again destroyed by the British in 1814. The first naval engagement of the Revolution was fought off the coast of Fort O'Brien in 1775, five days before the Battle of Bunker Hill.

MARYLAND

Maryland was begun when King Charles I cut a slice out of northern Virginia and gave it to his friend Lord Baltimore. Maryland became a haven for Irish and English Roman Catholics.

Maryland's delegates went to the Continental Convention, but they were instructed to hold out against independence. They shortly, however, recapitulated and joined the revolutionaries.

Maryland contains the burial place of John Paul Jones, naval hero of the Revolution, as well as other patriots, including Francis Scott Key, author of "The Star-Spangled Banner." Although the song was written during the War of 1812, his burial place is included here, as is the Star-Spangled Banner House, where the first flag was sewn by Mary Pickersgill.

Maryland also boasts Annapolis, one of the most historic towns in America.

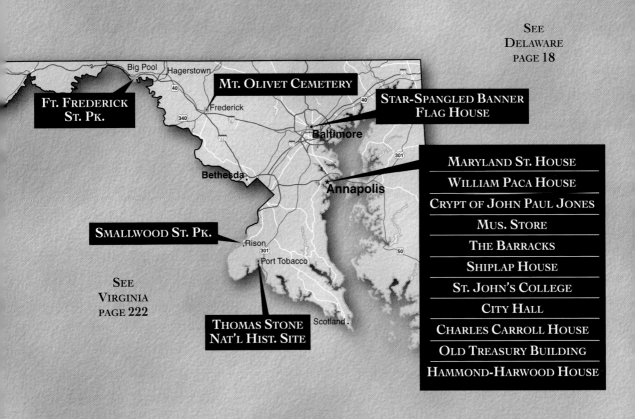

SEE PENNSYLVANIA PAGE 152

SEE
DELAWARE
PAGE 18

Big Pool

Hagerstown

**FT. FREDERICK
ST. PK.**

40

MT. OLIVET CEMETERY

Frederick

340

70

**STAR-SPANGLED BANNER
FLAG HOUSE**

40

95

270

Baltimore

95

301

Bethesda

Annapolis

MARYLAND ST. HOUSE

WILLIAM PACA HOUSE

CRYPT OF JOHN PAUL JONES

MUS. STORE

THE BARRACKS

SHIPLAP HOUSE

ST. JOHN'S COLLEGE

CITY HALL

CHARLES CARROLL HOUSE

OLD TREASURY BUILDING

HAMMOND-HARWOOD HOUSE

SMALLWOOD ST. PK.

Rison

301

Port Tobacco

50

SEE
VIRGINIA
PAGE 222

**THOMAS STONE
NAT'L HIST. SITE**

Scotland

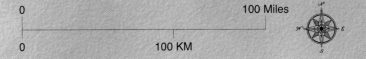

0   100 Miles

0   100 KM

FORT FREDERICK STATE PARK

11100 Fort Frederick Road, Big Pool, MD 21711

PHONE: 301-842-2155

HOURS: Open daily from April to October and Monday to Friday from November to March; closed Thanksgiving Day, Christmas Eve, and Christmas Day.

ADMISSION: A fee is charged.

Fort Frederick State Park commemorates the stone fort named in honor of Maryland's Lord Proprietor, Frederick Calvert, Sixth Lord Baltimore. The fort was completed in 1756 to protect English settlers from the French and their Indian allies. Whereas most forts of the period were built of wood and earth, Fort Frederick was unique because of its size and stone walls. Though the fort was never attacked by the French, it served as an important supply base for English campaigns and saved hundreds of lives of war refugees. During the American Revolution, the fort served as a prison for Hessian (German) and British soldiers. During the Great Depression, the Civilian Conservation Corps reconstructed the stone wall and located the foundations of the original buildings. Historic displays can be found in the fort, barracks, and visitor's center. The visitor's center also features an orientation film entitled *Fort Frederick*. The park annually holds military reenactments and other special events.

MOUNT OLIVET CEMETERY

515 South Market Street, Frederick, MD 21701

PHONE: 301-662-1164

HOURS: Open daily from dawn to dusk.

ADMISSION: Free.

Francis Scott Key Monument and grave site at Mount Olivet Cemetery

Mount Olivet Cemetery contains the graves of many of Maryland's patriots, as well as that of Francis Scott Key, who wrote "The Star-Spangled Banner," and his family. Revolutionary War patriots interred here include Richard Potts, delegate to the Continental Congress; General Roger Nelson, officer in the Revolutionary War; and Thomas Johnson, delegate to Continental Congress from Maryland. All of the soldiers and patriots interred here were removed from other cemeteries that at one time were within the city of Frederick.

STAR-SPANGLED BANNER FLAG HOUSE

844 East Pratt Street, Baltimore, MD 21202
PHONE: 410-837-1793
HOURS: Open Tuesday to Saturday.
ADMISSION: A fee is charged.
www.flaghouse.org

Star-Spangled Banner Flag House and Museum

The Star-Spangled Banner Flag House was originally the home of Mary Pickersgill, who sewed the flag that flew over Fort McHenry during the War of 1812. It was this flag that inspired Francis Scott Key to pen the words to our national anthem. Pickersgill's flag still survives and hangs at the Smithsonian Institution's National Museum of American History. The house, built in 1793, features federal period furniture and many original possessions. The garden features a footstone map of the United States.

MARYLAND STATEHOUSE

State Circle, Annapolis, MD 21401
PHONE: 410-974-3400
HOURS: Open daily; closed Christmas Day, Thanksgiving Day, and New Year's Day.
ADMISSION: Free.

The Maryland Statehouse, a stately Georgian building begun in 1772 and completed in 1779, is the oldest building in the U.S. to have continually remained an active seat of government. The building served as the nation's capitol from 1783-1784, and the Treaty of Paris that finally ended the Revolutionary War was ratified at this site by the Continental Congress. George Washington resigned his commission here, and the Annapolis Convention met here in 1765. From this meeting emerged the United States Constitutional Convention in Philadelphia.

To the right of the front door is the Old Senate Chamber where the Continental Congress met. This room has been restored to its original appearance and features a mannequin of George Washington dressed as he was when he resigned his commission. There are a number of portraits of early governors of Maryland by Charles Willson Peale, as well as Peale's celebrated portrait of Washington, Lafayette, and Tilghman at Yorktown. The President's desk, as well as some of the other desks and chairs in the room, are original pieces made for the Statehouse in 1796-97 by Annapolis cabinetmaker John Shaw.

WILLIAM PACA HOUSE

186 Prince George Street, Annapolis, MD 21401

PHONE: 410-263-5553

HOURS: Open daily from March to December and Friday and Saturday from January to February.

ADMISSION: A fee is charged.

www.annapolis.org

The William Paca House was built by Paca between 1763 and 1765. Paca was a lawyer and one of the most active Patriots of the war. He was a Maryland delegate to the first and second Continental Congresses, signed the Declaration of Independence, was elected to the first Maryland state Senate in 1776, and after the war served as governor of Maryland from 1782-85. Paca lived in this 37-room home until 1780. The house and garden have been restored to their eighteenth-century appearance. The house features a collection of antique furniture, silver, and paintings. The garden features five terraces, a pond, and a wilderness garden.

William Paca House and Garden

THE BARRACKS

43 Pinkney Street, Annapolis, MD 21401

PHONE: 410-263-8550

HOURS: By appointment.

The Barracks was one of the private homes rented out during the Revolutionary War period as a billet for soldiers. Annapolis was the center of Maryland's war effort during the Revolution and there was a need for places in the city to house the troops coming and going through the city. Many of the homes in the city were leased by the colonial government for this purpose. The house features a Revolutionary War exhibit on the first floor.

THE CRYPT OF JOHN PAUL JONES

USNA, 52 King George Street, Annapolis, MD 21402
PHONE: 410-263-6933
HOURS: Open daily.
ADMISSION: Free.

The remains of John Paul Jones lie in an elaborate marble sarcophagus in a crypt located in the Naval Academy Chapel and are guarded by a Navy guard. Inscribed in the floor are the names of all the ships commanded by Jones during the Revolutionary War. In 1778, Jones, aboard the American frigate *Ranger*, received a salute by the French fleet. This was the first recognition of the "Stars and Stripes" by a foreign government. In September of 1779, Jones commanded the *Bon Homme Richard*, on loan from the French government. The ship was named for Benjamin Franklin's "Poor Richard's Almanac." On September 23, 1779, Jones engaged and defeated the HMS *Serapis*. In the course of the action the American flag was shot away. When asked if he had

struck his colors, he replied, "Strike? I may sink, but I'm damned if I'll strike." Jones died in 1792 at the age of forty-five and was buried in Paris. In 1899, Horace Porter, then-ambassador to France, began a search for Jones's body, which was not discovered until 1905. Jones's remains were brought back to the Naval Academy and kept in Bancroft Hall until the completion of the crypt in 1913.

The Crypt of John Paul Jones

MUSEUM STORE

77 Main Street, Annapolis, MD 21401
PHONE: 410-268-5576
HOURS: Open daily; hours vary throughout the year.

The Museum Store is housed in the old Victualling Warehouse. During the Revolutionary War, the Victualling Warehouse was taken over by the government of Maryland and served as a storehouse for food supplies such as pork, flour, and molasses. These supplies were stored until they could be shipped to the Continental armies under Washington. The original building burned in the late eighteenth century but was rebuilt on its original site in 1811. Today, the Victualling Warehouse is home to the Historic Annapolis Foundation's Museum Store. Audio cassettes for Annapolis walking tours are available here, as are books and gifts relating to the city.

SHIPLAP HOUSE

18 Pinkney Street, Annapolis, MD 21401
PHONE: 410-267-7619
HOURS: Open Monday to Friday.
ADMISSION: Free.

Shiplap House was built about 1715 as the home and inn of Edward Smith. In addition to running an inn, Smith was also a "sawyer," meaning someone who cut lumber into lengths that could be used for building houses and ships. No doubt lawmakers coming to Annapolis for government affairs stayed at Smith's inn. In the 1750s, Nathan Hammond operated a shop on the site, and the building now houses an exhibit on trade in the eighteenth century.

Shiplap House

ST. JOHN'S COLLEGE

60 College Avenue, Annapolis, MD 21401
PHONE: 410-263-2371

McDowell Hall at St. John's College

St. John's College was established in 1696 and is the third oldest college in the United States after Harvard and The College of William and Mary. Patriots from Annapolis gathered on the grounds of St. John's to discuss current events. At the north end of the campus, overlooking College Creek, is the French Soldiers Monument that is dedicated to the French troops who died during the Revolutionary War.

ANNAPOLIS CITY HALL

160 Duke of Gloucester Street, Annapolis, MD 21401
PHONE: 410-263-7997 (Mayor's office)
HOURS: Open Monday to Friday.
ADMISSION: Free.

When first built in 1766, the Annapolis City Hall was called the Assembly Rooms. Upon its completion, the building became the site not only for government offices, but for balls and other city social events. George Washington attended balls there, and records indicate he also took his turn at the card tables that were in the ballroom.

CHARLES CARROLL HOUSE

107 Duke of Gloucester Street, Annapolis, MD 21401
PHONE: 410-269-1737
HOURS: Vary by season.
ADMISSION: A fee is charged; children and seniors discounted.

The Charles Carroll House was home to three generations of the Carroll family, including Charles Carroll of Carrollton, the only Catholic to sign the Declaration of Independence in 1776. Maryland is now the only state in which the homes of all of its signers still exist. The Carroll House features museum interpretive displays, living-history and musical performances, and terraced, waterfront boxwood gardens.

Charles Carroll House

OLD TREASURY BUILDING

State Circle, Annapolis, MD 21012
PHONE: 410-267-8149
HOURS: Call for hours.
ADMISSION: Free.

The Old Treasury Building was built between 1735 and 1737 and is the oldest public building in Maryland. It was built as a secured office for the storage of the state's currency and its records. The brick walls are thick, the windows are barred, and the wooden door is massive. When the building was used as the treasury, it was open only on Wednesdays, and furnishings included only two iron chests, one to hold the record books, and the other for the currency itself. The building has been restored by the state and is now the home of the Research Center for Historic Annapolis Foundation. It contains information on the historic buildings of Annapolis.

HAMMOND-HARWOOD HOUSE

19 Maryland Avenue, Annapolis, MD 21401
PHONE: 410-263-4683
HOURS: Open daily; closed Thanksgiving Day, Christmas Day, and New Year's Day.
ADMISSION: A fee is charged.

The Hammond-Harwood House epitomizes the elegant lifestyle of the eighteenth-century wealthy family in colonial Annapolis. The house was begun in 1774 for Patriot Mathias Hammond and today is a museum. The house features ornately carved moldings and is an excellent example of eighteenth-century Georgian architecture. It contains period furnishings and fine arts, including several portraits by the Peale family and one of the premier collections of John Shaw furniture in the nation.

Hammond-Harwood House

THOMAS STONE NATIONAL HISTORIC SITE

6655 Rose Hill Road, Port Tobacco, MD 20677
PHONE: 301-934-6027
HOURS: Open daily from Memorial Day to Labor Day and Wednesday to Sunday from Labor Day to Memorial Day.
ADMISSION: Free.

Thomas Stone National Historic Site features Haberdeventure, a five-part mansion built in 1773 by Maryland's youngest signer of the Declaration of Independence. Thomas and his wife, Margaret Brown, both from prominent Maryland families, were married in the late 1760s. Their three children were born at Haberdeventure. Thomas, a lawyer, first became involved in local

Haberdeventure at Thomas Stone National Historic Site

politics, then served in the Continental Congress. He later served as a Maryland state senator and delegate. He helped draft the Articles of Confederation, which bound the United States together prior to the adoption of the Constitution. Margaret died in June 1787 and Thomas died four months later. Both are buried in the family cemetery near the mansion.

SMALLWOOD STATE PARK

State Highway 224, Rison, MD 20658
PHONE: 301-743-7613
HOURS: Open daily.
ADMISSION: A fee is charged from April to October on weekends and holidays. Park is free at all other times.

The Smallwood State Park was named for patriot Major General William Smallwood, who fought and was wounded at White Plains, New York, in 1776. After the Revolution, Smallwood served as the fourth governor of Maryland, and during his term, the state ratified the U.S. Constitution. On the park grounds is Smallwood's retreat house, a small, brick plantation house. Restoration of the house, beginning from the remaining foundation and three partial walls, began in 1954. Today, the house is fully restored with a collection of period furnishings on display. Each year, on the second Sunday in December, demonstrations and candlelight tours of the home are given. The 628-acre park also features nature trails, periodic craft demonstrations, military exhibitions, and other special events.

MASSACHUSETTS

*B*oston, Massachusetts, was a hotbed of turmoil in the years leading up to the Revolution. One of its leading citizens, Samuel Adams, was a master of propaganda and stirred the pot of revolution through the symbolism of the Liberty Tree on Boston Common, where characters were hanged in effigy, and through the drafting of the Townshend Acts, a circular letter written by Adams that informed the public of the unconstitutionality of the British taxes being levied on the colonies. His crowning moment may have been the Boston Tea Party, in which Adams led a mob disguised as Mohawks down to the waterfront and emptied 342 chests of precious tea into the harbor. This act served to inflame the British.

Today, the Revolution still lives in Boston, as it does in other cities around the state, such as Lexington, Concord, and Cambridge.

SEE NEW YORK PAGE 100

.Pittsfield

SEE CONNECTICUT PAGE 10

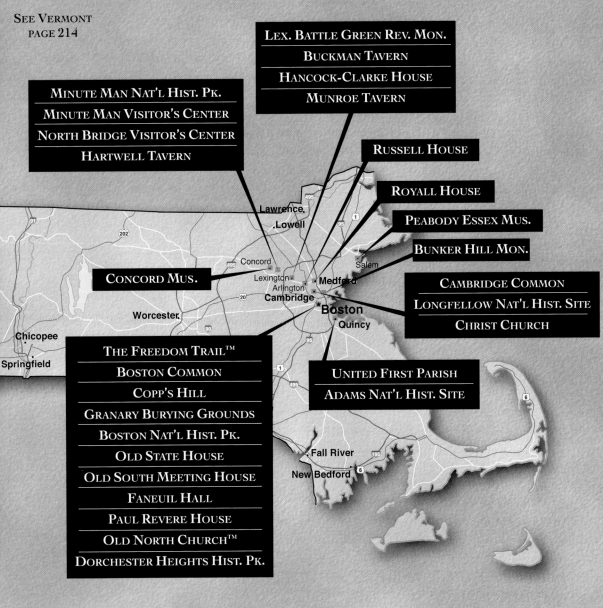

SEE
NEW HAMPSHIRE
PAGE 72

SEE VERMONT
PAGE 214

LEX. BATTLE GREEN REV. MON.

BUCKMAN TAVERN

HANCOCK-CLARKE HOUSE

MUNROE TAVERN

MINUTE MAN NAT'L HIST. PK.

MINUTE MAN VISITOR'S CENTER

NORTH BRIDGE VISITOR'S CENTER

HARTWELL TAVERN

RUSSELL HOUSE

ROYALL HOUSE

PEABODY ESSEX MUS.

BUNKER HILL MON.

CONCORD MUS.

CAMBRIDGE COMMON

LONGFELLOW NAT'L HIST. SITE

CHRIST CHURCH

THE FREEDOM TRAIL™

BOSTON COMMON

COPP'S HILL

GRANARY BURYING GROUNDS

BOSTON NAT'L HIST. PK.

OLD STATE HOUSE

OLD SOUTH MEETING HOUSE

FANEUIL HALL

PAUL REVERE HOUSE

OLD NORTH CHURCH™

DORCHESTER HEIGHTS HIST. PK.

UNITED FIRST PARISH

ADAMS NAT'L HIST. SITE

SEE RHODE ISLAND PAGE 178

0   50 Miles

0   50 KM

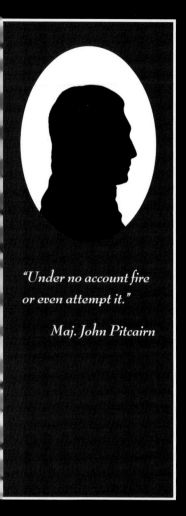

"Under no account fire or even attempt it."

Maj. John Pitcairn

BRITISH

COMMANDERS:
Gen. Thomas Gage,
Lt. Col. Francis Smith,
Brig. Gen. Earl Hugh Percy,
Maj. John Pitcairn

STRENGTH: 1,700

CASUALTIES: 238

THE BATTLE AT LEXINGTON AND CONCORD

April 19, 1775

After the Colonial Wars against the French in Canada, British Parliament decided that it was only fair for the colonists to pay for the quartering of the soldiers in the colonies, and the fairest way was through levying taxes. The colonists, on the other hand, did not want the soldiers in their towns in the first place and believed taxation without representation was tyranny. Britain could not understand the problem because they were treating the colonists as they did every other British colony. However, since the colonists were mostly British who left England for more freedom, they would not tolerate oppression from the government they left behind. After a series of acts by Parliament and responses from the colonists, the most famous of which was the Boston Tea Party, Boston Harbor was closed. Food and provisions poured in from sympathetic neighboring towns and colonies; and outside Boston, ammunition, weapons, and gunpowder began to be gathered and stored.

General Thomas Gage, the overall commander of all British forces in the American colonies and commander of the Boston garrison, was aware of the stores. On April 14, 1775, he was ordered to take immediate steps to disrupt any treasonable colonial plans. He, in turn, ordered Lieutenant Colonel Francis Smith to take 700 troops and seize the weapons and gunpowder. Because of spies on both sides, Gage knew where the weapons were stored and the colonists knew when the British were planning to get them. Paul Revere, William Dawes, and Dr. Prescott warned the colonists in the countryside of the approaching British. Revere and Dawes were stopped by British patrols, but Prescott made it to Concord in time for them to scatter most of the ammunition. Smith, hearing the church bells, knew that his march was no secret, so he sent word to Gage that he needed reinforcements.

En route to Concord, the British advance guard, commanded by Royal Marine Major John Pitcairn, was blocked by seventy minutemen from Lexington. Pitcairn ordered the men to lay down their arms and disperse. He also directed his men to hold their fire. Many of the militia began to drift away, but some-

One artist's conception of Lexington and Concord

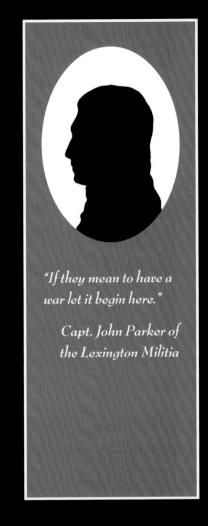

"If they mean to have a war let it begin here."

Capt. John Parker of the Lexington Militia

one fired a shot. The British fired off a volley and some of the Americans fired individually. After another volley the British charged with bayonets and the Americans fled. With only one man wounded, the British continued on toward Concord.

The stores of ammunition at Concord had already been dispersed by the time the British arrived, and what little ammunition was left they burned. Seeing the smoke, nearby residents believed that the British were burning Concord and made ready their muskets. Smith ordered his men to return to Boston, but as they left, militia commanded by Captain Isaac Davis opened fire, and the British hastily returned to Concord. Once again the British departed for Boston. En route, always out of musket range, the sharpshooting American militia picked off British troops. This continued with a brief respite when Gage's reinforcements of 1,000 men under Brigadier General Percy reached them. After giving Smith's men a few minutes to rest, he ordered them to continue to Boston. By this time, thousands of minutemen had joined in on both sides and the rear of the column, so the British force was in real danger. Percy then decided to march to Bunker Hill instead of attempting to cross a partially destroyed bridge that led to Boston. On the high ground, the British were safe and the Americans withdrew.

AMERICAN

COMMANDERS:
Col. James Barrett,
Capt. John Parker,
Capt. Isaac Davis

STRENGTH: 4,000

CASUALTIES: 95

LEXINGTON BATTLE GREEN REVOLUTIONARY MONUMENT

Lexington Green, Lexington, MA 02420
PHONE: 781-862-1703
HOURS: Open daily.
ADMISSION: Free.

On April 19, 1775, the seven minutemen slain by the British were buried in a common grave in Ye Old Burying Ground. Their boxes, "made of four large boards and nailed up," were put into two horse carts and brought to the graveyard. They were placed in a large trench, as near the woods as possible, and covered with soil. Then, for fear the British should find them, pine or oak boughs were spread over the grave so it looked like a heap of brush. In 1834, the bodies of the men were removed from the Burying Ground and set in a tomb at the foundation of the Revolutionary Monument on the Battle Green. The monument sits on a natural rise of land, formerly known as School House Hill. Their removal from Ye Old Burying Ground was prompted by a desire to honor them and their sacrifice. The men buried at the foundation of the monument are Jonas Parker, Robert Munroe, Samuel Hadley, Jonathan Harrington, Jr., Isaac Muzzey, Caleb Harrington, and John Brown. The Lexington Visitor's Center is located across from the Green.

BUCKMAN TAVERN

One Bedford Street on the Lexington Green, Lexington, MA 02420
PHONE: 781-862-5598
HOURS: Open daily.
ADMISSION: A fee is charged.

Buckman Tavern was built in 1709. In the early hours of April 19, 1775, eighty minutemen, after being aroused from their beds, waited at Buckman Tavern for the British to attack. Today, the tavern still bears the indentions from the British musket balls. It functions as a historical museum with costumed tour guides.

Buckman Tavern

HANCOCK-CLARKE HOUSE

36 Hancock Street, Lexington, MA 02420
PHONE: 781-861-0928
HOURS: Open daily.
ADMISSION: A fee is charged.

The Hancock-Clarke House was originally built in 1698 as a parsonage for the grandfather of John Hancock, who was a signer of the Declaration of Independence. On the night of Paul Revere's famous ride, Samuel Adams and John Hancock were staying at the house. Revere returned to the house after being captured on his way to Concord and released. He accompanied Hancock and Adams to the edge of the town before returning to the green to watch the shooting. They had been spirited out of Boston earlier to avoid being arrested by the British for treason. At the time of the Revolutionary War, the family of Parson Jonas Clarke was occupying the house. The house is now a museum and features the pistols of Major John Pitcairn, the commander of the British advance guard engaged on Lexington Green.

MUNROE TAVERN

1332 Massachusetts Avenue, Lexington, MA
PHONE: 781-674-9238
HOURS: Open daily.
ADMISSION: A fee is charged.

The Munroe Tavern was the command post for Lord Percy while his forces oversaw the withdrawal of the British from Concord by way of Lexington. During this time, the tavern served as a hospital for the wounded British. A bullet hole in the ceiling, a remnant of the Revolution, remains.

CONCORD MUSEUM

200 Lexington Road, Concord, MA 01742
PHONE: 978-369-9763
HOURS: Open daily; closed major holidays.
ADMISSION: A fee is charged.
www.concordmuseum.org

The Concord Museum collection began around 1850 and boasts one of the oldest and best-documented Americana collections. The museum features examples of seventeenth-, eighteenth-, and nineteenth-century artifacts. Revolutionary War items include the lantern which was hung in the Old North Church and signaled the British approach, powder horns, muskets, cannonballs, and fifes. A fifteen-minute film acquaints visitors with the rich history of Concord.

Lantern hung from the North Church on the night of Paul Revere's ride

MINUTE MAN NATIONAL HISTORICAL PARK ——————

Concord, Lincoln, and Lexington, MA
PHONE: 978-369-6993
HOURS: Open daily.
ADMISSION: Free.
www.nps.gov/mima

The Minute Man National Historical Park comprises over 900 acres of land and includes the Minute Man Visitor's Center, North Bridge Visitor's Center, Hartwell Tavern, and the Battle Road Trail. The Battle Road Trail winds for over five miles from Lexington through Lincoln to Concord and interprets the battle that began the American Revolutionary War on April 19, 1775. Visitors are guided by a series of outdoor exhibit panels and granite mile markers, historic homes, stone walls, and remnants of structure foundations that interpret the story of the Battle of Lexington and Concord. Trail highlights include: Meriam's Corner, where skirmishes between British and Americans occurred; Parker's Revenge, the site where Captain Parker led the Lexington militia to attack the British in retaliation for colonial deaths incurred earlier that morning on Lexington Green; the Paul Revere Capture Site, where Revere's midnight ride was ended by a British patrol; and the Wayside, home of Samuel Whitney, muster master of the Concord Minute Men, and later the home of Nathaniel Hawthorne, Bronson Alcott, and Margaret Sidney. Hartwell Tavern is also on the Battle Road Trail.

HARTWELL TAVERN

Within Minute Man National Historical Park
PHONE: 978-369-6993
HOURS: Open daily.
ADMISSION: Free.

The Hartwell Tavern was built in 1733 as the home of Ephraim and Elizabeth Hartwell and their children. It was operated as a farm and tavern. The tavern became a landmark as travelers to and from Boston stopped and shared the latest news of the day. Today the Hartwell Tavern offers an opportunity to observe colonial living with craft demonstrations by costumed interpreters.

NORTH BRIDGE VISITOR'S CENTER

174 Liberty Street, Concord, MA
PHONE: 978-369-6993
HOURS: Open daily.
ADMISSION: Free.

The North Bridge is the site of "the shot heard 'round the world." Standing next to the bridge is the Minute Man Statue by artist Daniel Chester French. The visitor's center features a thirty-minute program entitled "The Two Revolutions" and offers a walking guide.

North Bridge and Minute Man Statue at the Minute Man National Historical Park

MINUTE MAN VISITOR'S CENTER

Route 2A West, Lexington, MA
PHONE: 781-862-7753
HOURS: Open daily.
ADMISSION: Free.

The Minute Man Visitor's Center features a multimedia program, "The Road to Revolution," a forty-foot mural that portrays the fight between the British and colonial militia, and a bookstore. Maps of the Battle Road Trail are available at the visitor's center.

Visitor's Center at Minute Man National Historical Park

THE FREEDOM TRAIL™ ————————————

3 School Street, Boston, MA 02108
PHONE: 617-227-8800
HOURS: Open daily.
ADMISSION: Free.
www.thefreedomtrail.org

This two-and-a-half-mile walking tour links sixteen historic places in Boston via a red brick line in the street. Of the following, nine sites were of importance during the Revolutionary War and are in order of location from Boston Common through downtown to the North End and Charlestown.

GRANARY BURYING GROUNDS

Tremont Street next to Boston Common, Boston, MA
PHONE: 617-635-4505 (Freedom Trail Visitor's Center)
HOURS: Open daily.
ADMISSION: Free.

The Granary Burying Grounds was established in 1660. Notables buried here among the 1,600 graves include Paul Revere, his wife, and his father; Abiah and Josiah Franklin, the parents of Benjamin Franklin; Samuel Adams, Robert Paine, and John Hancock, all signers of the Declaration of Independence; patriot James Otis; and the five victims from the Boston Massacre.

COPP'S HILL BURIAL GROUND

Hull and Snowhill Streets, Boston, MA
PHONE: 617-635-4505 (Freedom Trail Visitor's Center)
HOURS: Open daily.
ADMISSION: Free.

Copp's Hill Burial Ground began as a cemetery in the 1660s. A century later, during the Battle of Bunker Hill, the British used the cemetery grounds to launch their artillery. Graves include Prince Hall, a Revolutionary soldier and head of the Black Masons; early settler Cotton Mather; and Edward Hartt, builder of the USS *Constitution*.

BOSTON COMMON

Tremont, Boylston, Charles, Beacon, and Park Streets, Boston, MA

Boston Common can be called the country's oldest public park. In the 1600s, it was used as a field for grazing cattle and as a drill field for the militia. Before and during the Revolution, the Common was a rallying point for the militia and the citizens of Boston. Patriots were called to arms and independence from the Common by Bostonian firebrands.

BOSTON NATIONAL HISTORICAL PARK

Visitor Center, 15 State Street, Boston, MA
PHONE: 617-242-5642
HOURS: Open daily.
ADMISSION: The visitor's center and all federally owned sites are free, but a small fee is collected at the privately owned and operated sites.
www.nps.gov/bost

Boston National Historical Park is an association of eight privately, municipally, and federally owned and managed historic sites which offer visitors an understanding of the city's role in the nation's history. Seven of the eight sites are connected by the Freedom Trail. In downtown Boston, Old South Meeting House, Old State House, Faneuil Hall, the Paul Revere House, and Old North Church bring to life the American ideals of freedom of speech, religion, government, and self-determination. In Charlestown, the Bunker Hill Monument is the site of the first major battle of the American Revolution, and in South Boston, Dorchester Heights is significant for its role in the evacuation of the British in March of 1776. The Boston National Historical Park's downtown visitor center offers free maps, brochures, and information on the Freedom Trail and the Boston area, as well as ranger-led programs along the Freedom Trail. The center also has a bookstore.

FANEUIL HALL

1 Faneuil Hall Square, Boston, MA 02109
PHONE: 617-242-5675
HOURS: Open daily.
ADMISSION: Free.

In Faneuil Hall's original design, the main floor served as a marketplace, with stalls leased by farmers and butchers, and the second floor was a large meeting room. The citizens of Boston turned this meeting room into a "Cradle of Liberty," where they debated the burning issues of the day. These public debates helped encourage the opposition to the Sugar Tax of 1764, the Stamp Act of 1765, and the Tea Act of 1773. Today, rangers give historical lectures about Faneuil Hall every half hour on the second floor.

Faneuil Hall

OLD STATE HOUSE, THE BOSTONIAN SOCIETY'S MUSEUM

206 Washington Street, Boston, MA 02109
PHONE: 617-720-1713
HOURS: Open daily; closed Thanksgiving Day, Christmas Day, and New Year's Day.
ADMISSION: A fee is charged.

The 1713 Old State House is the oldest surviving public building in Boston. It was the center for political life and thought in the colonies. The basement was rented by John Hancock and others as a warehouse. Upstairs was the Council Chamber of the Royal Governors, where in 1761 James Otis argued against the Writs of Assistance, the British Crown's policy of issuing general search warrants with neither charges nor individuals specified. John Adams wrote of him, "Otis was a flame of fire . . . then and there the child Independence was born." At one end of the building is Representatives Hall, where the Massachusetts Assembly convened. Here began the debates on Englishmen's rights that led to the secession from Britain. From the balcony over-looking King Street (now State Street), on July 18, 1776, the Declaration of Independence was read to Bostonians. Later that day, the lion, unicorn, and other symbols of royal authority were torn down from the Old State House and publically burned. The building boasts a museum dedicated to the history of the city with many Revolutionary War artifacts, paintings, and prints on display. An audio tour, available in English, Spanish, French, and Japanese, allows visitors to learn more about the building, the artifacts, and the history of the city. Outside the Old State House, a circle of cobblestones in the street marks the site of the Boston Massacre, where on March 5, 1770, British soldiers killed five patriots.

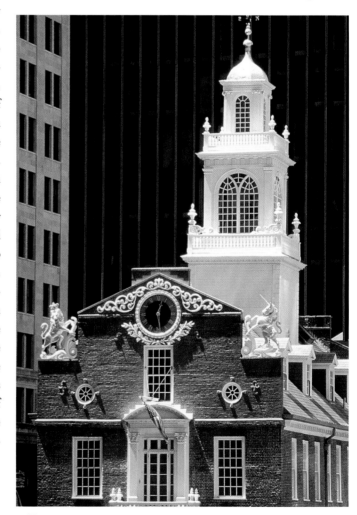

Old State House

PAUL REVERE HOUSE

19 North Square, Boston, MA 02113
PHONE: 617-523-2338
HOURS: Open daily; closed Mondays
from January to March.
ADMISSION: A fee is charged.
www.paulreverehouse.org

Although this house dates from 1680, Paul
Revere purchased it in 1770. His family
lived here during the Revolution and the
early years of the Republic. Revere sold
the house in 1800 and moved to a nearby
home. Revere died on May 10, 1818, at his
Charter Street home, which no longer   *Paul Revere House*
exists. Today the house has been restored to reflect its original seventeenth-century appearance
and the Revere period. It stands as an example of early colonial urban architecture.

OLD NORTH CHURCH™

193 Salem Street, Boston, MA 02113
PHONE: 617-523-6676
HOURS: Open daily; closed Thanksgiving Day
and Christmas Day.
ADMISSION: Free.
www.oldnorth.com

The Old North Church™ is one of the most famous
structures of the Revolutionary War, immortalized in
Henry Wadsworth Longfellow's 1861 poem "Paul
Revere's Ride." On April 18, 1775, the sexton hung
two lanterns in the belfry to tell the patriots that the
British troops were on their way by water to seize the
weapons stored in Concord. The church served the
British as well, for General Thomas Gage witnessed
the Battle of Bunker Hill from the church's spire on
June 17. During the occupation of Boston, British
troops worshiped in the church.

Old North Church™

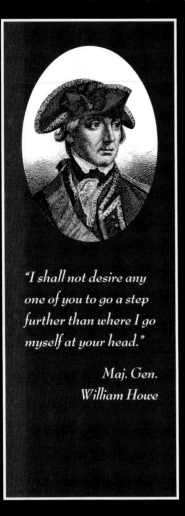

BRITISH

COMMANDER:
Maj. Gen. William Howe

STRENGTH: 2,200

CASUALTIES: 1,034

BATTLE OF BUNKER HILL

June 17, 1775

After the first shots of the Revolutionary War, militia units began to gather around Boston, Massachusetts and form an army. General Artemas Ward, a senior Massachusetts militia officer, wanted to contain the British by land in Boston. Near Boston on the Charlestown Peninsula were three hills that commanded an excellent strategic position of the approaches to the city. The Provincial Congress directed Ward to occupy Bunker Hill, the highest of the three hills, after learning of a British plan to seize Dorchester Heights and break the colonial army's siege lines in Roxbury. Accordingly, Colonel William Prescott and his force, accompanied by Brigadier General Israel Putnam of Connecticut, set out across the Charlestown Neck on the evening of June 16. When they reached Charlestown, Putnam insisted that Breed's Hill, which was lower but closer to Boston, was the better hill to occupy. Prescott again capitulated and the men dug in on Breed's Hill. They were spotted by a British sloop and were fired upon throughout the day.

On the British side, they could not ignore this occupation by the Americans. By entrenching on Breed's Hill, British shipping was now in range of militia artillery should the Americans place guns on the hill. Major General Sir Henry Clinton, a senior British officer in Boston, urged siege to drive them off the hill, but Major General William Howe successfully pressed for a frontal assault. Just after 1:00 P.M., Howe landed his troops in Charlestown and formed them at the base of Breed's Hill. To steady his largely undisciplined troops for the assault, legend has it that Prescott or Putnam advised the men not to fire until they saw the whites of the enemy's eyes. Although the British paused twice to fire as they mounted Breed's Hill, the militia held its fire. In fact, the British were within thirty yards before the colonists fired. Although the British rallied and assaulted the hill twice more, the surprising fortitude of the colonists brought British casualties to forty percent. On the third assault, the British fixed bayonets while the Americans, who were low on gunpowder, used their muskets as clubs and threw rocks to slow the British. Prescott soon called retreat, and his men fled across the Charlestown Neck to safety.

Despite the loss, the colonists sent a clear message to the British government that they were united and committed to fight. After this battle there was no turning back—it completely banished any thoughts of a conciliation between England and the colonies.

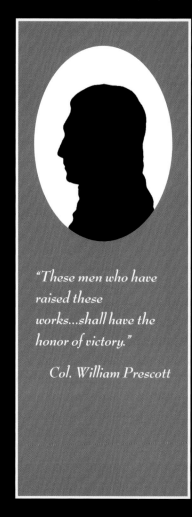

"These men who have raised these works...shall have the honor of victory."

Col. William Prescott

The Battle of Bunker Hill, a Chappel engraving

AMERICAN

COMMANDER:
Col. William Prescott

STRENGTH: 2,500-4,000

CASUALTIES: 400-600

Bunker Hill Monument

Monument Square, Charlestown, MA 02129

Phone: 617-242-5641

Hours: Open daily; closed Thanksgiving Day, Christmas Day, and New Year's Day.

Admission: Free.

The Bunker Hill Monument is an obelisk that commemorates the Battle of Bunker Hill. Although the battle was technically an American defeat, it provided a psychological victory for the Americans. The obelisk marks the approximate center of the American redoubt that repulsed two attacks before falling to the third. The peak of the obelisk can be reached by climbing the 294 stairs to the top. The monument also features a statue of Colonel William Prescott. An exhibit lodge with visitor information is located near the monument.

Bunker Hill Monument

USS Constitution and the Bunker Hill Monument in the distance

OLD SOUTH MEETING HOUSE

310 Washington Street, Boston, MA 02108
PHONE: 617-482-6439
HOURS: Open daily; closed major holidays.
ADMISSION: A fee is charged.

Built in 1729 and home to a Puritan congregation, the Old South Meeting House was the largest building in colonial Boston. Benjamin Franklin was baptized here, and patriots William Dawes and James Otis worshiped here. Old South provided the stage for much of the drama leading up to the Revolutionary War. On December 16, 1773, five thousand angry colonists gathered at Old South to protest a tax—and started a revolution with the Boston Tea Party. When Samuel Adams proclaimed, "This meeting can do nothing more to save this country!," the Sons of Liberty marched to the harbor and dumped the tea. Visitors can explore "Voices of Protest," the multi-media exhibition that

Old South Meeting House

tells the story of the Old South Meeting House and the people who have spoken here.

DORCHESTER HEIGHTS NATIONAL HISTORICAL PARK —

Thomas Park, South Boston, MA
PHONE: 617-242-5675
HOURS: Open daily for grounds. Call for monument hours.
ADMISSION: Free.

In November 1775, Bostonian Henry Knox was charged with the task of moving badly-needed cannon from Fort Ticonderoga, New York, to Boston, Massachusetts. As Knox and his men neared the city, they wrapped their wagon wheels with straw to deaden the sound. They moved the cannon into place on the hills of Dorchester Heights, south of Boston, in order to attack the British. Within only a few days, British General Howe, his troops, and a thousand colonial loyalists set sail for Nova Scotia, abandoning the city to Washington's troops. The monument that stands in Dorchester Heights commemorates the 1776 victory.

CAMBRIDGE COMMON

Massachusetts Avenue and Garden Streets, Cambridge, MA

The sixteen-acre Cambridge Common is only about one quarter of the original Common where the citizens of Cambridge trained their militia and held public meetings. The Common was the main camp and training ground for the Continental army and the location where General George Washington assumed command of the Continental army on July 3, 1775. The Common also boasts three British cannon captured in 1775.

LONGFELLOW NATIONAL HISTORIC SITE ——————

105 Brattle Street, Cambridge, MA 02138
PHONE: 617-876-4491
HOURS: Interior is closed for renovation.
ADMISSION: A fee is charged.

The house on the grounds of the Longfellow National Historic Site is known as the Vassal-Craigie-Longfellow House. It was built in 1759 by British Major John Vassal. The provisional government during the Revolution confiscated the house. During the siege of Boston, General George Washington made the home his headquarters for nine months in 1775-76. Also during the siege, Washington supervised the construction of three earthenwork forts along the Cambridge side of the Charles River. The remains of one, Fort Washington, can still be seen in Cambridgeport. In 1843, Henry Wadsworth Longfellow received the home as a wedding gift from his father-in-law, hence its name. The huge manuscript collection includes letters from George Washington and Thomas Jefferson. In addition, the house sponsors special tours and programs that focus on Washington and the Revolution as it affected Cambridge.

Longfellow House

> *Listen, my children, and you shall hear*
> *Of the midnight ride of Paul Revere,*
> *On the eighteenth of April, in Seventy-Five;*
> *Hardly a man is now alive*
> *Who remembers that famous day and year.*
>
> *Excerpt from* Paul Revere's Ride
> *by Henry Wadsworth Longfellow, 1860*

CHRIST CHURCH

Zero Garden Street, Cambridge, MA 02138
PHONE: 617-876-0200
HOURS: Open daily.
ADMISSION: Free.

In 1775, colonial troops from Wethersfield, Connecticut used Christ Church as their barracks. When Martha Washington joined her husband in December, the troops had moved out, and the church was opened for a service on December 31. After the British defeat at Saratoga in October 1777, the captured British troops were held in Cambridge. In June 1778, the funeral service for a young British officer in Christ Church enraged a mob of Cambridge patriots. They damaged the church so badly that services were not held for another twelve years. A plaque marks Washington's pew and one of the bullet holes that is said to date from the Continental army's encampment.

ROYALL HOUSE

15 George Street, Medford, MA 02155
PHONE: 781-396-9032
HOURS: Open for tours from Wednesday to Sunday from May 1 to October 1.
ADMISSION: A fee is charged.

Isaac Royall extensively modified an original, older brick house to create this handsome house. Several officers used the house during the siege of Boston. General John Stark occupied it while his regiment was camped in Medford before the Battle of Bunker Hill. General Washington visited it often after he arrived and took command of the Continental army. On display is a tea chest from the Boston Tea Party of 1773, one of only two or three that survived.

West and south exterior of the Royall House

RUSSELL HOUSE

7 Jason Street, Arlington, MA 02476

PHONE: 781-648-4300

HOURS: Open Friday to Sunday from April to October; other times by appointment.

ADMISSION: A fee is charged.

The Jason Russell House was the site of a fierce battle between locals and retreating British regulars on the night of April 19, 1775. Russell, who was crippled, took his family to safety and then returned to protect his house and shoot the British. Unfortunately, Russell was shot in his doorway and eleven militiamen were killed in the house. Eight additional militiamen held out successfully in the basement. Russell's descendants occupied the house for the next 120 years. Today, it serves as a museum. The furnishings are from the seventeenth and eighteenth centuries.

Russell House

United First Parish Church

1306 Hancock Street (Quincy Center), Quincy, MA 02169
PHONE: 617-773-1290
HOURS: Open daily from April 19–November 10.
ADMISSION: A fee is charged.

The United First Parish Church is the burial place of President John Adams and First Lady Abigail Adams, as well as President John Quincy Adams and First Lady Louisa Catherine Adams. The church began in 1636 as a branch of the Congregational Church in Boston and became an independent church in 1639. The Adamses were life-long members of the church, and their tombs are in a crypt inside the church. The Hancock family was also prominent in the church. John Hancock was baptized in this church by his father, Reverend John Hancock, who was the minister from 1726 to 1744.

Peabody Essex Museum

East India Square, Salem, MA 01970
PHONE: 978-745-9500
HOURS: Open daily from April to October and Tuesday to Sunday from November to March; closed major holidays.
ADMISSION: A fee is charged.
www.pem.org

Peabody Essex Museum contains one of the most important collections of Revolutionary War memorabilia in existence. The museum's holdings include Revolutionary War ship models and relics, uniforms from the original second corps cadets, and a vast collection of portraits depicting the Patriots.

Adams National Historic Park

135 Adams Street, Quincy, MA 02169
PHONE: 617-773-1177
HOURS: Open daily from mid-April to mid-November.
ADMISSION: A fee is charged.

The fourteen-acre Adams National Historic Park commemorates the Adams family and their service to the United States. The main Revolutionary War features include the birthplaces of John Adams and John Quincy Adams, which are the oldest presidential birthplaces in the U.S. It was in the John Quincy Adams Birthplace that John Adams, Samuel Adams, and James Bowdoin wrote the Massachusetts Constitution, a document that greatly influenced the United States Constitution. Another feature of the park is The Old House, home to four generations of the Adams family. The house contains 78,000 artifacts and the grounds include an eighteenth-century garden and a historic orchard.

NEW HAMPSHIRE

Many Revolutionary War sites are preserved in the southern part of New Hampshire. John Paul Jones lived in Portsmouth while his ship Ranger *was being built and again while he waited for his ship* America *to be completed. Today, the Jones House is the headquarters for the Portsmouth Historical Society.*

Tobias Lear also lived in Portsmouth. Lear was George Washington's private secretary through the war and was at Mount Vernon when Washington fell ill and died. Historians owe much to Lear's account of Washington's final hours.

Many of the sites in New Hampshire are connected with General John Stark, who commanded the colony's troops at the Battle of Bennington. Stark is credited with the words that today are the state's motto and that, no doubt, was the motto for Americans during the Revolution: "Live free or die."

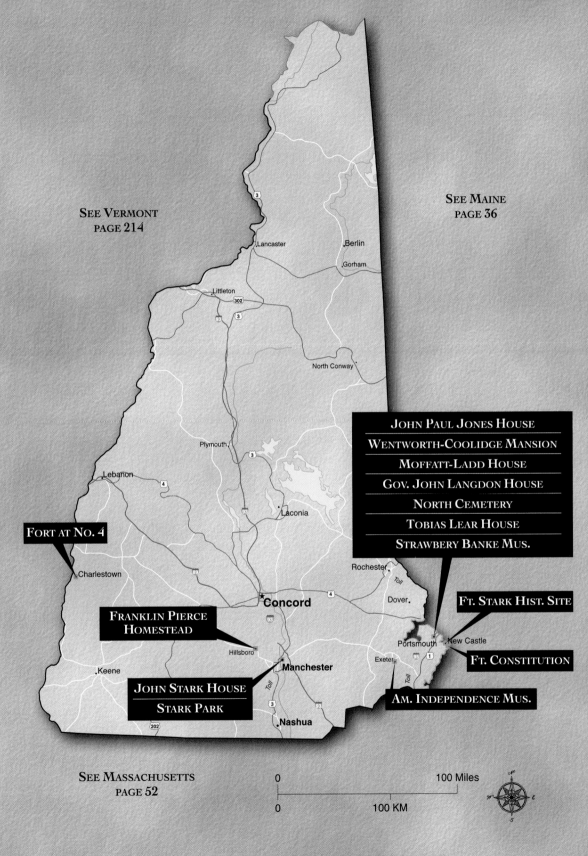

SEE VERMONT
PAGE 214

SEE MAINE
PAGE 36

Lancaster

.Berlin

.Gorham

Littleton

302

North Conway.

Plymouth.

Lebanon

Laconia

JOHN PAUL JONES HOUSE

WENTWORTH-COOLIDGE MANSION

MOFFATT-LADD HOUSE

GOV. JOHN LANGDON HOUSE

NORTH CEMETERY

TOBIAS LEAR HOUSE

STRAWBERY BANKE MUS.

FORT AT NO. 4

Charlestown

Rochester.

Dover.

FT. STARK HIST. SITE

★ **Concord**

**FRANKLIN PIERCE
HOMESTEAD**

Hillsboro

Portsmouth. New Castle

Exeter.

FT. CONSTITUTION

.Keene

Manchester

JOHN STARK HOUSE

STARK PARK

AM. INDEPENDENCE MUS.

Nashua

202

SEE MASSACHUSETTS
PAGE 52

0   100 Miles

0   100 KM

JOHN PAUL JONES HOUSE

43 Middle Street, Portsmouth, NH 03801

PHONE: 603-436-8420

HOURS: Open Monday to Sunday from mid-May to mid-October.

ADMISSION: A fee is charged.

The John Paul Jones House was built in 1758 by Gregory Purcell; and after his death, his widow operated the house as a boarding house. John Paul Jones stayed there in 1777 while his ship, *Ranger,* was being constructed, and again from August 31, 1781 to November 7, 1782 while his ship *America* was being readied in the Langdon shipyards. Today, the house is the headquarters of the Portsmouth Historical Society.

John Paul Jones House

WENTWORTH-COOLIDGE MANSION

375 Little Harbor Road, Portsmouth, NH 03801

PHONE: 603-436-6607

HOURS: Open Tuesday to Sunday from May to mid-October.

ADMISSION: A fee is charged; children free.

The Wentworth-Coolidge Mansion, originally a working farm and the home of New Hampshire's first Royal Governor, Benning Wentworth, overlooks Little Harbor and was built between 1720 and 1760. Highlights of the mansion's tour include original flocked wallpaper, a French stewing kitchen, and the council chamber where the state's first provincial government conducted affairs during the pre-Revolutionary War period.

MOFFATT-LADD HOUSE

154 Market Street, Portsmouth, NH 03801
PHONE: 603-436-8221
HOURS: Open Monday to Sunday from mid-June to mid-October.
ADMISSION: A fee is charged.

The Moffatt-Ladd House was built in 1763 by John Moffatt, a successful merchant. General William Whipple, a signer of the Declaration of Independence and the husband of Katherine Moffatt, also lived in this house. Portraits, letters, manuscripts, fine furnishings, and textiles, many from the Moffatt family, record 150 years of family history at this site. The house also contains a secret underground passageway.

Moffatt-Ladd House

GOVERNOR JOHN LANGDON HOUSE

143 Pleasant Street, Portsmouth, NH 03801
PHONE: 603-436-3205
HOURS: Open Wednesday to Sunday from June to mid-October.
ADMISSION: A fee is charged.
www.spnea.org/visit/homes/langdon/htm

The Governor John Langdon House was built in 1783 for Revolutionary War Major John Langdon. Langdon rose from modest origins to become a merchant and shipbuilder, a representative to the Continental Congress, and an advocate for the creation of a navy. In addition, Langdon served as a three-term governor of New Hampshire and hosted George Washington in his home in 1789. After Langdon's death in 1819, the house was occupied by other prominent families. At the end of the nineteenth century, descendants of Governor Langdon purchased the house and restored it. The garden has also been restored and features perennial flower beds, a rose and grape arbor, and a pavilion.

Governor John Langdon House

TOBIAS LEAR HOUSE

51 Hunking Street, Portsmouth, NH 03801
PHONE: 603-661-4117
HOURS: Open Wednesday during summer months or by appointment.
ADMISSION: A fee is charged; children discounted.

The Lear house was built in 1740 and was the birthplace of Tobias Lear, who in 1786 became the

private secretary for General George Washington. Lear managed the accounting of Mount Vernon, tutored Washington's adopted children, and handled Washington's correspondence. Washington visited the Lear house in 1789 as part of his tour of the Eastern states. The South Parlor has been reconstructed as a representation of that time. Tobias Lear was at Mount Vernon when Washington fell ill and died, and Lear's eyewitness account of Washington's final hours has been invaluable to historians. The house is presently undergoing restoration.

Tobias Lear House

NORTH CEMETERY

Maplewood Avenue, Portsmouth, NH 03801
PHONE: Not available.
HOURS: Open daily dawn to dusk.
ADMISSION: Free.

The Old North Cemetery was set aside in Portsmouth in 1753. Buried here are General William Whipple, a signer of the Declaration of Independence; Governor John Langdon, a signer of the U.S. Constitution; and Captain Thomas Thompson, commander of the Continental ship *Raleigh*.

STRAWBERY BANKE MUSEUM

64 Marcy Street, Portsmouth, NH 03802
PHONE: 603-433-1100
HOURS: Open daily from May to October; guided walking tours are offered from November to April.
ADMISSION: A fee is charged; seniors, groups, and children discounted.
www.strawberybanke.org

Strawbery Banke is a ten-acre waterfront living-history neighborhood and museum. The area features restored historic houses where visitors can converse with costumed role players. Some of the houses are used for exhibits on special themes such as architecture or archeology, and still others serve as shops for artisans practicing traditional trades.

Herb garden at Strawbery Banke

CHASE HOUSE

Chase House was built about 1762 by John Underwood, a mariner. He later sold the house to his in-laws, the Dearings, but four years later repurchased it from them at a considerably higher price. The house is noted for elaborately carved woodwork, both inside and out, crafted by Ebenezer Dearing, a noted local shipcarver. George Washington, on his visit to Portsmouth in 1789, attended a reception in this house.

WILLIAM PITT TAVERN

The William Pitt Tavern was built in 1766 by John Stavers, a suspected loyalist. He was called before Portsmouth's Committee of Safety and testified against Parliament's recent actions. The committee certified that he should be left alone. Eight months later the Declaration of Independence was signed and promulgated. The following January 29, 1777, Mark Noble tried to chop down Stavers' tavern sign. Within two days, the Portsmouth Committee of Safety arrested Stavers along with fifteen others. When the committee released all in exchange for parole and a promise to appear before them the following Wednesday, they kept Stavers confined because they believed his life would be endangered if he were liberated. On February 5, Stavers was among twelve who were released on condition of a year's good behavior and posting bond of £500 each. Stavers remained under a cloud of suspicion. The following May the state committee issued an order to the Portsmouth committee to bring before them fifteen people suspected "to be inimical to the American States" to sign another oath of loyalty. Stavers and two others signed the oath and were released. Stavers subsequently renamed his tavern the William Pitt Tavern in honor of the British statesman who advocated the American cause in Parliament. Newspapers thereafter referred to it simply as Stavers Tavern. Subsequent visitors to the tavern reputedly included the Marquis de Lafayette in 1782, John Hancock, William Whipple, General Henry Knox, and supposedly George Washington in 1789. Strawbery Banke has restored the tavern to its original condition.

STOODLEY'S TAVERN

In the 1770s, Stoodley's Tavern, owned by James Stoodley, was a gathering place for the patriots in the area. Stoodley's son-in-law, Elijah Hall, eventually inherited the tavern and lived in it until his death in 1830. During the Revolution, Hall had served as a lieutenant under John Paul Jones aboard the Portsmouth-built *Ranger*, named for the New Hampshire Revolutionary militia, Rogers Rangers.

WHEELWRIGHT HOUSE

Wheelwright House was built during the American Revolution and is an excellent example of a classical Georgian house. Captain John Wheelwright made his living at sea, as evidenced by an inventory of his estate taken after his death in 1784. During the five years preceding the American Revolution, Wheelwright commanded the brig *Abigail* on eight consecutive voyages to the West Indies. The war, however, brought hardships. In September of 1775 the *Abigail*, laden with a cargo of lumber, was seized off the New Hampshire coast by a squadron of British ships and taken to Boston, then under British control. Wheelwright served as second lieutenant aboard the continental ship *Raleigh*, and later as commander of several privateers in Boston. The disruption of his trade and the wartime inflation resulted in debts he could not pay. When he died a year after the peace treaty was signed, he owed his creditors over £400. To pay the debts his house was sold at a public auction.

FORT STARK HISTORIC SITE

End of Wild Rose Lane, New Castle off Route 1B, New Castle, NH 03854
PHONE: 603-436-1552
HOURS: Open daily.
ADMISSION: Free.

Fort Stark is located on a ten-acre site that overlooks Little Harbor, New York. This active fort has been in use in every war from the Revolutionary War to World War II. The fort is named in honor of General John Stark, the commander of New Hampshire forces at the Battle of Bennington, New York. Stark is credited with the words that eventually became the state motto, "Live free or die." A self-guided walking tour overlooks the Piscataqua River, Little Harbor, and the Atlantic Ocean.

FORT CONSTITUTION

Route 1B, at U.S. Coast Guard Station, New Castle, NH 03854
PHONE: 603-436-1552
HOURS: Open daily.
ADMISSION: Free.

Fort Constitution was originally named Fort William and Mary and was a British fort overlooking Portsmouth Harbor. On December 13, 1774, Paul Revere, four months before his famous Boston ride, rode from Boston to Portsmouth with the news that the British were on their way to New Castle with reinforcements. The next day, colonists captured the fort in one of the first overt acts against the Crown. The supplies inside the fort were sent to Boston and used at Bunker Hill. Today, the base of the original walls are intact. Interpretive panels are throughout the park, and a self-guided tour is available.

AMERICAN INDEPENDENCE MUSEUM

1 Governors Lane, Exeter, NH 03833
PHONE: 603-772-2622
HOURS: Open Wednesday to Sunday from May to October.
ADMISSION: A fee is charged; children discounted.

The American Independence Museum includes the Ladd-Gilman House, Folsom Tavern, and more than an acre of landscaped property. The focus of the museum is research and study of the American Revolution and colonial life in New Hampshire, particularly focusing on the lives of three prominent New Hampshire families: the Ladds, the Gilmans, and the Folsoms. Exhibits feature memorabilia of the Gilman family, including that of Captain Nicholas Gilman, Jr., who served on Washington's staff. Museum holdings also include papers of Washington, Lafayette, and John Hancock.

Ladd-Gilman House

LADD-GILMAN HOUSE

The Ladd-Gilman House was built circa 1721 by Captain Nathaniel Ladd and his third wife, Mercy Hilton. During the Revolution, Exeter was the state capital of New Hampshire, and the Ladd-Gilman House served as the state's treasury. The historical collection of the house includes the Dunlap Broadside of the Declaration of Independence; two drafts of the U.S. Constitution (Committee of Style and Committee of Detail); portraits of George Washington and Nicholas Gilman, Jr.;

letters and documents by George Washington and Nicholas Gilman, Jr.; furnishings, tableware, silver, and decorative arts from the period; and textiles, military uniforms, and weaponry of the Revolution.

FOLSOM TAVERN

The Folsom Tavern was built around 1775 and was probably originally named "The Raleigh" after the country's newest naval ship built at the Portsmouth Naval Shipyard. Revolutionary officers met at the Folsom Tavern on November 18, 1783 and formed the first veterans' and patriotic organization in the country. President George Washington stopped for breakfast at the tavern on November 4, 1789. The tavern is currently being restored.

STARK HOUSE

2000 Elm Street, Manchester, NH 03104
PHONE: 603-666-6600 (Manchester Chamber of Commerce)
HOURS: Open by appointment.
ADMISSION: A fee is charged.

The Stark House was built in 1737 by John Stark's father, Archibald Stark. This house is where General John Stark spent his boyhood and early married life. The house was moved to its present site in 1969 and was restored. Stark was an officer at Bunker Hill but is most famous for his victory at Bennington, where he took a position on the high ground later named Stark's Knob, New York.

Stark House

STARK PARK

North River Road, Manchester, NH 03104
PHONE: Not available.
HOURS: Open daily.
ADMISSION: Free.

Stark Park is the family cemetery of Revolutionary War hero John Stark. Stark's grave is marked by an obelisk, and other family members' graves are marked by one large headstone.

PIERCE HOMESTEAD

Junction of routes 9 and 31, Hillsboro, NH 03244
PHONE: 603-478-3165
HOURS: Open Friday to Sunday in June, September, and early October; Saturday and Sunday from July to Labor Day.
ADMISSION: A fee is charged.

Pierce Homestead

The Pierce Homestead is the birthplace of Franklin Pierce, the fourteenth president of the United States. The president's father, General Benjamin Pierce, built this home in 1804. General Pierce served in the Revolution, then twice served as New Hampshire's governor. The Pierce home has been restored in the late Federal style.

FORT AT NO. 4

State Route 11, Charlestown, NH 03603
PHONE: 603-826-5700
HOURS: Open daily from Memorial Day to October.
ADMISSION: A fee is charged.

The Fort at No. 4 was built as a fortified village during the French and Indian Wars in 1744. During the Revolutionary War, the fort was used as a military base by John Stark before his expedition to Bennington, New York. Fortifications and living quarters have been reconstructed to the period. Exhibits include colonial and Native American artifacts, as well as costumed interpreters who demonstrate eighteenth-century crafts and skills.

NEW JERSEY

New Jersey saw fighting early. In December of 1776, Washington kept one step ahead of the British as he went across New Jersey, yet the British took Fort Lee that same year. The British and the Hessians spent the winter in New Jersey.

Perhaps the most desperate move of Washington's career was the crossing of the Delaware River into Trenton on December 25. In a bid for one victory before the enlistment of his army expired on December 31, Washington's army woke up the Hessians early on the morning after Christmas, recovered the Jerseys, and saved the American cause.

Today, many places of interest remain preserved in New Jersey, including Washington Crossing State Park in Titusville, the Old Barracks Museum in Trenton, Monmouth Battlefield State Park in Manalapan, and Rockingham Historic Site in Princeton, where General Washington wrote "Farewell to the Armies" while the Continental Congress met at Nassau Hall in Princeton.

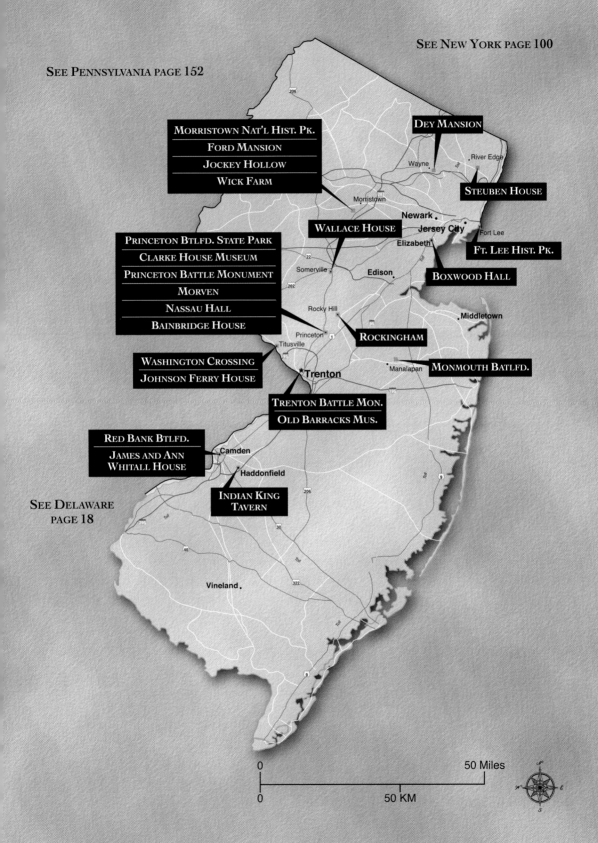

SEE NEW YORK PAGE 100

SEE PENNSYLVANIA PAGE 152

DEY MANSION

River Edge

Wayne

MORRISTOWN NAT'L HIST. PK.
FORD MANSION
JOCKEY HOLLOW
WICK FARM

STEUBEN HOUSE

Morristown

Newark

Jersey City

Fort Lee

WALLACE HOUSE

Elizabeth

FT. LEE HIST. PK.

PRINCETON BTLFD. STATE PARK
CLARKE HOUSE MUSEUM
PRINCETON BATTLE MONUMENT
MORVEN
NASSAU HALL
BAINBRIDGE HOUSE

Somerville

Edison

BOXWOOD HALL

Rocky Hill

Middletown

Princeton

ROCKINGHAM

Titusville

WASHINGTON CROSSING
JOHNSON FERRY HOUSE

Manalapan

MONMOUTH BATLFD.

Trenton

TRENTON BATTLE MON.
OLD BARRACKS MUS.

RED BANK BTLFD.
JAMES AND ANN
WHITALL HOUSE

Camden

Haddonfield

INDIAN KING
TAVERN

SEE DELAWARE
PAGE 18

Vineland

0   50 Miles

0   50 KM

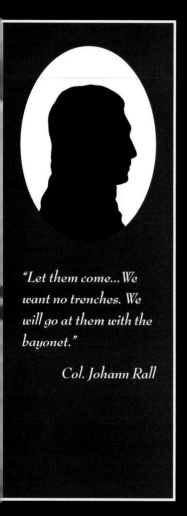

"Let them come... We want no trenches. We will go at them with the bayonet."

Col. Johann Rall

BRITISH

COMMANDERS:
Col. Johann Rall,
Gen. Lord Charles Cornwallis

STRENGTH: 1,500

CASUALTIES:
114 killed; 948 prisoners

BATTLE OF TRENTON

December 26, 1776

At the close of 1776, General George Washington was desperate for a victory. Three-quarters of his army would disappear on December 31 as their recruits' enlistments were up on that day. Washington knew that perhaps before they could be replaced, the British and Hessians might come across the Delaware River and attack Philadelphia.

Although he was risking his whole army, Washington became convinced that he must attack across the Delaware before his army disappeared. If he failed, he would be cut off from retreat by the river and there would be no hope of another crossing.

Washington resolved to attack Trenton where British and Hessian troops were quartered. There were to be three separate divisions crossing the river in three places. The plan called for the army, after taking Trenton, to push on to Princeton and then New Brunswick.

They used Durham boats that were forty to sixty feet long, eight feet wide, and two feet deep. The boats were keeled and pointed at each end, which meant they could travel in either direction. Each boat carried a mast with two sails and required a crew of four. The larger boats could carry fifteen tons while drawing only twenty inches and could carry artillery, horses, and many men.

Today, we cannot fully appreciate the Revolution without understanding the crossing of the Delaware. Washington's army was poorly clad. Few had proper shoes; many had no shoes at all. One of his staff officers wrote in his diary before they embarked: "Christmas 6:00 P.M. . .It is fearfully cold and raw and a snowstorm setting in. The wind is northeast and beats in the faces of the men. It will be a terrible night for the soldiers who have no shoes. Some of them have tied old rags around their feet, but I have not heard a man complain."

The crossing began at 5:00 P.M., but the night was bitterly cold and the river was full of blocks of ice. They had planned to be across the river by midnight, leaving five hours in which to cover the nine miles to Trenton before daybreak. Instead, Washington's army completed the crossing at 3:00 A.M., and it took another hour to assemble the troops and begin the march

Washington at the Battle of Trenton

toward Trenton. Washington divided his force and moved with one section toward Trenton from the northwest, leaving the second section, commanded by General Sullivan, on River Road from the west. At 5:30 A.M., Sullivan sent word that his muskets could not fire because of the sleet. Washington replied, "...use the bayonet. I am resolved to take Trenton."

The staff officer who wrote in his diary before the crossing also wrote, "I have never seen Washington so determined as he is now. He stands on the bank of the stream, wrapped in his cloak, superintending the landing of his troops. He is calm and collected, but very determined. The storm is changing to sleet and cuts like a knife."

Washington reached Trenton at 8:30 A.M., three hours behind schedule. He expected to find the 1,400 Hessians waiting as a result of an earlier, unauthorized Continental raid on the outposts. Because of heavy drinking and celebrating the night before, however, the Hessians and British were not prepared for the two-pronged attack on the city. After an hour of fighting from house to house and in hand-to-hand bayonet fighting, the Hessians surrendered to Washington.

The Hessian commander, Colonel Johann Gottlieb Rall, had gone to a Christmas Eve supper at the home of a town merchant, where he enjoyed wine and a game of cards. In the middle of the night, a visitor requested to speak with Rall. The servant would not admit the stranger, who then wrote a note that was delivered to Rall. The note contained the message that the Americans were marching on Trenton. Rall probably never read it. If he did read it, he discounted the message, for two days later it was found in his pocket upon his death.

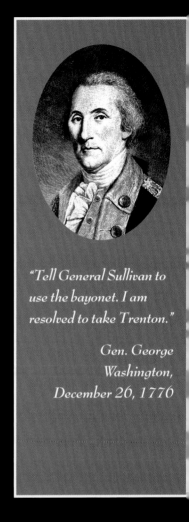

"Tell General Sullivan to use the bayonet. I am resolved to take Trenton."

Gen. George Washington, December 26, 1776

AMERICAN

COMMANDER: Gen. George Washington

STRENGTH: 2,400

CASUALTIES: 4

BRITISH

COMMANDERS:
Gen. Lord Charles Cornwallis,
Lt. Col. Charles Mawhood

STRENGTH: 1,200

CASUALTIES:
28 killed; 58 wounded;
187 missing

BATTLE OF PRINCETON

January 3, 1777

After his victory at Trenton, General George Washington learned that General Lord Charles Cornwallis, who was in New York at the time of the attack on Trenton, had begun to advance toward Trenton. Because of their precarious position with their backs to the Delaware, the Continentals used delaying tactics to detain Cornwallis from entering Trenton until night. When he saw Continental fires lighting up their trenches, Cornwallis decided to wait until daylight to attack. In the morning, however, the British discovered that all American trenches were empty and Washington had escaped to Princeton using the old Quaker Road. Cornwallis had left Princeton with about 1,200 troops commanded by Lieutenant Colonel Charles Mawhood to guard supplies.

Just outside Princeton, Washington ordered General Hugh Mercer and his force to destroy a bridge on the more direct Post Road to Princeton. At the bridge, Mercer ran into the British troops and cavalry led by Mawhood. Both commanders thought they had encountered a patrol, and both raced to the high ground now called Mercer Heights. After exchanging fire, Mawhood ordered his troops to charge with bayonets. The Americans were in trouble because only a few had muskets and bayonets. Washington, hearing the assault, ordered 600 Pennsylvania militia under General Cadwalader to reinforce Mercer. They arrived just as Mercer's men had begun a retreat with Mercer mortally wounded. Cadwalader's men began confidently, but fled when the British fired a volley into the force. At this time, Washington took command, rallied the terrorized men, and led his men against an unflinching British line. This action turned an American retreat into a British rout—they began fighting their way south to Cornwallis and retreating to Princeton. Washington then turned toward Princeton, where he learned that the Americans had already defeated the regiment left to guard supplies—they had a cannon brought up and fired two shots at Nassau Hall, where the British had attempted to take shelter.

Following this, Washington called off pursuit so that he could keep the army together and begin marching north before

Cornwallis could move on his rear. The last Americans were heading out of Princeton as Cornwallis's men entered from the south.

This forty-five-minute battle was a great American victory—Washington had now succeeded in driving the British from most of New Jersey.

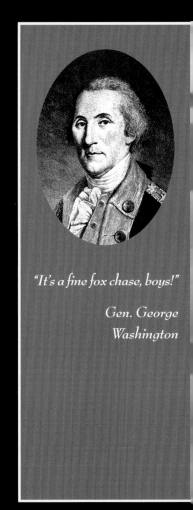

"It's a fine fox chase, boys!"

Gen. George Washington

AMERICAN

COMMANDER:
Gen. George Washington

CASUALTIES:
40 killed or wounded

An engraving after John Trumbull's painting of the American victory at Princeton

FORT LEE HISTORIC PARK ———————

Hudson Terrace, Fort Lee, NJ 07024
PHONE: 201-461-1776
HOURS: Open Wednesday to Sunday.
ADMISSION: A parking fee.

George Washington ordered the building of Fort Lee along the Hudson River to prevent the British from sailing up the river and to protect New York City. Across the river from Fort Lee stood Fort Washington, where British troops were stationed. On November 20, 1776, the Patriots abandoned Fort Lee and retreated into Pennsylvania. Fort Lee Historical Park includes reconstructed cannon batteries and a visitor's center that features exhibits on the Revolutionary War.

PRINCETON BATTLEFIELD STATE PARK ———

500 Mercer Road, Princeton, NJ 08540
PHONE: 609-921-0074
HOURS: Open daily.
ADMISSION: Free.

Princeton Battlefield State Park is now designated as a National Historic Landmark and covers eighty-five acres. The site commemorates the conclusion of Washington's ten-day offensive commencing with the crossing of the Delaware on Christmas night and ending with the Battle of Princeton. It was at Princeton that Washington had his first victory against British Regulars in the field. On the grounds are the Thomas Clarke House Museum, which features a Revolutionary War firearms and sword display. The Quaker Meeting House is nearby. Princeton Battlefield is noted for the Mercer Oak, which once stood in the middle of the battlefield and marks the spot where General Hugh Mercer was mortally wounded. The oak collapsed in March of 2000.

CLARKE HOUSE MUSEUM

PHONE: 609-921-0074
HOURS: Open Wednesday to Sunday.
ADMISSION: Free.

The Clarke House, built by Thomas Clarke in 1772, is on the battleground and served as a sanctuary for General Mercer, who died there nine days after being mortally wounded. A grave with both British and American dead from the Battle of Princeton is also within the park. The house has been restored with period furniture and contains exhibits related to the Revolutionary War.

PRINCETON BATTLE MONUMENT ———————

Stockton and Bayard Streets, Princeton, NJ 08540
The Princeton Battle Monument, located on park property in the borough of Princeton, was dedicated in 1922 by President Warren G. Harding. The monument consists of a figure which represents "Liberty" rallying General Washington and his troops and the death of General Hugh Mercer.

Nassau Hall

1 Nassau Hall, Princeton University, Princeton, NJ 08540
PHONE: 609-258-3603
HOURS: Open daily; closed mid-December to early January.
ADMISSION: Free.

Nassau Hall was built in 1756. At the time, it was not only the largest academic building in the colonies, but it also housed the entire College of New Jersey—now Princeton University—for nearly fifty years. During the Revolution, both British and American troops were at different times quartered there. They plundered the library, ruined the organ in the prayer hall, and broke up the furniture and woodwork for fuel. During the Battle of Princeton, Nassau Hall changed hands three times. While the British were in charge, Washington's artillery shot a cannonball through a window in the prayer hall. This shot destroyed a portrait of George II, while another hit the south wall of the west wing and left a scar which is still visible. Between June and November of 1783,

Nassau Hall served as the nation's capital, during which time the Continental Congress met there. Today, the building houses Princeton's administration offices. Visitors are allowed to see the Memorial Room, but access to other parts of the building is only offered through Orange Key Tours, which begin at Frist Campus Center.

Nassau Hall

Bainbridge House

158 Nassau Street, Princeton, NJ 08542
PHONE: 609-921-6748
HOURS: Open Tuesday to Sunday.
ADMISSION: Free.

Bainbridge House was built in 1766 by Job Stockton, a prosperous tanner and cousin of Richard Stockton, a signer of the Declaration of Independence. The house was the birthplace of William Bainbridge, a hero of the War of 1812, and hence the house received its name. In 1783, members of the Continental Congress stayed here. The house has been restored to its original appearance by the Historical Society of Princeton. Almost all of the 1766 structure is intact, and most

Bainbridge House

of its original woodwork remains, including the paneled walls and flooring. The interior trim was restored to original paint colors, the pine flooring was refinished, and portions of the brick facade were replaced with eighteenth-century bricks and repainted. The Bainbridge House is the headquarters for the historical society and contains a museum and library.

ROCKINGHAM HISTORIC SITE ———

108 County Road 518, Princeton, NJ 08540
PHONE: 609-921-8835
HOURS: Open Wednesday to Sunday.
ADMISSION: Free.

Rockingham, the estate belonging to Judge John Berrien, served as Washington's final wartime headquarters. George and Martha Washington rented the two-story farmhouse from Berrien's widow in 1783. While Congress met in Princeton to await the signing of the treaty with England, Washington wrote his "Farewell Address to the Armies" here. The site is furnished with period pieces and will be closed until late 2001 for relocation and restoration.

Rockingham Historic Site

MORVEN ———

55 Stockton Street, Princeton, NJ 08540
PHONE: 609-683-4495
HOURS: House is closed temporarily for renovation; garden open in spring, summer, and fall.
ADMISSION: Not available.

The original mansion on this site was built by Richard Stockton III, signer of the Declaration of Independence, and his wife Annis Boudinot Stockton, a published poet. Stockton was captured and imprisoned by the British for a month at the end of 1776. During his imprisonment, British officers resided in Morven in order to oversee the occupation of New Jersey. When Stockton was released and returned home, he found that his estate had been looted and the library and furniture pillaged by British troops. Although Stockton died in 1781, his wife, Annis, continued to live at Morven. In 1783, while the Continental Congress was meeting in Princeton, she and her brother Elias, who was president of the Congress, hosted George and Martha Washington. Morven was one of Princeton's social hubs during the eighteenth century, and the original dwelling dates from the 1750s, though research indicates that little of the original structure remains. The home is presently being restored; the exterior of the house, the interior and exterior of the servants' quarters, and the historic gardens are completed. Morven will be closed for tours until the second phase of restoration has been completed. During the spring, summer, and fall, the gardens are open for tours.

INDIAN KING TAVERN MUSEUM

233 Kings' Highway East, Haddonfield, NJ 08033
PHONE: 856-429-6792
HOURS: Open Wednesday to Sunday; closed on Tuesday and Wednesday following a Monday holiday.
ADMISSION: Free guided tours.

The Indian King Tavern, named for local Lenape Indians, was built in 1750 and is an example of eighteenth-century colonial tavern architecture. The tavern became a Revolutionary War meeting place for New Jersey's Legislature, and it was at this site, in 1777, that the state's Great Seal was adopted and New Jersey officially became a state. Guided tours are available by appointment for groups of ten or more.

Indian King Tavern Museum

MORRISTOWN NATIONAL HISTORICAL PARK

Morristown Avenue and Route 287 Washington Place, Morristown, NJ
PHONE: 973-539-2085
HOURS: Open daily; closed Thanksgiving Day, Christmas Day, and New Year's Day.
ADMISSION: A fee is charged.

The Morristown National Historical Park encompasses 1,700 acres and preserves those sites in the Morristown area that Washington and the Continental army occupied during the Revolutionary War from 1779 to 1780. Washington chose the Morristown area for its logistical, geographical, and topographical military advantages, in addition to its proximity to New York City, which was occupied by the British in 1779. Also on the park grounds are the Jacob Ford Mansion, General Washington's military headquarters; the Upper Redoubt site; the historic Wick House and Farm, headquarters of General Arthur St. Clair; and the Guerin house, home of a local farmer who did not take kindly to the commandeering of his sheep and rations. This house is a private residence and is not open to the public. There are also over twenty-seven miles of hiking trails in the Jockey Hollow where Washington's men built their winter huts. Replica huts are open to the public. A two-mile loop is open to automobiles.

Morristown National Historical Park

FORD MANSION

The Ford Mansion was one of the finest homes in Morristown. Mrs. Ford invited General George Washington to make his headquarters at the mansion, and he did so during the winter of 1779–80. Washington brought with him such a large contingent of aides-de-camp and servants that Mrs. Ford and her four young children were forced to live in only two rooms of the house. Guided tours feature rooms in which Washington conducted his daily briefings and worked out military strategy.

JOCKEY HOLLOW

Jockey Hollow features five soldier huts that are replicas of those built in the winter of 1779–80, which by most accounts was the worst winter in New Jersey in 100 years. When the Continental soldiers arrived for winter quarters, they had to build the huts. General Washington directed that the enlisted huts be built first. The first huts were ready to be occupied by Christmas, and the last of the officers' huts were completed by mid-February.

WICK FARM

The Wick family was prosperous, their home comfortable, and their farm large, including 1,400 acres of timber and open fields. This farm was the perfect place for winter quarters of 13,000 American soldiers in 1779-80. The Wick farmhouse served as the headquarters for General Arthur St. Clair.

WASHINGTON CROSSING STATE PARK ———

355 Washington Crossing-Pennington Road, Titusville, NJ 08560
PHONE: 609-737-0623
HOURS: Open daily.
ADMISSION: A fee is charged from Memorial Day to Labor Day.

Washington Crossing State Park commemorates the crossing of the ice-clogged Delaware River by General Washington and his 2,400 troops on December 25, 1776 to attack the Hessian garrison at Trenton. After crossing the rough winter river at night, General George Washington and the Continental army landed at Johnson's Ferry, at the site now known as Washington Crossing State Park. At 4:00 A.M., they began their march to Trenton, where they defeated the Hessian troops in an unexpected attack. This battle was quickly followed by the second Battle of Trenton on January 2, 1777, and the Battle of Princeton on January 3, 1777. Markers along the Continental Lane in the park mark the beginning of Washington's route to Trenton. After the crossing, Washington took shelter in the Ferry House, which is now a museum and restored tavern. The visitor's center interprets events surrounding the Battle of Trenton. The 841-acre park features trails and interpretive signs.

JOHNSON FERRY HOUSE

Washington Crossing State Park, NJ
PHONE: 609-737-2515
HOURS: Open Wednesday to Sunday.
ADMISSION: Free.

This early eighteenth-century farm-house near the Delaware River was built by Garret Johnson, who operated a 490-acre colonial plantation and a ferry service along the river. General Washington and other officers likely used the house briefly during the crossing of the Delaware on Christmas night. The keeping room, bedchamber, and textile room are furnished with period pieces similar to those used by the Johnson family from 1740 to 1770.

Sitting room at Johnson Ferry House

Bedchamber at Johnson Ferry House

JAMES AND ANN WHITALL HOUSE

6 Blackwood-Barnsboro Road, Sewell, NJ 08080
PHONE: 856-468-0100
HOURS: Open Wednesday to Friday all year; open on weekends in the spring and fall.
ADMISSION: Free.

Whitall House was built in 1748 by James and Ann Whitall and served as both the headquarters for the Americans during the Revolutionary War and later as a field hospital.

STEUBEN HOUSE

1209 Main Street, River Edge, NJ 07661
PHONE: 201-487-1739
HOURS: Open Wednesday to Sunday.
ADMISSION: A fee is charged.

The Steuben House was presented to Baron von Steuben in 1783 by the state of New Jersey in gratitude for his assistance to the colonies during the Revolutionary War. The house contains a fine collection of colonial and early New Jersey furnishings. Because the site of the home saw so much of the fighting during the Revolutionary War, the Steuben House boasts that it has seen more of the Revolution than any other house in America.

Steuben House

WALLACE HOUSE

71 Somerset Street, Somerville, NJ 08876
PHONE: 908-725-1015
HOURS: Open Wednesday to Sunday; closed state and federal holidays.
ADMISSION: Free.

The Wallace House was built in 1776 by John Wallace, who named it Hope Farm. Wallace was a successful Philadelphia merchant and leased the house to General Washington during the Middlebrook winter encampment from December 1778 to June 1779. The house is a fine example of Georgian architecture and is furnished with eighteenth-century pieces.

BOXWOOD HALL

1073 East Jersey Street, Elizabeth, NJ 07201
PHONE: 973-648-4540
HOURS: Open Monday to Saturday.
ADMISSION: Free.

Boxwood Hall was built around 1750, then later became the residence of Elias Boudinot, president of the Continental Congress that ratified the Peace Treaty with Great Britain. George Washington visited here in 1789 on his way to New York for his first inauguration. The house has an incredible collection of American furniture from the period of 1760 to 1840.

NEW YORK

New York was settled by the Dutch West India Company in 1621; but in 1664, the British went to war to gain control of the area. At the start of the Revolution, General Howe planned to use New York as the British base during the war. But Washington understood the importance of holding New York against the British when he said, "It is the Place that we must use every Endeavour to keep from them. For should they get that Town, and the Command of the North River, they can stop the Intercourse between the northern and southern Colonies, upon which depends the Safety of America."

The British landed on Long Island in August 1776, and throughout the war occupied much of the state. They would not evacuate the state until late in 1783, after the Treaty of Paris was signed.

Today, many sites remain in New York, from the Thomas Paine House in New Rochelle to the von Steuben Memorial in Remsen, from the Great Chain at West Point Military Academy to Fort Ticonderoga and Fort Stanwix. The Revolutionary War sites in New York are numerous. Even in New York City there are sites like Fraunces Tavern, where Washington bid farewell to his officers, and Trinity Church, the final resting place of Alexander Hamilton.

CROWN PT.

SEE VERMONT PAGE 214

Ft. TICONDEROGA

Crown Point
Ticonderoga

STEUBEN MEM.

ORISKANY BTLFD.

SARATOGA
NAT'L HIST. PK.

SKENESBOROUGH MUS.

Ft. STANWIX NAT'L MON.

Remsen

Whitehall

REV. WAR CEMETERY

Rochester

Rome • Oriskany

Salem

Utica

SEE MASSACHUSETTS
PAGE 52

Syracuse

Stillwater

Walloorvisac

BENNINGTON BTLFD.

Albany

WASHINGTON'S HEADQTRS.

VAN WYCK HOMESTEAD

Binghamton

MOUNT GULIAN

SEE CONNECTICUT
PAGE 10

GEN. H. KNOX'S HEADQTRS.

CONSTITUTION IS.

NEW WINDSOR CANTONMENT

Newburgh
Fishkill
Vails Gate
Beacon
Highland Falls
West Point

U. S. MILITARY ACADEMY

WEST POINT MUS.

STONY POINT BTLFD.

Stony Point
Katonah

SEE PENNSYLVANIA
PAGE 152

Yonkers
Tarrytown
New Rochelle

JOHN JAY HOMESTEAD ST. HIST. SITE

PHILIPSE MANOR HALL

New York

TARRYTOWN MUS.

Staten Island

THOMAS PAINE COTTAGE

SEE NEW JERSEY
PAGE 82

CONFERENCE HOUSE

THOMAS PAINE MUS.

FRAUNCES TAVERN MUS.

MORRIS-JUMEL MANSION

TRINITY CHURCH

ST. PAUL'S CHURCH

FEDERAL HALL NAT'L MEM.

WESTERN NEW YORK

OLD Ft. NIAGARA

Youngstown

Niagara Falls

Buffalo

0   100 Miles

0   100 KM

OLD FORT NIAGARA

Fort Niagara State Park, Youngstown, NY 14174
PHONE: 716-745-7611
HOURS: Open daily.
ADMISSION: A fee is charged.

Old Fort Niagara was begun by the French in 1726 and captured by the British in 1759. When the Revolution broke out in 1775, British-controlled Old Fort Niagara was instrumental in the defense of Canada and in the control of the Great Lakes. In addition, Fort Niagara was the main point of contact between the British and the Iroquois, as it became the destination of many Loyalists fleeing the western parts of the former colonies. The fortress served as a defense for the British-dominated Great Lakes and was a launching point for Loyalist raids on the frontiers of New York and Pennsylvania. The Treaty of Paris, ending the Revolution, placed the boundary between the United States and Canada through the Great Lakes. Fort Niagara fell on the American side of the line. The transfer of the fort from the British to the United States was accomplished in the summer of 1796. Old Fort Niagara offers self-guided tours of such original eighteenth-century buildings as the French Castle, two British redoubts, a bakehouse, and a large powder magazine. It also features historic fortifications and museum exhibits.

Old Fort Niagara

Old Fort Niagara

FORT STANWIX NATIONAL MONUMENT ━━━━━━

112 East Park Street, Rome, NY 13440

PHONE: 315-336-2090

HOURS: Open daily April to December; closed Thanksgiving Day and Christmas Day.

ADMISSION: Free.

Fort Stanwix was built in 1758 by the British. It fell into disrepair after 1763 until American troops under Elias Dayton began rebuilding it. In 1777, Fort Stanwix was held by 800 Americans commanded by Colonel Peter Gansevoort. The British lay siege to the fort and successfully repulsed attempts to relieve the fort, including what some call the bloodiest battle of the war at the Battle of Oriskany. Benedict Arnold led a successful expedition that relieved Fort Stanwix on August 23, 1777.

On October 22, 1784, representatives of the United States and the Iroquois Confederacy signed a peace treaty negotiated on the site of Fort Stanwix. The 1783 Treaty of Paris, which ended the American Revolutionary War fought between the United States, Great Britain, and France, did not include provisions for Great Britain's American Indian allies. This Fort Stanwix Treaty ended the war fought between the United States and the Iroquois Confederacy and served as a precedent for future United States treaties negotiated with other American Indian nations to end the war in other regions of the country. In the treaty, the Iroquois Confederacy ceded claims to land in Ohio to the United States. Following treaty negotiations, Pennsylvania representatives purchased land from the Iroquois nations up to its present northern border.

Fort Stanwix National Monument maintains an extensive archeological collection and a nearly complete reconstruction of the fort. The visitor's center is located inside the Gregg Barracks and includes an orientation diorama, theater, and bookstore. The monument also has three short trails that encircle the fort. One follows a portion of the Oneida Carrying Place, the strategic Iroquois Confederacy portage that bridged the waterways between the Atlantic Ocean and the Great Lakes. The other two trails interpret the siege of 1777.

Oriskany Battlefield State Historic Site ────────

7801 Route 69, Oriskany, NY 13424
Phone: 315-768-7224
Hours: Open Wednesday to Sunday from mid-May to mid-October.
Admission: Free.
www.nysparks.state.ny.us

The Battle of Oriskany, fought on August 6, 1777, was not only a turning point in the Revolutionary War, but it has been described as one of the bloodiest battles of the war. American General Nicholas Herkimer, 800 Colonial troops, and sixty Oneida warriors were on their way to Fort Stanwix to relieve the siege of the fort. British troops with their Native American allies, led by Mohawk Joseph Brant, attacked them in a ravine west of Oriskany Creek. The fighting was hand-to-hand. Although Herkimer was wounded in the leg and his horse killed, he continued to issue commands while propped against a tree. The Colonials suffered heavy losses, but still caused the Seneca, Mohawks, and British to retreat. The wound to Herkimer's leg resulted in his death ten days later. This battle contributed to the British defeat at Saratoga. The battlefield contains a visitor's center, tours, self-guided paths, and interpretive signs.

The wounded American Brigadier General Nicholas Herkimer at Oriskany

STEUBEN MEMORIAL STATE HISTORIC SITE

Starr Hill Road, Remsen, NY 13438
PHONE: 315-768-7224
HOURS: Open Wednesday to Sunday from mid-May to mid-October.
ADMISSION: Free.
www.nysparks.state.ny.us

The Steuben Memorial honors Frederich Wilhelm Augustus, Baron von Steuben, known as "the drillmaster of the American Revolution." The Prussian General Steuben was at Valley Forge, the location of the main body of American troops during the winter of 1777-78, and acted as advisor to the poorly trained American army. With little knowledge of English, Steuben, through interpreters, converted the ragged and starving army into a well-trained fighting force. The American army learned to inspect arms, mount guard, act as sentries, march in columns, and use bayonets in combat. Steuben's manual, *Regulations for the Order and Discipline of the Troops of the United States*, known as the "Blue Book," is still basic to military training and organization. After the war, Steuben became an American citizen and New York granted him 1,600 acres of land in the Mohawk Valley in gratitude of his work with the military. A replica of his cabin is at the Steuben Memorial State Site, which contains period pieces. In a five-acre wooded area, known as the Sacred Grove, a plain, large monument marks Steuben's burial spot.

CROWN POINT STATE HISTORIC SITE

Route 903, Crown Point, NY 12928
PHONE: 518-597-4666
HOURS: Open Wednesday to Saturday from mid-May to October.
ADMISSION: A fee is charged.

The ownership of Crown Point was disputed by both the French and British until it was finally abandoned by the French in 1759. The British began reconstruction of the fort as a fortification complex in the British conquest of Canada and control of Lake Champlain. Seth Warner and some of the Green Mountain Boys captured the fort on May 11, 1775, along with needed cannons and heavy ordnance. In 1777, General John Burgoyne's army occupied Crown Point after the American evacuation to Mount Independence. Crown Point remained under British control until the end of the war. The ruins of the fort include the remains of the moat, stonework, bastions, and barracks. A visitor's center includes historical exhibits to explain the fort and its significance.

Capt. William Delaplace

BRITISH

COMMANDER:
Capt. William Delaplace

STRENGTH: 50

CASUALTIES:
50 taken prisoner

BATTLE OF FORT TICONDEROGA

May 10, 1775

Where Lake George empties its waters into Lake Champlain, the lake narrows to one-half mile, and at one point, the passage is less than a quarter mile. At this point, on a high bluff overlooking the water, stands Fort Ticonderoga. The French built the first fort here in 1755. In 1758 they held off a British attack, but a year later, the British attacked again with 11,000 men and overcame the 400 French soldiers. The French blew up the fort and retreated. When the British rebuilt the fortifications, they named it Fort Ticonderoga.

Benedict Arnold and Ethan Allen had both expressed the belief that, when the American revolt finally came, Fort Ticonderoga would be the key to the invasion route between Canada and the American colonies. When Arnold heard the news of the events at Lexington and Concord, he headed toward Boston. On the way, he heard of the critical shortage of artillery for the siege of Boston. Arnold knew Fort Ticonderoga held a large store of heavy cannon, twenty brass pieces, a dozen large mortars, and several small arms and stores. Arnold proposed an attack on Fort Ticonderoga to the Massachusetts Congress and received orders to proceed.

Meanwhile, on May 7, two hundred men from Connecticut, Massachusetts, and the New Hampshire Grants, what is

Capture of Fort Ticonderoga: Ethan Allen and Captain Delaplace

Cannon at Fort Ticonderoga

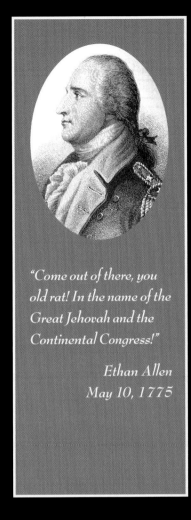

now modern day Vermont, met at Castleton, New York. They chose a Committee of War and elected Ethan Allen as commander. Arnold met up with Allen and his men.

The fort was barely defended and had twenty-four women and children as military personnel; it was taken without a shot fired. After the surrender of the fort, the next and perhaps most difficult task was to transport the guns to Boston. Henry Knox, a former bookseller who became commander of artillery, directed the transportation of the cannon the following winter. Oxen dragged them by sled for three hundred miles from New York to Massachusetts. The guns were just what the army besieging Boston needed, and the success of Ticonderoga and the eventual transportation of the guns led directly to the British evacuation of Boston. In 1777, British forces led by General John Burgoyne forced the Americans to abandon Fort Ticonderoga, but the Americans regained the fort after Burgoyne's surrender at Saratoga.

AMERICAN

COMMANDERS:
Benedict Arnold,
Ethan Allen

STRENGTH: 83

CASUALTIES: 0

FORT TICONDEROGA

Route 74 East, Ticonderoga, NY 12883

PHONE: 518-585-2821

HOURS: Open daily from May to October.

ADMISSION: A fee is charged.

The reconstruction of Fort Ticonderoga began in 1908, and President William Howard Taft celebrated the opening of the fort and a new museum in 1909. The fort was restored according to early plans. Today, the museum contains items that offer a glimpse into the reality of life during the time of the Revolution. Items displayed include personal possessions, entrenching tools, ice creepers, camp stoves, and medical equipment. Visitors can also see reproduced barracks built first of logs and reinforced with earth that would hold a winter garrison of 400 men. Other items that bring to mind the past include one of the gun barrels brought from Fort Ticonderoga to Boston and a shattered mortar hauled from Lake Champlain. The fort offers drills, fife and drum corps performances, and demonstrations of cannon firings.

Fort Ticonderoga

Cannon at Fort Ticonderoga

SKENESBOROUGH MUSEUM

Route 22, Whitehall, NY 12887
PHONE: 518-499-0716
HOURS: Open Monday to Saturday from mid-June to Labor Day and Saturday and Sunday from Labor Day to mid-October.
ADMISSION: Free.

The Skenesborough Museum features a sixteen-foot diorama of the 1776 shipyard of Whitehall, New York. The ships built in Skenesborough were under the command of Benedict Arnold. For this reason, the city of Whitehall considers itself the birthplace of the American navy. During the spring of 1776, British forces planned to take control of Lake Champlain. American forces hurriedly built a fleet of ships to defend the lake. Benedict Arnold commanded the fleet of fifteen warships that was defeated by the British during the Battle of Valcour Island on October 11, 1776. Arnold planned a nighttime retreat past the British blockade. Arnold's remaining gunboats slipped past the British fleet and fought three more days before retreating to Fort Ticonderoga. This battle is exhibited at the museum, which also displays models of the first naval yard and the hull of the USS *Ticonderoga* which was sunk during the War of 1812 and raised from Lake Champlain in 1958. Recently the remains of what is believed to be one of Arnold's gunboats have been discovered at the bottom of Lake Champlain.

REVOLUTIONARY WAR CEMETERY

Corner of Archibald Street and State 22, Salem, NY 12865
PHONE: Not available.
HOURS: Open daily.
ADMISSION: Free.

The Revolutionary War Cemetery at Salem is on an old burial ground that was begun with the first burial in 1769. Legend tells that after the Battle of Saratoga in 1777, 100 soldiers were brought to Salem for burial in a common grave. In addition, the cemetery can document the burials of 101 Revolutionary War soldiers.

"The fortune of war, General Gates, has made me your prisoner."

Maj. Gen. John Burgoyne

BRITISH

COMMANDER:
Maj. Gen. John Burgoyne

FREEMAN'S FARM
STRENGTH: 7,500
CASUALTIES: 600

BEMIS HEIGHTS
STRENGTH: 6,800+
CASUALTIES: 600

BATTLES OF SARATOGA—
FREEMAN'S FARM AND BEMIS HEIGHTS

September 19 and October 7, 1777

On the morning of September 19, 1777, British General John Burgoyne began moving his three divisions toward Stillwater, New York. American General Horatio Gates was firmly ensconced behind fortifications on Bemis Heights on the Hudson River and commanded a superior force of seasoned Continental soldiers and skilled riflemen. Despite his advantage, Gates waited for the British to attack. Posted about a mile ahead of this line, American scouts—Colonel Daniel Morgan's rifle corps—had taken position in buildings on the John Freeman farm. From there, they could clearly see the red coats of advancing British soldiers.

Surprising the advance guard of Burgoyne's center column, Morgan's men inflicted heavy casualties on the British and pursued the survivors. Encountering the rest of the center column, the American scouts were scattered, but not before sending word of the British arrival back to Bemis Heights. American forces continued to pressure the British center column, and the fight swayed back and forth well into the afternoon.

Burgoyne had split his army into three prongs. One prong, led by German General von Riedesel, was significantly delayed. Once it arrived, von Riedesel sent his Brunswickers against Arnold's right flank, cheering and playing drums as they marched. The Americans, though still outnumbering their enemy, saw the fresh troops arrive and, with dusk falling, chose to pull back to their position on Bemis Heights.

After the battle at Freeman's Farm, technically a British victory, Burgoyne had 6,800 troops but little hope of reinforcements or food, whereas Gates had reinforcements from the militia of New England and New York flocking to Bemis Heights and bringing food, artillery, and ammunition.

Four months in the wilderness had reduced the British uniforms to rags, and they were almost out of food. Their horses and oxen were beginning to die of starvation, and soldiers were deserting—some to the American side. Night after night, the Americans fired on the British.

Surrender of General Burgoyne at Saratoga, painting by John Trumbull

Burgoyne insisted on one last offensive. He attempted, on October 7, a "reconnaissance in force" to test the strength of the Americans. The reconnoitering party formed three columns and moved southwest from Freeman's Farm. After less than a mile, they stopped in the middle of a wheat field and waited. The troops' line extended about one thousand yards across the fields, with their east flank in thick woods and their west flank at the base of a far hill.

Gates got wind of the British action and ordered Colonel Morgan's corps to attack the British right, while General Poor's brigade came against the enemy's left. The two detachments moved through the dense forest to surprise and attack the British at the same time. Poor's men arrived first, fired upon the British grenadiers, and captured their general. Morgan's men moved into position and attacked the right. The British center, left unprotected, withdrew to the fortifications. American forces attacked the British fortifications during the night, and the British fell back to their river fortifications.

By October 8, Burgoyne began to retreat northward to Saratoga, but the Americans pursued. Burgoyne held out another nine days and then surrendered 5,700 soldiers, six generals, thirty guns, and 5,000 small arms. With Burgoyne's surrender, all British outposts in the north were withdrawn to Canada. All but New York City, Rhode Island, and Philadelphia now belonged to the Americans.

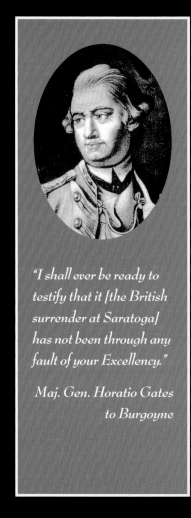

"I shall ever be ready to testify that it [the British surrender at Saratoga] has not been through any fault of your Excellency."

Maj. Gen. Horatio Gates to Burgoyne

AMERICAN

COMMANDER:
Maj. Gen. Horatio Gates

FREEMAN'S FARM
STRENGTH: 8,500
(3,000 engaged)
CASUALTIES: 300

BEMIS HEIGHTS
STRENGTH: 14,000
CASUALTIES: 150-200

SARATOGA NATIONAL HISTORICAL PARK ——

648 Route 32, Stillwater, NY 12170

PHONE: 518-664-9821 ext. 224

HOURS: Open daily; closed Thanksgiving Day, Christmas Day, and New Year's Day. Tour Road open April to mid-November as weather permits.

ADMISSION: A fee is charged.

www.nps.gov/sara

Neilson House

Saratoga National Historical Park spreads over 3,500 acres and contains the Saratoga Battlefield, the Saratoga Monument in the town of Victory, and the Schuyler House. The visitor's center at the park shows a twenty-minute introductory film every half-hour. A small museum contains artifacts from the time of the battles, including original cannon from the defeated British army. A self-guided tour is marked along a single-lane, one-way road that passes through the American and British defensive positions. Along the way are ten interpretive stops, including the Neilson House, which served as the headquarters for the American forces. Maps are available at the visitor's center. There are also hiking trails in the north part of the park for which maps are available. The park offers many varied programs and activities throughout the year, including encampments and living history demonstrations. In February, His Majesty's 24th Regiment of Foot hosts its annual recruitment for portraying the life of a British soldier in eighteenth-century America. In June, many eighteenth-century American reenactors show daily life in an American camp. The Frost Faire in January displays colonial winter activities. The anniversary of the Battles of Saratoga is celebrated annually with an encampment and other activities.

SCHUYLER HOUSE

Route 4, Schuylerville, NY 12871

PHONE: 518-664-9821 ext.224 (Saratoga NHS)

HOURS: Open Wednesday to Sunday from late June to Labor Day.

ADMISSION: Free.

The Schuyler House, burned by the retreating British after the Battles of Saratoga, was rebuilt within thirty days of Burgoyne's surrender. This house was the country estate of General Philip Schuyler, a noted statesman and military leader. Schuyler directed the Canada invasion of 1775, organized the caravan that carried cannon from Fort Ticonderoga to Boston, and kept General Burgoyne at the Schuyler family's Albany mansion after Burgoyne surrendered at Saratoga. Schuyler was twice a delegate to the Continental Congress, and his daughter married Alexander Hamilton in 1780 in the drawing room of the house. Volunteers in period-style clothing offer guided tours of the house during the summer. In mid-October, the house reopens for one evening of candlelight tours.

Schuyler House

SARATOGA MONUMENT

Burgoyne Street, Victory, NY 12884
PHONE: 518-664-9821 ext. 224
HOURS: Open daily.
ADMISSION: Free.

The obelisk of the Saratoga Monument rises 154½ feet to commemorate the Battles of Saratoga and General John Burgoyne's surrender on October 17, 1777. On each face of the obelisk is a niche for a bust of each of the commanding officers: Horatio Gates, Philip Schuyler, Daniel Morgan, and Benedict Arnold. Arnold's niche, however, is empty in testimony to his later treason and escape to England.

Saratoga Monument

BENNINGTON BATTLEFIELD

Route 67, Walloomsac, NY
PHONE: 518-686-7109
HOURS: Not available.
ADMISSION: Not available.

In August 1777, British General Burgoyne directed Lieutenant Colonel Friedrich Baum to raid the storehouses at Bennington in what is now Vermont. The Americans attacked the British at Walloomsac, New York and defeated them in a two-hour battle led by Brigadier General John Stark. Two hundred British were killed and the rest were captured. At the battlefield, relief maps and markers help to explain the battle to visitors.

VAN WYCK HOMESTEAD MUSEUM AND LIBRARY

P.O. Box 133, 504 Route 9, Fishkill, NY 12524-0133
PHONE: 845-896-9560
HOURS: Museum open Saturday and Sunday; library open Tuesday, Wednesday, and Saturday from Memorial Day to October.
ADMISSION: Free.

The Van Wyck Homestead was built in 1732 by Dutch settlers and today is the site of a library and museum rich in Revolutionary War material. The homestead site was the headquarters for the supply depot for General Washington's army from 1776 through 1783. The house features Revolutionary War items as well as artifacts relating to the history of Fishkill. The house also features lectures and guided tours.

Van Wyck Homestead Museum and Library

MOUNT GULIAN

Near Newburgh/Beacon Bridge, Fishkill, NY 12524
PHONE: 845-831-8172
HOURS: Open Wednesday to Sunday from April to December or by appointment.
ADMISSION: A fee is charged.

Mount Gulian, built circa 1730 by Dutch merchant Gulian Verplanck, became the Revolutionary War headquarters of General Friedrich von Steuben, who was instrumental in changing the ragtag Patriot volunteers into the Continental army. The Society of the Cincinnati, a fraternal organization of Revolutionary War officers and the country's first veterans' organization, was founded here in May

Mount Gulian

1783. Today, Mount Gulian is headquarters for the New York State Society of the Cincinnati. Additionally, the site is historically connected to the Native Americans and nineteenth-century African American culture. Forty-four acre Mount Gulian overlooks the Hudson River and consists of the reconstructed homestead, an eighteenth century Dutch barn, and a restored garden.

WASHINGTON'S HEADQUARTERS STATE HISTORIC SITE

84 Liberty Street, Newburgh, NY 12551
PHONE: 845-562-1195
HOURS: Open Wednesday to Sunday from mid-April to October.
ADMISSION: A fee is charged.

Washington's Headquarters

Washington's Headquarters is the former home of Jonathan Hasbrouck. The house was built sometime between 1750 and 1770 and functioned as the headquarters for General Washington from April 1782 until August 1783. The home features period furnishings, firearms, and military artifacts; guided tours are available. Washington's Headquarters Museum is in a separate building on the grounds and features colonial artifacts.

GENERAL HENRY KNOX'S HEADQUARTERS STATE HISTORIC SITE

Route 94 and Old Forge Hill Road, Vails Gate, NY 12584
PHONE: 845-561-5498
HOURS: Open Wednesday to Sunday from Memorial Day to Labor Day.
ADMISSION: A fee is charged.

American Major General Henry Knox established his military headquarters at this house several times during the war. Knox, who at one time was joined at the house by his wife and children, occupied the headquarters the longest of any of the generals, but he was not the only general to establish his headquarters here. Major General Horatio Gates also occupied the home, as did General Nathanael Greene. The elegant 1754 Georgian-style home has been restored with period furniture and portable camp equipment that the Continental officers used.

NEW WINDSOR CANTONMENT STATE HISTORIC SITE

Route 300, Vails Gate, NY 12584
PHONE: 845-561-1765
HOURS: Open Wednesday to Sunday from mid-April to October.
ADMISSION: A fee is charged.

At the site of the New Windsor Cantonment, seven thousand troops of the Continental army, accompanied by about five hundred women and children, transformed the 1,600 acres of forest and meadows into a military enclave or cantonment. This was their home from October 1782 to June 1783. Today, the visitor's center offers exhibits on the history of the site. There is a living-history exhibit, featuring musket and artillery demonstrations and a blacksmith. Also on the site is a recreated camp and a temple building that is a reproduction of the original Temple of Virtue. At the Temple of Virtue, Washington addressed his officers in 1783 with the intent of defusing a possible riot.

Reconstructed Temple at the New Windsor Cantonment

UNITED STATES MILITARY ACADEMY ————————

West Point Highway, Highland Falls, NY 10996
PHONE: 845-938-2638
HOURS: Visitor's Center open daily; closed Thanksgiving Day, Christmas Day, and New Year's Day.
ADMISSION: Free.
www.usma.edu

Washington called this area of the Hudson the "key to America" and ensured that the highlands of West Point were fortified with cannon and defenses overlooking the Hudson River. In 1778, Washington ordered Colonel Thaddeus Kosciuszko to design and build the fortifications, which included numerous forts and redoubts, and a Great Chain that stretched across the Hudson River from West Point to Constitution Island. In 1780, Benedict Arnold, the commander at West Point, attempted to smuggle the plans of West Point's fortifications to the British through Howe's aide-de-camp, Major John Andre. Andre was caught and hanged, whereas Arnold escaped to the British. In 1802, the United States Military Academy was established at West Point. Today, the academy includes many Revolutionary sites and monuments of interest.

FORT PUTNAM

USMA, West Point, NY

Fort Putnam was built in 1778 by Colonel Rufus Putnam's 5th Massachusetts Regiment and became the key to the network of forts and redoubts that provided West Point's defenses. The approaches to the Great Chain and the Plain were protected from this fort. Fort Putnam was originally a wood and earthen fortification but evolved into a stone fort that still stands. The trail to Fort Putnam is clearly marked but does entail a hike through the woods.

WEST POINT CEMETERY AND OLD CADET CHAPEL

Washington Road, USMA, West Point, NY

The West Point Cemetery overlooks the Hudson River and Constitution Island. Many of the more than six thousand graves are from the Revolutionary War, including America's first heroine, Margaret "Molly" Corbin, known as "Captain Molly." Margaret Corbin was with her husband at the Battle of Long Island in November 1776. After he was fatally shot, Molly manned his gun and continued to fight until she too was wounded. Many unknown Revolutionary soldiers are also buried here. A map of the cemetery is available at the Old Cadet Chapel on the grounds of the cemetery. Mounted on the inside walls of the Old Cadet Chapel are plaques representing the heroes of the Revolutionary War, including one for traitor Benedict Arnold. The information on Arnold's plaque has been scratched out.

KOSCIUSZKO MONUMENT

East of Trophy Point, USMA, West Point, NY

The Kosciuszko Monument stands on the Fort Clinton redoubt and honors Thaddeus Kosciuszko, a Polish artillery officer who assisted in the American victory at the Battle of

Saratoga. Kosciuszko came to West Point in 1778 and spent two years designing and overseeing the construction of the fortifications.

Washington Monument

On the Plain, USMA, West Point, NY

The Washington Monument commemorates George Washington, the commander in chief of the Continental army, who recognized the importance of the military position of West Point. The Plain on which the monument stands was used by Baron von Steuben as a training ground for Washington's troops. Today, as the monument of General Washington stands guard over the Plain, cadets still practice military drills here.

Great Chain

At Trophy Point, USMA, West Point, NY

The Great Chain was a five-hundred-yard chain that floated on logs and stretched across the Hudson River at West Point during the Revolutionary War. The chain was a key element in the defense of West Point and was used from 1778 until 1782. Thirteen of the links are on display at Trophy Point.

The Great Chain at Trophy Point

Constitution Island

Across the river from West Point, NY

Hours: Tour boat by appointment.

Admission: A fee is charged.

The first Revolutionary War fortifications in the West Point area were located on Constitution Island. In 1777, the British overran the fortifications, but the Americans returned in 1778. The Revolutionary fortifications are still standing and are available for tours.

WEST POINT MUSEUM

West Point Highway, Highland Falls, NY 10928
PHONE: 845-938-2203
HOURS: Open daily; closed Thanksgiving Day, Christmas Day, and New Year's Day.
ADMISSION: Free.

The West Point Museum calls itself the "oldest and largest military museum in the country." In the History of the U.S. Army gallery, there are military small arms, cannon, and uniforms from the Revolutionary War.

JOHN JAY HOMESTEAD STATE HISTORIC SITE

400 State Route 22, Katonah, NY 10536
PHONE: 845-232-5651
HOURS: Open Wednesday to Sunday from April to October.
ADMISSION: A fee is charged.

John Jay served as president of Continental Congress in 1774 and as minister to Spain during the Revolutionary War. Jay, along with Benjamin Franklin and John Adams, penned and negotiated the Treaty of Paris. Jay was later appointed the first chief justice of the United States Supreme Court. The John Jay Homestead was Jay's retirement home during the last twenty-eight years of his life. Today, visitors may tour the house, which is restored to the period of Jay's occupancy. Visitors may also take self-guided tours of the gardens and grounds and can visit the farm exhibit in the newly-restored main barn. Public events and programs are offered throughout the year.

John Jay Homestead State Historic Site

"[the American attack] would have done honor to the most veteran soldiers."

British Publication of the time

Lt. Col. Henry Johnson (pictured above)

BRITISH

COMMANDER:
Lt. Col. Henry Johnson

STRENGTH: 564

CASUALTIES: 63

BATTLE OF STONY POINT

July 15-16, 1779

During the winter of 1778-79, the Americans, now in control of the area around New York City, blockaded the city by both land and sea. To regain control of the main north-south highway across the Hudson River, British General Clinton took Stony Point and Verplanck's Point with little overall resistance.

At Stony Point, Clinton built a citadel surrounded by artillery batteries connected with trenches and an abatis, a wall of sharpened tree trunks. At high tide, this fortress became an island. Seven hundred men were left to guard Stony Point with a smaller number at Fort Lafayette, located just across the Hudson River. The sloop HMS *Vulture* provided gun support.

In spite of the seemingly impregnable fortifications, General Washington proposed a plan for Brigadier General Anthony Wayne and his men to retake Stony Point. Wayne's men with unloaded muskets (to prevent their firing) and fixed bayonets silently marched one-half mile to the fort. They approached in two columns led by twenty men with axes to cut through the abatis. Because the men had to march through the swamp created by the high tide, they were not totally silent, but the British were not alerted until the Americans began chopping the abatis. Ignoring the British fire, they made their way in. As soon as there were two large gaps, a small force outside the abatis began firing their muskets at the fort. As planned, Johnson sent half of his small garrison out of the abatis toward the shooting. Meanwhile the two columns of bayonetted forces silently moved through the abatis, over the parapet, and into the citadel. Once inside, they began shouting "The fort's our own!" Panic and confusion set in with the British, who began surrendering in droves before Johnson could get his force outside to regroup. The Americans then turned the fort's guns onto the *Vulture*, which hastily moved downstream. The fort was captured in thirty minutes.

No real military advantage was gained by the Battle of Stony Point, but the morale advantage to the Americans was huge. For the first time, the American forces were successful upon British regulars inside a fortified position. Congress applauded the news of the fall of Stony Point and heaped great praise upon General Wayne. In fact, Congress gave Wayne a gold medal and awarded silver medals to two other commanders on the American side. In addition, they gave the troops money equivalent to the value of the captured British stores.

The British, for their part, praised the Americans for their clemency to their British prisoners. The after-action assessment of the Americans included, "The rebels had made the attack with a bravery never before exhibited, and they showed at this moment a generosity and clemency, which during the course of the rebellion had no parallel."

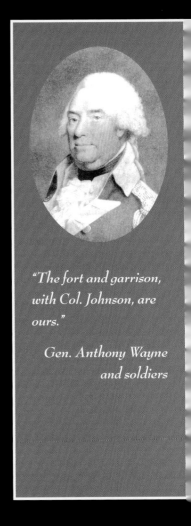

"The fort and garrison, with Col. Johnson, are ours."

Gen. Anthony Wayne and soldiers

The Stony Point Lighthouse

AMERICAN

COMMANDER:
Brig. Gen. Anthony Wayne

STRENGTH: 1,450

CASUALTIES: 15

STONY POINT BATTLEFIELD STATE HISTORIC SITE —

Park Road off NY Highway 9W (north), Stony Point, NY 10980

PHONE: 845-786-2521

HOURS: Open Wednesday to Sunday from mid-April to October.

ADMISSION: Free.

Stony Point Battlefield covers eighty-seven acres with the earthen fort that is still intact and may be seen on a self-guided walking tour. Historical markers show the spots of Wayne's action. The site features an eighteenth-century military camp with the firing of cannon and muskets. A museum of eighteenth-century items is in the visitor's center.

HISTORICAL SOCIETY OF TARRYTOWN MUSEUM HEADQUARTERS

1 Grove Street, Tarrytown, NY 10591

PHONE: 845-631-8374

HOURS: Open Tuesday to Saturday.

ADMISSION: A fee is charged.

The Historical Society of Tarrytown Museum features exhibits and weapons from the Revolutionary War, with an emphasis on the capture, trial, and execution of British Major John Andre. Andre was captured behind American lines and, in his boot, carried information on the forts and ordnance at West Point. He also carried dozens of confidential orders issued by Washington.

PHILIPSE MANOR HALL STATE HISTORIC SITE

Warburton Avenue and Dock Street, Yonkers, NY 10701

PHONE: 845-965-4027

HOURS: Open Wednesday to Sunday from April to October.

ADMISSION: Free.

Philipse Manor Hall

Philipse Manor Hall was the home of Frederick Philipse III, who, on November 28, 1776, signed the Declaration of Dependence. This declaration, signed the same year as the Declaration of Independence, proclaimed the loyalty of the signers to their sovereign, George III, King of Great Britain. The Philipses lived in luxury from the rents paid by the tenant farms on their property. Philipse was such a known loyalist that General George Washington ordered him arrested in 1776. Philipse later fled to British-occupied New York City and then on to England. His lands and mansion were confiscated by the New York State Legislature and sold. Philipse Manor Hall features a priceless collection of presidential portraits, including five portraits of Washington.

THOMAS PAINE COTTAGE

20 Sicard Avenue, New Rochelle, NY 10804
PHONE: 845-633-1776
HOURS: Open daily except Wednesday and
Monday.
ADMISSION: A fee is charged.

The Thomas Paine Cottage is all that remains of several
buildings built by Paine on 300 acres of land granted to
him by the State of New York in 1784 in recognition of
his services to the nation. The cottage was moved to its

Thomas Paine Cottage

present location from the south side of what is now Paine Avenue by the Huguenot Association
that owns the cottage. Paine left few furnishings, so many of the exhibits have little to do with the
patriot's life, but are instead centered around Huguenot history and early New Rochelle. At the
rear of the house on the ground floor is the Paine Room. Here, on Christmas Eve in 1805, an assas-
sination attempt was made on Thomas Paine. The would-be assassin was caught but never prose-
cuted. In the room are two chairs used by Paine at a local tavern and a life-size wax figure of Paine.
In addition, a stove that was given to Paine by Benjamin Franklin is on display.

THOMAS PAINE MEMORIAL MUSEUM

983 North Avenue, New Rochelle, NY 10804
PHONE: 845-632-5376
HOURS: Open Friday to Sunday from April to October.
ADMISSION: A fee is charged.
www.thomas-paine.com

The Thomas Paine Museum is the home of the Thomas Paine Historical Association that was
formed for the purpose of providing a permanent home for the manuscripts and artifacts of
Paine. The mission of the Association is "to perpetuate the memory of Thomas Paine, dissemi-
nate the record of his public service, and to preserve and make accessible to the public memorials
of his life and work." Today, the museum contains a fine collection of books, pamphlets, and pic-
tures, including many first editions of Paine's works, rare prints, and several original manuscripts. Tours are available.

MORRIS-JUMEL MANSION

65 Jumel Terrace at West 160th Street, New York, NY 10032
PHONE: 212-923-8008
HOURS: Open Wednesday to Sunday.
ADMISSION: A fee is charged.

The Morris-Jumel Mansion was built in 1765 as a summer retreat for British Lieutenant
Colonel Roger Morris and his wife. Morris was George Washington's friend and comrade dur-

ing the French and Indian War. With the outbreak of the war, however, Morris, a Loyalist, left for England. Subsequent inhabitants included Washington, British Lieutenant General Sir Henry Clinton, and Baron Wilhelm von Knyphausen, the Hessian commander. Each was drawn to the mansion because of its views of downtown Manhattan, New Jersey, and Westchester and because of its military vantage point. When the war ended, the house was confiscated and became a popular tavern along the Albany Post Road known as Calument Hall. The house features twelve restored period rooms. Research is underway for a reinterpretation of the room believed to have been used by Washington.

FEDERAL HALL NATIONAL MEMORIAL

Corner of Wall and Broad Streets, New York, NY 10005
PHONE: 212-825-6888
HOURS: Open daily July to August and Monday to Friday during the rest of the year; closed major holidays.
ADMISSION: Free.

Federal Hall National Memorial

The City Hall of New York originally stood on the site of the Federal Hall National Memorial. This is where the Stamp Act Congress met in 1765, where Congress sat during the period from 1785 to 1790, and where the first U.S. Congress was convened. George Washington's inauguration took place on the balcony of the old building, and the Departments of State, War, and the Treasury, as well as the Supreme Court, were created within its walls. The Bill of Rights was adopted here by Congress. The Federal Hall National Memorial exhibits documents and artifacts interpreting the role of old City Hall in early American history.

FRAUNCES TAVERN MUSEUM

54 Pearl Street, New York, NY 10004
PHONE: 212-425-1778
HOURS: Open Monday to Friday.
ADMISSION: A fee is charged.

The Fraunces Tavern Museum was originally built as a residence, but in 1763 Samuel Fraunces opened the building as a tavern. After the Revolutionary War, Fraunces became George Washington's steward; and on December 4, 1783, the tavern was the setting for a farewell dinner Washington hosted for his officers. Only the brick in the west wall of the museum is original, but the museum features mementoes from General Washington's farewell dinner and colonial life. The downstairs of the Fraunces Tavern is a restaurant.

Saint Paul's Church National Historic Site ———

Broadway at Fulton Street, New York, NY
PHONE: 212-602-0874
HOURS: Open daily.
ADMISSION: Free.

Saint Paul's Church was completed in 1766 and during the Revolution was the worship place for British Generals Cornwallis and Howe. After President Washington's inauguration, a special service was held here on April 30, 1789, and a memorial service was held for Washington in the chapel in 1799, as was the funeral of President James Monroe in 1831. Many patriots are buried at Saint Paul's, and America's first war monument honors General Montgomery. An oil painting of the first rendition of the Great Seal of the United States hangs over Washington's pew. In the graveyard is a mass grave of 100 Hessians who used the church as a barracks and hospital.

Trinity Church and Graveyard ————

Broadway at Wall Street, New York, NY 10006
PHONE: 212-602-0800
HOURS: Open daily for tours.
MUSEUM HOURS: Open daily.
ADMISSION: Free.

The original building of Trinity Church was destroyed by a fire in September 1776 that swept through New York City, but some early patriots are buried in the graveyard. The most well-known of these is Alexander Hamilton, who, during the Revolutionary War, was captain of the Provincial Company of New York Artillery. Hamilton led the company through the New Jersey Campaign and saw action at Trenton and Princeton. In 1777, he became secretary to General Washington and was later promoted to Lieutenant Colonel. Hamilton was fatally shot by Aaron Burr in a duel on July 11, 1804.

Conference House ————

7455 Hylan Boulevard, Staten Island, NY 10307
PHONE: 718-984-2086
HOURS: Open Friday to Sunday from March to December.
ADMISSION: A fee is charged, seniors and children discounted.

The Conference House was built around 1680 by Captain Christopher Billopp and was the site of a fateful conference on September 11, 1776. On that date, Benjamin Franklin, John Adams, and Edward Rutledge met here with the British Vice Admiral Lord Richard Howe. In an effort to avoid an American Revolution, Admiral Howe offered clemency to "all repentant rebels." The offer was refused since the Declaration of Independence had already been signed and there was no turning back for the Patriots.

NORTH CAROLINA

The colony of North Carolina was settled by Irish and Scottish immigrants who fled to the New World for economic reasons.

Up until 1768, there were only minor clashes between the British and the farmers. In the spring of that year, however, an association of "Regulators," poor frustrated farmers who objected to taxation without representation, was formed. Colonial Governor Tryon was determined to break up the loosely formed Regulators. On May 14, 1771, his militia reached the Alamance River where the Regulators were camped. The Regulators outnumbered Tryon's force two to one, but the rebels had no leaders, no artillery, and few rifles.

Tryon opened fire, and after more than an hour of resistance, the British drove the Regulators from the field. Many Regulators fled to the as yet undeveloped lands of Kentucky and Tennessee.

Many Revolutionary War sites in North Carolina have been preserved, from historic towns on the Atlantic coast to the Alamance Battleground in the middle of the state to Fort Defiance and the Old English Cemetery in the western part of the state.

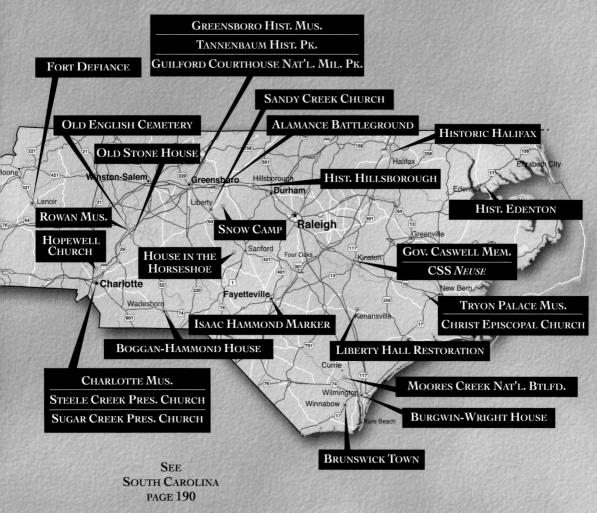

SEE
TENNESSEE
PAGE 210

SEE VIRGINIA PAGE 222

GREENSBORO HIST. MUS.

TANNENBAUM HIST. PK.

GUILFORD COURTHOUSE NAT'L. MIL. PK.

FORT DEFIANCE

SANDY CREEK CHURCH

OLD ENGLISH CEMETERY

ALAMANCE BATTLEGROUND

HISTORIC HALIFAX

OLD STONE HOUSE

HIST. HILLSBOROUGH

ROWAN MUS.

HIST. EDENTON

SNOW CAMP

HOPEWELL
CHURCH

HOUSE IN THE
HORSESHOE

GOV. CASWELL MEM.

CSS *NEUSE*

TRYON PALACE MUS.

CHRIST EPISCOPAL CHURCH

ISAAC HAMMOND MARKER

LIBERTY HALL RESTORATION

BOGGAN-HAMMOND HOUSE

CHARLOTTE MUS.

STEELE CREEK PRES. CHURCH

SUGAR CREEK PRES. CHURCH

MOORES CREEK NAT'L. BTLFD.

BURGWIN-WRIGHT HOUSE

BRUNSWICK TOWN

SEE
SOUTH CAROLINA
PAGE 190

0   100 Miles

0   100 KM

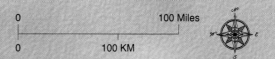

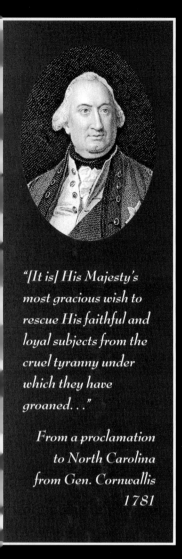

BRITISH

COMMANDER:
Gen. Lord Charles Cornwallis

STRENGTH: 1,900

CASUALTIES: 532 reported

BATTLE OF GUILFORD COURTHOUSE

March 15, 1781

The Battle of Guilford Courthouse was technically a British victory, but it came at such a high price of troop loss that it was instrumental in the British defeat at Yorktown seven months later.

American General Nathanael Greene, commanding both a veteran militia and continental troops, managed to evade the British until reinforcements arrived and made the American army twice that of the British. Greene decided to fight at Guilford Courthouse, which would force the British to march ten miles to him. Greene situated his men west of the courthouse to take full advantage of the woods and fields over which the British troops would have to advance.

Greene deployed his men in three lines with the North Carolina militia, the least reliable of the troops, in front. Because of the terrain, his second line, composed of Virginia militia, was far behind the first, and his third line, of continentals, was farther back behind the right wing of the first two lines. Greene placed sharpshooters on both flanks of the first line with the continental cavalry units on the two flanks under the commands of Colonel Henry "Light-Horse Harry" Lee and Colonel William Washington.

Cornwallis was bivouacked ten miles southwest of Guilford when he learned of Greene's location. He marched his men at 3:30 A.M., without breakfast, to the battle site. American cannon began firing upon seeing the British arrive on the field just after noon. Cornwallis quickly deployed his troops and replied to the fire with his own artillery. The North Carolina militia fired the two rounds Greene had requested then fell back, as the American marksmen on either flank kept up a steady fire. Cornwallis broke the first line, hitting hard on the right and left. On his left, Colonel James Webster struck the second line and drove it back, allowing him to advance to engage Greene's third line. On the American left, the Hessian regiment under von Bose and the first guards drove Lee, his Virginia riflemen, and the North Carolina militia back and away from the action in the center. Lee held out, depriving

American 6-pounder cannon on the Guilford Courthouse Battlefield

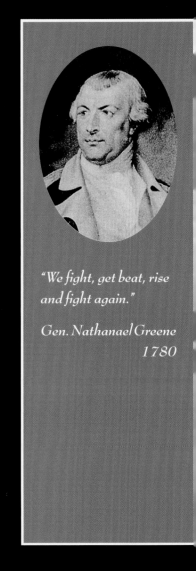

Cornwallis of men to assist in the advance on the second line. Meanwhile, the second American line was being slowly pushed backward. The right flank, in particular, was forced back to the point of making a right angle to the center of the line. Finally, the right flank crumbled while the left held for awhile before giving way. Webster's wing, the British left, advanced to the third line and was repulsed twice by the continentals on their right. In the center, the guards emerged into the open fields and ravines in front of the third line. Advancing against the 2nd Maryland, an untried continental unit, they broke through until hit in a counterattack by the cavalry under Colonel Washington and the infantry of the 1st Maryland. Forced back, the guards were saved by the firing of the Royal Artillery's three-pounder guns. Arriving British on the American left prompted Greene to withdraw from the field.

The Battle of Guilford's Courthouse was the largest, most hotly-contested action of the Revolutionary War's Southern Campaign. The serious loss of British manpower suffered at Guilford Courthouse foreshadowed final American victory at Yorktown seven months later.

AMERICAN

COMMANDER:
Gen. Nathanael Greene

STRENGTH: 4,400

CASUALTIES: 261
reported

GUILFORD COURTHOUSE NATIONAL MILITARY PARK

2332 New Garden Road, Greensboro, NC 27410-2355
PHONE: 336-288-1776, Ext. 28
HOURS: Open daily; closed New Year's Day, Thanksgiving Day, and Christmas Day.
ADMISSION: Free.

The 220-acre Guilford Courthouse National Military Park commemorates the battle of March 15, 1781, between the Patriots and the British. At the visitor's center, an eighteen-minute film is available that tells of the campaign through the words of a soldier, and museum exhibits are also available. A two-and-one-quarter mile self-guided auto tour features seven informational stops. A restored historic road and two miles of paved foot trails provide access to important points of the battlefield. Twenty-eight monuments stand throughout the park honoring men and women of the Revolutionary period, including the Nathanael Greene Monument and the Signers Monument, where two of North Carolina's three signers of the Declaration of Independence (William Hopper and John Penn) are buried. Each year on March 15, the park hosts special events to commemorate the anniversary of the battle. Special living-history programs are featured on Memorial Day and Independence Day.

General Nathanael Greene Monument

Monument to Lieutenant Colonel James Stuart, a British officer killed at Guilford Courthouse

OLD STONE HOUSE

Old Stone House Road, Granite Quarry, NC 28072

PHONE: 704-633-5946

HOURS: Open Saturday and Sunday from April to November.

ADMISSION: A fee is charged.

The Old Stone House was built by Michael Braun in 1766 and today stands as a memorial to the Germans, who settled in Rowan County in the early 1700s. Braun was a wheelwright by profession, a planter, and a land owner. He held various political offices before and during the Revolution. The house underwent a six-year restoration in the early sixties. It is furnished with period furnishings from both North Carolina and Pennsylvania, to where Braun originally immigrated. Each December, an eighteenth-century folk Christmas is recreated at the house featuring decorations, trades, and crafts of the period, as well as musket firings and cooking demonstrations.

HOUSE IN THE HORSESHOE STATE HISTORIC SITE

324 Alston House Road, Sanford, NC 27330

PHONE: 910-947-2051

HOURS: Open daily; closed Monday from November to March.

ADMISSION: Free.

The House in the Horseshoe, built by Whig colonel Philip Alston, was a site of fighting during the American Revolution and still bears the scars of the war. Late in the summer of 1781, while Alston and his band of Patriots were camped at the house, they were attacked by a larger group of Tories led by David Fanning. During the ensuing skirmish, the Tories attempted to set the house on fire by rolling a cart filled with burning straw against it. Alston surrendered after both sides took several casualties. The house remains riddled with bullet holes.

House in the Horseshoe

HOPEWELL PRESBYTERIAN CHURCH AND CEMETERY —

Beatties Ford Road, Huntersville, NC 28078
PHONE: 704-875-2020
HOURS: Open for tours Monday to Friday.
ADMISSION: Free.

Hopewell Presbyterian Church

The Hopewell Presbyterian Church offers tours of both the church and cemetery. Although the buildings of the church only date back to the 1830s, its cemetery contains the graves of many Revolutionary War patriots. Among these is General William Lee Davidson, who was killed at Cowan's Ford. Light-Horse Harry Lee observed, "A promising soldier, was lost to his country, in the meridian of life, and at a moment when his services would have been highly beneficial to her." There are also four graves of the signers of the Mecklenburg Declaration of Independence. The original gravestone of Francis Bradley is preserved in the Heritage Room at Hopewell Presbyterian; an identical stone now marks his grave. Bradley was well-known throughout the state as a terrorizer of Tories. In fact, he was so well known as a Tory hater that four Tories ambushed and killed him at his plantation.

THE CHARLOTTE MUSEUM OF HISTORY AND HEZEKIAH ALEXANDER HOMESITE ——

3500 Shamrock Drive, Charlotte, NC 28215
PHONE: 704-568-1774
HOURS: Open Tuesday, Wednesday, Saturday, and Sunday for tours; closed major holidays.
ADMISSION: A fee is charged; children and seniors discounted.
www.charlottemuseum.org

The Hezekiah Alexander Homesite, also known as the "Rock House," was built in 1774 and is the oldest surviving structure

Hezekiah Alexander Homesite

in Mecklenburg County. Hezekiah Alexander was chosen in 1775 by the Fifth Provincial Congress to serve on the committee charged with drafting the first North Carolina constitution and bill of rights. During the war, Alexander supervised the raising, supplying, and financing of Patriot forces. Costumed interpreters lead tours throughout the house, including a springhouse, a reconstructed log kitchen, and the gardens. The Charlotte Museum of History features changing exhibits from the eighteenth, nineteenth, and twentieth centuries.

Charlotte Museum of History

STEELE CREEK PRESBYTERIAN CHURCH

7407 Steele Creek Road, Charlotte, NC
PHONE: 704-588-1290
HOURS: Open daily.
ADMISSION: Free.

Steele Creek Presbyterian Church began in 1760, and the graves in the cemetery adjacent to the church date from that time. Robert Irwin, an elder in the church and a signer of the Mecklenburg Declaration, is buried here. A marker in the cemetery lists the names of thirteen soldiers of the Revolution interred here. There are also some noted heroines of the War.

SUGAR CREEK PRESBYTERIAN CHURCH

101 Sugar Creek Road West, Charlotte, NC 28213
PHONE: 704-596-4466
HOURS: Open Monday to Friday for tours.
ADMISSION: Free.

Organized in 1755, Sugar Creek Presbyterian Church is the oldest church in the county. In the cemetery of the church lie two of the signers of the Mecklenburg Declaration: Hezekiah Alexander and Abraham Alexander. A tombstone in the cemetery honors Captain Joseph Graham, who led the stand against the British army at the site during the Battle of Charlotte. The twenty-year-old officer was engaged in hand-to-hand combat when his horse backed into a tree limb, knocking the young man to the ground. He sustained three bullet wounds in the thigh, a saber thrust in the side, and a gash on the neck that almost decapitated him. He was left to die on the battlefield. However, he regained consciousness and managed to crawl to a spring near the church. A woman discovered him as she came for water. She ran to Graham's mother, who helped carry him home. Five months later, Graham was again fighting the British. The woman who saved Graham, Susan Wilson Alexander, also lies buried in the church cemetery. A museum in the church features archival material significant to the history of Sugar Creek Presbyterian Church.

BOGGAN-HAMMOND HOUSE

210 East Wade Street, Wadesboro, NC 28170
PHONE: 704-694-6694 (Anson County Historical Society)
HOURS: Open Monday to Friday; closed major holidays.
ADMISSION: Free.

The Boggan-Hammond House was built by Patrick Boggan for his daughter Nellie around 1783. Boggan was an officer of the North Carolina militia during the Revolutionary War. The militia was engaged in several raids against local Loyalists, sometimes in collaboration with Patriots from South Carolina. The Boggan-Hammond House, which is the oldest structure in Wadesboro, was restored in the late 1960s and completed in 1970. It is now operated as a historic museum. The house was placed on the National Register of Historic Places in 1972. It is owned and operated by the Anson County Historical Society, Inc.

ISAAC HAMMOND MARKER

Corner Cool Spring and Meeting Streets, Fayetteville, NC

Isaac Hammond was a free black man who served as a soldier in the American Revolutionary War and later served as a musician in the local militia unit, the Fayetteville Independent Light Infantry. In 1797, shortly after the F.I.L.I. was organized, Isaac Hammond became its first fifer. According to North Carolina colonial records, Isaac Hammond was a member of Captain Jones's Company in the 10th Regiment of the North Carolina Continental Line. He is buried on the F.I.L.I. Parade Ground.

SNOW CAMP COMMUNITY

I-85/40, exit 145, 15 miles south on North Carolina Highway 49
PHONE: 800-726-5115 or 336-376-6948
HOURS: Open daily from June to August.
ADMISSION: A fee is charged.

Log dwelling at Snow Camp Community

Snow Camp was a Quaker community where British soldiers camped after the Battle of Guilford Courthouse. Visitors to the area can see local residents perform a drama entitled *Sword of Peace,* which depicts the role of the Quakers in the American Revolution.

ALAMANCE BATTLEGROUND STATE HISTORIC SITE ——

5803 South NC 62, Burlington, NC 27215
PHONE: 336-227-4785
HOURS: Open daily; closed major holidays.
ADMISSION: Free

The Battle of Alamance, a precursor of the Revolutionary War, was fought on this site in 1771. The visitor's center offers a 25-minute film entitled *The War of the Regulation*, which relates the history of the Battle of Alamance and the North Carolina back country in the eighteenth century. A walking trail features a three-quarter-mile nature trail, the James Hunter Monument, and a granite column commemorating the battle. Colored pennants mark battle positions as well as the Regulator campsite. The John Allen House is also on the grounds and may be toured with guides. John's sister, Amy, was the wife of Herman Husband, the pamphleteer and prominent instigator in the Regulator movement. Husband was an admirer of Ben Franklin and escaped to Pennsylvania after the Battle of Alamance. The house was built in 1780 and moved to the battleground and restored in 1966.

James Hunter Monument

John Allen House

SANDY CREEK BAPTIST CHURCH

4736 Sandy Creek Church Road, Liberty, NC 27298-8116
PHONE: 336-622-7414
HOURS: Open daily from dawn to dusk.
ADMISSION: Free.

Sandy Creek Baptist Church was established in 1755. Most of the members of the church sympathized with the farmers who opposed the taxes of the King's government. The church, however, had passed a resolution that any members who took up arms against the local authority would be excommunicated. As a result of the Regulators, there was a mass exodus of Sandy Creek Baptist members. In the church's cemetery lie several Revolutionary War soldiers in marked graves.

HISTORIC HILLSBOROUGH

150 East King Street, Hillsborough, NC 27278
PHONE: 919-732-7741
HOURS: Open daily.
ADMISSION: Free.

Hillsborough, site of the 1775 Provincial Congress, was occupied by both the American and British armies during the Revolution. Colonel David Fanning's Tory raiders captured Governor Thomas Burke in September 1781, precipitating the Battle of Lindley's Mill. Hillsborough is also the site of the North Carolina Constitutional Convention of 1788, where delegates demanded a Bill of Rights before they would ratify the U.S. Constitution. A Revolutionary War tour, beginning at the Orange County Visitors Bureau, is offered.

HISTORIC HALIFAX STATE HISTORIC SITE

Corner of St. David's and Dobbs Streets, Halifax, NC
PHONE: 252-583-7191
HOURS: Open daily; closed major holidays.
ADMISSION: Free.

The town of Halifax was founded in 1760 and today stands as a restored village. The Historic Halifax Visitor Center features a short film, exhibits, and displays showing the history of the town. Throughout the day, free guided walking tours of the restored buildings begin at the visitor center. This tour includes visits to several authentically restored and furnished buildings. Maps for self-guided tours are also available, but the interiors of the sites are only open on guided tours.

Like other colonial towns, Halifax was planned with an open space in its center to be used as a town common and market. Market Square, also called Market Green, became the economic center of Halifax. Farmers brought their produce to sell and often camped overnight on the square before beginning the long trip home. During the American Revolution, a barracks was constructed near the market house and militia troops paraded and drilled on these grounds.

A marker is on the site where the original Halifax County Courthouse stood—this is the most historic spot in the town. On April 4, 1776, delegates throughout the state assembled in Halifax to attend the Fourth Provincial Congress at the county courthouse. Four days later, the delegates adopted a declaration reading: "Resolved, That the delegates of the colony in the Continental Congress be empowered to concur with the delegates of the other colonies in declaring independence, and forming foreign alliances, reserving to this colony the sole and exclusive right of forming a constitution and laws for this colony." On April 12, the delegates approved unanimously the Halifax Resolves. Its enactment by the Provincial Congress represented the most revolutionary official act taken by an American colony to that date. Thus North Carolina became the first colony to issue an official declaration of independence along with a request that its sister colonies follow suit.

The North Carolina state flag displays two dates. One, April 12, 1776, commemorates the Halifax Resolves. When the Halifax Resolves were read in the Continental Congress, the delegates at Philadelphia sent copies home with the request that their constituents follow this example. On May 15, Virginia became the first colony to follow North Carolina's lead. Less than two weeks later, the delegates from North Carolina and Virginia presented their instructions to the Continental Congress. On June 7, Richard Henry Lee moved "that these United Colonies are and of right ought to be free and independent states."

News reached Halifax on July 22 that the Continental Congress had approved the final draft of the Declaration of Independence. Upon receiving a copy of the Declaration, the council voted that it should be read in public for the first time in North Carolina on August 1. The place chosen for the momentous event was the lawn of the courthouse where the first seeds had been sown only months earlier.

The site also contains a colonial cemetery where the oldest known grave dates back to 1766. Two women of the Revolutionary War era are buried here. Adjacent to the cemetery is the Joseph Montfort Amphitheater. The play, *First for Freedom*, has been presented every summer since its premier in 1976. It dramatizes the events of 1776 that culminated in the Halifax Resolves. King Street ends at the river overlook. Here, on the banks of the Roanoke River, Cornwallis was forced to stop in Halifax because floodwaters along the river at this point delayed his crossing.

THE HALIFAX JAIL

The Halifax Jail presently on the site was not built until 1838, but it stands on the exact site occupied by two previous wooden jails. The first, built in 1760, was destroyed when escaping prisoners set it on fire. The second housed prisoners of war during the Revolutionary War, including Allan MacDonald, a Scottish Highlander taken prisoner at the Battle of Moore's Creek Bridge in February 1776. Allan was the husband of the famed Flora MacDonald.

Halifax Jail

THE OWENS HOUSE

The Owens House was built about 1760 and was moved to its present site in the mid-1800s. The house was occupied during the eighteenth and nineteenth centuries by wealthy Halifax residents. Today, the house is furnished as the home of a typical merchant of the late Colonial period.

Owens House

EAGLE TAVERN

Eagle Tavern was built in the late 1700s by William Barksdale, who expanded his lodging and entertainment business by adding the tavern to his hotel. Cornwallis was believed to have lodged in the Eagle Hotel.

HISTORIC EDENTON STATE HISTORIC SITE

108 North Broad Street, Edenton, NC 27932
PHONE: 252-482-2637
HOURS: Open daily from April to October; closed Monday from November to March. Guided walking tours are available four or five times daily, depending on the season. Trolley tours are also available three to four times daily, depending on the season.
ADMISSION: Free for self-guided tours; a fee is charged for guided tours.

Historic Edenton offers guided tours that include many points of interest from the Revolutionary War. Included on the tour are the Chowan County Courthouse, James Iredell House, Barker House, Cupola House, and Saint Paul's Church. The visitor's center offers maps for a self-guided tour of Historic Edenton, but entrance to the buildings is allowed only on the guided tours.

Chowan County Courthouse State Historic Site

117 East King Street, Edenton, NC 27932

Historic Edenton is one of North Carolina's oldest communities. It was established in the late seventeenth century and incorporated in 1722. The Chowan County Courthouse, built in 1767, with its green running to the waters of Albemarle Sound, stands as one of the finest examples of Georgian architecture in the South. During the Revolutionary War, local Patriots used the building to plot their strategy. The Chowan County Courthouse is considered to be the most intact colonial courthouse in America.

Chowan County Courthouse

Historic Cannon

Edenton's Waterfront

Three Revolutionary War cannon stand on Edenton's waterfront facing Albemarle Sound. These cannon are part of a shipment of twenty-three cannon purchased by two Edenton patriots with the help of Benjamin Franklin for the defense of the town against the British. The cannon were brought to Edenton in 1778 aboard the ship *The Holy Heart of Jesus*. One half were for Virginia and one half for North Carolina. When the ship docked at the port of Edenton, however, the captain tried to extract a charge for transportation equal to 150 pounds of tobacco for every 100 pounds of the cannon. Virginia paid for their cannon, as their warehouses had plenty of tobacco, but all the tobacco in all the warehouses of Edenton did not equal the combined weight of the cannon. Legend has it that Captain Boritz dumped them into the bay. Six were recovered during the Civil War, three of which remain in Edenton. The other three stand on Capitol Square in Raleigh.

JOSEPH HEWES MONUMENT

This monument is dedicated to Joseph Hewes, a Colonial patriot and distinguished citizen of Edenton. Hewes was both a ship owner and merchant who traded with England and the West Indies. Although the Revolutionary War would mean a financial sacrifice to Hewes, he nonetheless signed the Declaration of Independence and placed his entire fleet at the disposal of the Continental forces. In 1775, Hewes was appointed to the Naval Board, making him virtually the first secretary of the U.S. Navy. Hewes procured John Paul Jones's commission in the Continental navy, and Jones wrote Hewes, "You are the Angel of my happiness; since to your friendship I owe my present enjoyments, as well as my future prospects. You more than any other person have labored to place the instruments of success in my hands." Joseph Hewes died in Philadelphia and was buried in that city's Christ Church, but North Carolina honors this distinguished member of our founding fathers with this monument.

THE EDENTON TEAPOT

Adjacent to the Courthouse Green

This whimsical monument marks what is known as the "Edenton Tea Party" of October 25, 1774. On this date, fifty-one local women executed resolutions in support of the Provincial Congress, which had banned the import and consumption of British tea. After the resolution was signed, the women offered a toast with a drink brewed from raspberry leaves. The teapot sits atop one of the cannon brought to Edenton in 1778.

BARKER HOUSE ———————————————

505 South Broad Street, Edenton, NC 27932
PHONE: 252-482-7800
HOURS: Open daily.
ADMISSION: Free.

The Barker House was built in 1782 by Thomas and Penelope Barker. Although the house was built after the Revolution, its owners were well-known North Carolina patriots. Mrs. Barker

was the principle figure in the Edenton Tea Party, and Mr. Barker handled the international trade for the colony in London. When the war began, Barker, who was in London at the time, was able to return home only by obtaining a French passport.

Barker House

Saint Paul's Episcopal Church

101 West Gale Street, Edenton, NC 27032

Phone: 252-482-3522

Hours: Not available.

Admission: Available through the guided walking tour from Historic Edenton State Historic Site Visitor's Center.

Saint Paul's Episcopal Church, built between 1736 and 1766, stands in silent testimony to the Revolution. The Vestry of St. Paul's recorded their protest on June 19, 1776, prior to the signing of the Declaration of Independence, in a written document called "The Test." The document ends: "We, the subscribers, professing our allegiance to the King and acknowledging the constitutional executive power of Government, do solemnly profess, testify and declare that we do absolutely believe that neither the Parliament of Great Britain nor any member of a constituent branch thereof, have a right to impose taxes upon these colonies to regulate the internal policy thereof; that all attempts by fraud or force to establish and exercise such claims and powers are violations of the peace and security of the people and

Saint Paul's Episcopal Church

ought to be resisted to the utmost, and that the people of this Province, singly and collectively, are bound by the Acts and Resolutions of the Continental and Provincial Congresses, because in both they are freely represented by persons chosen by themselves. And we do solemnly and sincerely promise and engage under the sanction of Virtue, Honor and the Sacred Love of Liberty and our Country, to maintain and support all the Acts, Resolutions and Regulations of the said Continental and Provincial Congresses, to the utmost of our power and ability."

JAMES IREDELL HOUSE STATE HISTORIC SITE

1105 East Church Street, Edenton, NC 27932
PHONE: 252-482-2637
HOURS: Open daily.
ADMISSION: Available through the guided walking tour from Historic Edenton State Historic Site Visitor's Center.

The James Iredell House was built in 1773 and purchased by James Iredell, Sr. in 1778. Iredell came from England, and his early career included a stint as a British tax collector. He served as attorney general of North Carolina during much of the war and was instrumental in punishing Loyalists who interfered with the war effort. President George Washington appointed Iredell as an associate justice of the first U.S. Supreme Court. He served from 1791 until his death in 1799. Iredell's friend, James Wilson, from Pennsylvania, was a signer of the Declaration of Independence and the U.S. Constitution and a fellow associate justice of the Supreme Court. Wilson died in the house in 1798.

CUPOLA HOUSE

408 South Broad Street, Edenton, NC 27932
PHONE: 252-482-2637 (Historic Edenton)
HOURS: Not available.
ADMISSION: Available through the guided walking tour from Historic Edenton State Historic Site Visitor's Center.

The Cupola House was built in 1758 in the Jacobean style by Francis Corbin, a land agent for Lords Proprietor Lord Granville. Samuel Dickinson, a physician and loyal patriot, bought the house in 1777. His wife participated in the Edenton Tea Party. The house features large chimneys, decorative finials, and a second story overhang. The vegetable garden and formal gardens in the front were restored according to a 1769 map of the house.

Cupola House

CSS *Neuse* Historic Site and Governor Caswell Memorial

2012 West Vernon Avenue, Kinston, NC 28502

Phone: 252-522-2091

Hours: Open Monday to Saturday from April to October and Tuesday to Saturday from November to March.

Admission: Free.

The Governor Richard Caswell Memorial honors Caswell, one of the Colonial militia who was at the Battle of Alamance and fought against the Regulators. In 1754 he was elected to the Colonial assembly, a post he held for seventeen years. Caswell was elected to the Continental Congress; and during the American Revolution, he commanded Patriot forces at the Battle of Moores Creek Bridge in 1776. Caswell became North Carolina's first elected governor and headed the committee that wrote the new state's constitution. He would eventually serve six one-year terms as governor both during and after the war. Caswell suffered a fatal stroke while presiding over the state senate in Fayetteville. His body was returned to Kinston for burial in the family cemetery.

Christ Episcopal Church

320 Pollock Street, New Bern, NC 28563

Phone: 252-633-2109

Hours: Open Monday to Friday.

Admission: Free.

The present Christ Episcopal Church stands on the foundation of the original structure, King's Chapel, built in 1750. President George Washington worshiped at the original structure when he visited New Bern in 1791. The existing church houses artifacts from the colonial period, including a silver communion service given to the church by King George II in 1752, eight years before his death. Each piece bears the royal arms of England. Royal Governor Josiah Martin tried to take the communion service with him when he fled New Bern in 1775. Other gifts from King George II on display include a Bible and a Book of Common Prayer. In the church cemetery are graves from the colonial period. A marble slab in the churchyard honors Patriot John Wright Stanly, whose ship defeated the HMS *Lady Blessington* and captured its cannon during the Revolutionary War. Just outside the church fence sits those cannon from the *Lady Blessington*.

Christ Episcopal Church

Tryon Palace Historic Sites and Gardens —

610 Pollock Street, New Bern, NC 28560

Phone: 252-514-4900; toll free: 1-800-767-1560

Hours: Open daily; closed major holidays.

Admission: A fee is charged.

The Tryon Palace Historic Sites and Gardens includes the reconstructed Georgian buildings of the palace and the fourteen-acre grounds surrounding it. The palace itself was constructed between 1767 and 1770 as a meeting place for the Colonial assembly and as a residence for

Tryon Palace

British Royal Governor William Tryon. The central building contained public rooms for government functions on the ground floor, with family living quarters upstairs. Cooking and laundry facilities were in a wing, or "office," to the left of the main structure; stables were to the right. Designed by English architect John Hawks, the palace was praised for its elegance and beauty. The landscape of the palace was also much admired. The formal garden as it is today is laid out in the geometric style typical of eighteenth-century Europe. After just thirteen months in his new home, William Tryon was appointed governor of the colony of New York. His successor, Josiah Martin, took office when anti-British feelings were running high in New Bern. In May 1775, patriots forced Martin to flee the palace; many of his belongings were left behind. He was the second and last British colonial governor to live at the palace. During and after the Revolutionary War, the palace continued to be used for meetings of the General Assembly and as a residence for elected governors of the new state of North Carolina. But the building fell into disrepair, and in 1798 the main structure burned to the ground. The palace was reconstructed in the 1950s from the original architect's plans. Today it is furnished with rare eighteenth-century English and American antiques, reflecting the world of Governor Tryon during the decade of the American Revolution.

JOHN WRIGHT STANLY HOUSE

On his southern tour in 1791, President George Washington dined and danced at Tryon Palace. But his two nights in New Bern were spent at the nearby home of John Wright Stanly, which Washington described as "exceeding good lodgings." The elegance of the Stanly house, built in the Georgian style circa 1780, reflects the wealth of its owner, whose merchant ships plied the waters as privateers, raiding British vessels to aid the American cause during the Revolutionary War. When Union forces occupied New Bern in 1862, the Stanly house served as headquarters for their commander, General Ambrose Burnside. Distinctive American furniture of the period complements the elegant interior woodwork of the Stanly house. Stanly family history provides a fascinating chronicle of father and son, epidemic and duel, war and wealth.

LIBERTY HALL RESTORATION ———————————

409 South Main Street, Kenansville, NC 28349
PHONE: 910-296-2176
HOURS: Open Tuesday to Sunday.
ADMISSION: A fee is charged.

Liberty Hall Restoration is a two-story, eleven-room Greek revival house built by Thomas Kenan around 1810. The original Liberty Hall was built by James Kenan, who was a leader in the organized protest against the Stamp Act in Wilmington and fought in the Revolutionary War. Elected a militia colonel by the Third Provincial Congress in September 1775, he orchestrated the defense of the Duplin County area throughout the war and was instrumental in the American victory at the Battle of Moores Creek Bridge.

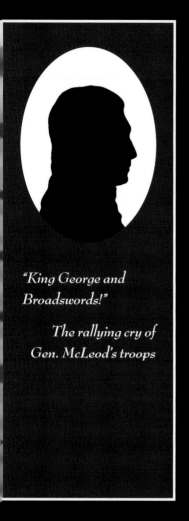

BRITISH

COMMANDERS:
Brig. Gen. Donald McDonald,
Gen. Donald McLeod

STRENGTH: 1,600

CASUALTIES: 50 killed;
850 captured

BATTLE OF MOORES CREEK BRIDGE

February 27, 1776

After Lexington and Concord, the North Carolina patriots were so filled with the fires of rebellion that within a few months Royal Governor Josiah Martin fled and a provincial congress was organized. North Carolina was preparing for war, but the state also had a strong Loyalist element.

In February 1776, sixteen hundred Scottish Loyalists banded together with the intent of establishing North Carolina as a British coastal base. Their commander, Brigadier General Donald McDonald, wanted to avoid a fight with his poorly equipped men on his march to the coast. He successfully evaded the 1,100 troops under Colonels James Moore, Richard Caswell, and Alexander Lillington until the morning of February 27 at Moores Creek Bridge.

Lillington had reached Moores Creek Bridge on February 25 and first set up earthworks, which were abandoned when a better idea surfaced. The Americans removed some of the board flooring from the bridge, leaving a gap where the Scots would have to cross on the logs. They then greased the logs and placed a cannon and swivel gun at the end of the bridge and aimed their muskets at the bridge.

The Tories had walked for three days through rough terrain and approached the creek at dawn. They saw the abandoned earthworks and thought their bridge was unguarded.

Patriot reenactors with a ½ pound swivel gun

The reconstructed Moores Creek Bridge

The Scots charged with the braying of bagpipes, the beat of drums, and the emitting of blood-curdling screams that had frightened opposing armies for centuries.

The rebels opened fire and killed several of the Tories instantly, including General McLeod. Others lost their balance and fell into the water, where they drowned. The Scots quickly retreated, only to be pursued by the rebels who hastily replaced the bridge's floor. General McDonald was taken prisoner, along with thirteen wagons, 1,500 rifles, 350 muskets, 150 swords, and £15,000.

This quick and decisive victory early in the war delayed any further action by the British in the Carolinas until 1780. The battle ended Royal Governor Josiah Martin's hopes of regaining control of the colony for the British. The Loyalist defeat ended British plans for an invasionary force to land in Brunswick, North Carolina. The victory raised the morale of the Patriots throughout all the colonies.

The reconstructed Moores Creek Bridge

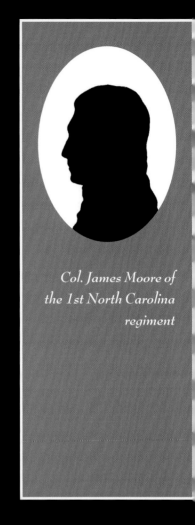

Col. James Moore of the 1st North Carolina regiment

AMERICAN

COMMANDERS:
Col. James Moore,
Col. Richard Caswell,
Col. Alexander Lillington

STRENGTH: 1,100

CASUALTIES: 1 killed; 1 wounded.

MOORES CREEK NATIONAL BATTLEFIELD

200 Moores Creek Drive, Currie, NC 28435

PHONE: 910-283-5591

HOURS: Open daily; closed New Year's Day and Christmas Day.

ADMISSION: Free.

Moores Creek National Battlefield is an eighty-six-acre park set aside to commemorate the 1776 victory of 1,000 Patriots over 1,600 British Loyalists at the Battle of Moores Creek Bridge. The visitor's center has exhibits depicting the Revolutionary period and a video. Self-guided trails include a one-mile history trail that explains the battle and includes the site where the Patriots and Loyalists clashed. Each year the park hosts an observance and battle commemoration on the last full weekend of February. The celebration features a living-history encampment, tactical demonstrations, folk singing, and a formal commemoration program that includes a speaker, military band, and wreath-laying ceremony. Within the park are the remains of fortifications at the site of the battle, partially restored earthworks, wayside exhibits, and markers.

BURGWIN-WRIGHT MUSEUM HOUSE

224 Market Street, Wilmington, NC 28401

PHONE: 910-762-0570

HOURS: Open daily.

ADMISSION: A fee is charged.

Burgwin-Wright Museum House

The Burgwin-Wright Museum House was built in 1770 by John Burgwin, colonial treasurer under the Royal Governor. The foundation of the house consists of the massive stone walls of a former jail that was located on the site. Burgwin, loyal to the Crown, fled Wilmington at the outbreak of the war and remained in England until the cessation of hostilities. In January 1781, Major Craig commandeered Burgwin's house as his headquarters. When Cornwallis's army limped into Wilmington on April 12, 1781, after its costly "victory" over Nathanael Greene's Americans at Guilford Courthouse, the British commander made his headquarters at Burgwin's House. It is sometimes known as "the Cornwallis House."

Cornwallis rested his army almost two weeks in Wilmington while he took on supplies for his march north to Yorktown. The floorboards inside the Burgwin-Wright House still have the marks reputedly left by British muskets during Cornwallis's stay. A separate building houses the restored colonial kitchen, known to have been in use during the Revolutionary War.

The Parlor of the Burgwin-Wright Museum House

BRUNSWICK TOWN HISTORIC SITE

8884 Saint Philip's Road Southeast, Winnabow, NC 28479
PHONE: 910-371-6613
HOURS: Open daily from April to October; closed Monday from November to March.
ADMISSION: Free.

This archeological site features the foundations of twenty-three of the town's buildings, including the foundations of the Royal Governor's house and the walls of Saint Philip's Anglican Church dating back to 1754. Brunswick was a major pre-Revolutionary port on North Carolina's Cape Fear River; but in 1776, the British troops razed the town. It was never rebuilt, but in 1861, the Confederates built a fort on the site, making Brunswick Town/Fort Anderson a unique view of two periods of American history. The visitor's center features exhibits from the pre-Revolutionary War period to the Civil War.

FORT DEFIANCE

4555 Fort Defiance Drive, Lenoir, NC 28645
PHONE: 828-758-1671
HOURS: Open Saturday and Sunday from June to October.
ADMISSION: A fee is charged.

Fort Defiance is the home of Revolutionary War hero William Lenoir, who completed the house in 1788. Although the house is post-war, Lenoir held the Patriot rank of captain at the Battle of Kings Mountain and was wounded there. Following the war, he was in the state legislature. Lenoir is buried near the house. The house is furnished with over 300 pieces of the original furnishings; Lenoir's eyeglasses are on display.

OLD ENGLISH CEMETERY

Corner of Council and Church Street, Salisbury, NC
PHONE: 704-638-3000 (Rowan Public Library)
HOURS: Open daily from dawn to dusk.
ADMISSION: Free.

The Old English Cemetery was established on land granted to the city by the British in 1770. During the month of February in 1781, British General Cornwallis encamped his army in the vicinity of the cemetery and several soldiers, casualties of the recent fighting with the American militia, were buried in the graveyard. American Revolutionary soldiers are also interred here.

GREENSBORO HISTORICAL MUSEUM

130 Summit Avenue, Greensboro, NC 27401
PHONE: 336-373-2043
HOURS: Open Tuesday to Sunday; closed major holidays.
ADMISSION: Free.
www.greensborohistory.org

The Greensboro Historical Museum features maps, weapons, and documents that chronicle the Revolution and North Carolina's role in it. Special attention is given to the Battle of Guilford Courthouse. Some of the archival material relates to Generals Greene and Washington.

Tannenbaum Historic Park

2200 New Garden Road, Greensboro, NC 27410

Phone: 336-545-5315

Hours: Open Tuesday to Sunday.

Admission: Free.

Tannenbaum Historic Park is located on the eighteenth-century farmstead of Joseph Hoskins. Hoskins served the Guilford County community as a constable, tax collector, and as sheriff. During the Battle of Guilford Courthouse, Hoskins' land served as a staging area for British troops under Cornwallis's command. The park also features the Colonial Heritage Center, with exhibits depicting life before, during, and after the Battle of Guilford Courthouse. Living history programs are scheduled throughout the year. The park also contains a museum store and picnic area.

Tannenbaum Historic Park

PENNSYLVANIA

*I*f Massachusetts was the hotbed of colonial resistance to the crown, Pennsylvania–specifically Philadelphia–was the voice of reason, planning, and government. After the Battle of Lexington and Concord, the Continental Congress met in Philadelphia and adopted the militia besieging the British in Boston as the "Army of the United Colonies," appointed George Washington commander in chief, sent Benedict Arnold across the Maine wilderness to try to bring in Canada as the fourteenth colony, and authorized other war-like acts. But it would be another fourteen months before the Declaration of Independence was signed.

Nowhere in America is the Revolution so alive as in Philadelphia. The Liberty Bell is on display. Independence Hall still stands, and the room where the Continental Congress met and signed the Declaration of Independence is still set up and furnished as it was on July 4, 1776. Visitors can stroll through Washington Crossing Park, where Washington made his desperate crossing Christmas night in 1776. The city also has several churches where the patriots worshiped and are buried in the graveyards. And there are battlefields: Brandywine, Fort Mifflin, and the fabled Valley Forge, where General von Steuben transformed ragged troops into a fighting army.

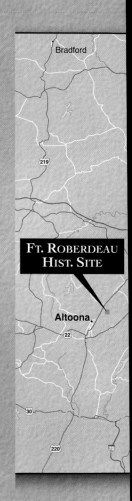

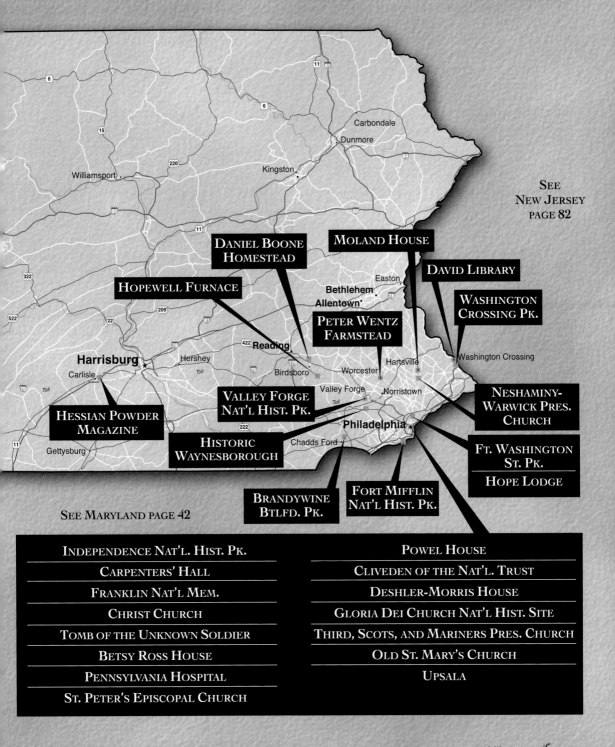

SEE NEW YORK PAGE 100

6

15

220

Williamsport

Carbondale

Dunmore

Kingston

15

SEE
NEW JERSEY
PAGE 82

322

522

22

209

81

11

DANIEL BOONE
HOMESTEAD

MOLAND HOUSE

DAVID LIBRARY

Easton

HOPEWELL FURNACE

Bethlehem

Allentown

WASHINGTON
CROSSING PK.

PETER WENTZ
FARMSTEAD

422 Reading

Harrisburg

Hershey

Toll

76

Birdsboro

Carlisle

HESSIAN POWDER
MAGAZINE

11

Gettysburg

VALLEY FORGE
NAT'L HIST. PK.

Worcester

Hartsville

Washington Crossing

222

Valley Forge

Toll

Norristown

NESHAMINY-
WARWICK PRES.
CHURCH

HISTORIC
WAYNESBOROUGH

Chadds Ford

Philadelphia

FT. WASHINGTON
ST. PK.

HOPE LODGE

SEE MARYLAND PAGE 42

BRANDYWINE
BTLFD. PK.

FORT MIFFLIN
NAT'L HIST. PK.

INDEPENDENCE NAT'L. HIST. PK.	POWEL HOUSE
CARPENTERS' HALL	CLIVEDEN OF THE NAT'L. TRUST
FRANKLIN NAT'L MEM.	DESHLER-MORRIS HOUSE
CHRIST CHURCH	GLORIA DEI CHURCH NAT'L HIST. SITE
TOMB OF THE UNKNOWN SOLDIER	THIRD, SCOTS, AND MARINERS PRES. CHURCH
BETSY ROSS HOUSE	OLD ST. MARY'S CHURCH
PENNSYLVANIA HOSPITAL	UPSALA
ST. PETER'S EPISCOPAL CHURCH	

0   50 Miles

0   50 KM

FORT ROBERDEAU HISTORIC SITE

Off I-99 at Bellwood exit, 8.5 miles NE, Altoona, PA 16601
PHONE: 814-946-0048
HOURS: Open daily from May 1 to October 31.
ADMISSION: A fee is charged.

Fort Roberdeau was built in 1778 in the middle of a fertile valley with lead deposits and a good water supply. Fort Roberdeau has also been called the Lead Mines Fort, which reveals its primary purpose: to protect those who mined and smelted lead for bullets during the Revolutionary War. Although the British never attacked the fort, by 1779, the Loyalists had managed to stop the lead mine through bribery and terrorism. Fort Roberdeau Historic Site features reconstructed stockades and cabins in the midst of forty-eight acres of fields and forest through which nature trails are marked. The fort features exhibits and special programs on the fort's history.

HESSIAN POWDER MAGAZINE

On the grounds of Carlisle Barracks, PA 17013
PHONE: 717-245-4101
HOURS: Open daily.
ADMISSION: Free.
carlisle-www.army.mil

In December 1776, the Continental Congress authorized establishment of an ordnance center at Carlisle to support the war effort. In 1777 the Hessian Gunpowder Magazine was constructed on Carlisle Barracks, originally called Washingtonburg, for use as a magazine to store gunpowder, cannon shot, and small arms. Local histories indicate that some of the construction work may have been performed by Hessian prisoners sent to this area after capture by George Washington's forces at the Battle of Trenton in December 1776. The Hessian Gunpowder Magazine was officially opened to the public in 1948 as a museum. Today, the history of Carlisle Barracks is recounted in the Hessian Magazine with displays from the Revolutionary War, Cavalry School, Civil War, Indian School, and the Army War College. The magazine is also the starting point for walking tours of historic Carlisle Barracks.

DANIEL BOONE HOMESTEAD

400 Daniel Boone Road, Birdsboro, PA 19508
PHONE: 610-582-4900
HOURS: Open Tuesday to Sunday.
ADMISSION: A fee is charged.

Daniel Boone was born on the site of the Daniel Boone Homestead on November 2, 1734. Boone not only forged new territories for a new country, but he held the rank of colonel in the Virginia militia during the American Revolution and fought in several engagements in the present state of Kentucky. The Daniel Boone Homestead includes 579 acres of land, seven eighteenth-century

Daniel Boone Homestead

structures, and recreational facilities. One of these, the Boone House, began as a one-room, one-story log house built by Squire Boone in 1730. Here, Daniel Boone was born. John DeTurk, a later owner of the property, was also a veteran of the American Revolution and is buried on the homestead. Six other reconstructed buildings tell the history of the Boone Family. Every three to four years, the Daniel Boone Homestead hosts one of the largest Revolutionary War reenactments in the country, drawing up to 1,500 participants and thousands of visitors.

HOPEWELL FURNACE

2 Mark Bird Lane, Elverson, PA 19520
PHONE: 610-582-8773
HOURS: Open daily; closed New Year's Day, Martin Luther King, Jr. Day, Presidents' Day, Veterans' Day, Thanksgiving Day, and Christmas Day.
ADMISSION: A fee is charged.

Hopewell Furnace operated from 1771 until 1883, casting such diverse items as stoves, kettles, machinery, flat irons, and sash weights. Until America won its independence, all of these items were against England's Act of 1750, prohibiting the manufacture of finished iron products. During the Revolutionary War, Hopewell supplied cannon, shot, and shells for the Continental army. Maps for self-guided tours are available at the visitor's center.

The Cast House at Hopewell Furnace National Historic Site

PETER WENTZ FARMSTEAD

Shearer Road off Route 73, Worcester, PA 19490
PHONE: 610-584-5104
HOURS: Open Tuesday to Sunday; closed Easter, Thanksgiving Day, Christmas Eve and Day, New Year's Eve and Day.
ADMISSION: Free.
www. montcopa.org/culture/history.htm

Peter Wentz Farmstead

Peter Wentz Farmstead is a restored Germanic-Georgian farmhouse used by General George Washington as he planned the Battle of Germantown. The fear of threats against Washington's life were so intense that his personal cook locked himself in the kitchen day and night, guarding the food supply against the possibility of poison. The 97-acre estate includes an eighteenth-century German kitchen, a garden, farm animals, and a farmhouse that dates to 1758. The house is fully furnished with period antiques and features unique wall decorations. Special events are provided year-round.

MOLAND HOUSE

1641 Old York Road, Hartsville, PA
PHONE: 215-343-6852
HOURS: By appointment only until restoration is complete.
ADMISSION: A fee is charged.

Moland House

The Moland House was George Washington's headquarters from August 10 to August 23, 1777. While here, Washington eagerly awaited news that the British were headed toward Philadelphia as eleven thousand troops encamped nearby in the countryside. It was from Moland House that Washington moved to Chads Ford on the Brandywine. And here, the Marquis de Lafayette joined the Continental army. At the present time, the Warwick Township Historical Society is restoring the Moland House to its eighteenth-century appearance.

NESHAMINY-WARWICK PRESBYTERIAN CHURCH ———

1401 Meetinghouse Road, Warminster, PA 18974
PHONE: 215-343-6060
HOURS: Open Monday to Friday; cemetery open from dawn to dusk.
ADMISSION: Free.
www.nwpc.net

The Neshaminy-Warwick Presbyterian Church was organized in 1726, and the first building was built in 1727. After George Washington crossed the Delaware River in August of 1777, he stopped his troops near what is now Hartsville and began a thirteen-day encampment. During this time, Washington issued orders to hold a general court martial. The court martial was held in the church sanctuary and included the trial of Captain Henry "Light-Horse Harry" Lee. Lee was charged with "disobedience of orders." The court, however, unanimously agreed that the charges were groundless, and he was "acquitted with honor." Lee was later governor of Virginia, congressman, and father of Robert E. Lee. Revolutionary War soldiers lie buried in the church graveyard.

Neshaminy-Warwick Presbyterian Church

DAVID LIBRARY OF THE AMERICAN REVOLUTION ——

1201 River Road, Washington Crossing, PA 18977
PHONE: 215-493-6776
HOURS: Open Tuesday to Saturday; closed holidays. Appointments are encouraged.
ADMISSION: Free.

The David Library of the American Revolution is a research facility dedicated to the period from 1750 to 1800. It is primarily a microform archive of approximately 10,000 reels that contain an estimated eight million pages of documentation. The collection is supported by a reference collection of 40,000 books and pamphlets in both bound volumes and microcards. The library is particularly strong in materials from British sources, some of which are not available elsewhere in this country. In addition to the complete Loyalist claims series, the library also has other materials from Canada and Britain on Americans who opposed the Revolution such as American Loyalist Muster Rolls; Ward Chipman Papers; and documents relating to refugees. Information on German troops may be found in British records and Hessian documents of the American Revolution. The library has an extensive collection of American government records on the state and national levels from the U.S. National Archives, the Library of Congress, and other repositories. The library offers a series of lectures and seasonal exhibits.

WASHINGTON CROSSING PARK ——

Washington Crossing, PA 18977
PHONE: 215-493-4076
HOURS: Open Tuesday to Sunday; closed major holidays.
ADMISSION: A fee is charged.

Washington Crossing Park is dedicated to the perpetuation and preservation of the site from which the Continental army, led by General George Washington, crossed the Delaware River and marched into Trenton on the morning of December 26, 1776. A visitor's center features a documentary film, taped narration, exhibits, and information about the park. A Durham boat house on the grounds features replicas of the Durham, a type of boat that Washington and his men used for the crossing. McConkey's Ferry Inn served as a guardpost during the Continental army's encampment in Bucks County in December 1776, with earthworks and cannon to defend the ferry landing. Tradition has it that Washington and his aides ate their Christmas dinner here prior to crossing the river. The Thompson-Neely House was the home of Robert and Hannah Thompson in December 1776. It became the headquarters of General Lord Stirling (William Alexander), who was in charge of the troops stationed along the Delaware to prevent a British crossing. Stirling and his staff spent nearly the entire month of December at the house. The park also contains other historical buildings dating prior to the Revolution, as well as the graves of America's first unknown soldiers and the grave of Captain James Moore, who died on December 25, 1776, at the Thompson-Neely House.

FORT WASHINGTON STATE PARK

500 Bethlehem Pike, Fort Washington, PA 19034
PHONE: 215-591-5250
HOURS: Open daily.
ADMISSION: Free.

Fort Washington State Park takes its name from the fort built here by soldiers of the American Revolution in the fall of 1777. Whitemarsh, as the area was called then, was the scene of the encampment of 12,000 soldiers of General Washington's army from November 2 until December 11, 1777. Following the unsuccessful battle of Germantown, Washington chose the heights of the Whitemarsh Valley as an easily defendable position.

Fort Washington State Park

From here he pondered the possibility of launching an attack against General Howe's British army in Philadelphia. Although Washington decided against an attack, the British marched out from Philadelphia on December 5 to engage the Americans in battle. Because of Washington's strong position, only local skirmishes took place. After much marching back and forth, Howe led his army back to Philadelphia on December 8. Washington knew his poorly-clad men needed better quarters than the Whitemarsh, so he headed to Valley Forge on December 11, 1777.

Fort Washington State Park

HOPE LODGE

553 South Bethlehem Pike, Fort Washington, PA 19034
PHONE: 215-646-1595
HOURS: Open Tuesday to Sunday; closed major holidays.
ADMISSION: A fee is charged.

Hope Lodge was built by Samuel Morris, a prosperous Quaker entrepreneur, in the colonial era of 1743 to 1748. He resided here until 1770. Another Philadelphia merchant, William West, purchased the house from Morris's heirs, and the Wests lived at Hope Lodge from 1776 to 1782. The house was then known as Whitemarsh Farms and as Whitemarsh Estate. The Wests were in residence during the Whitemarsh Encampment, a six-week period of the American Revolution when the Continental army camped in

Hope Lodge

the surrounding fields after the Battle of Germantown and before encamping at Valley Forge. During that time the house was used as headquarters by George Washington's Surgeon General, John Cochran. The house is open for guided tours only.

INDEPENDENCE NATIONAL HISTORICAL PARK

Visitor's Center, Third and Chestnut Streets, Philadelphia, PA 19106
PHONE: 215-597-8974
HOURS: Open daily.
ADMISSION: Free except for a few sites.
www.nps.gov/inde

Independence National Historical Park comprises forty-four acres of eighteenth-, nineteenth-, and twentieth-century buildings that commemorate the founding of the nation. These buildings mark the physical place where the United States began. At the visitor's center the movie *Independence*, an award-winning short film directed by John Huston, can be seen. Maps and guides are available in thirteen languages at the information desk. Below are the individual sites that compose Independence National Historical Park.

INDEPENDENCE HALL

Chestnut Street between Fifth and Sixth Streets,
Philadelphia, PA 19106
PHONE: 215-597-8974
HOURS: Open daily.
ADMISSION: Free.

Independence Hall, originally built as the Pennsyl-
vania State House, is where the Declaration of
Independence was adopted and the United States
Constitution written. Admission to Independence
Hall is by a park ranger-led tour.

LIBERTY BELL PAVILION

Market Street between Fifth and Sixth Streets,
Philadelphia, PA 19106
PHONE: 215-597-8974 (Visitor's Center)
HOURS: Open daily.
ADMISSION: Free.

Independence Hall

The bell, now called the Liberty Bell, was created for the Pennsylvania State House and probably
rang on July 8, 1776, to announce the first public reading of the Declaration of Independence. In
the 1830s abolitionists named it the Liberty Bell based on its inscription from Leviticus: "Proclaim
liberty throughout all the land, unto all the inhabitants thereof." While no one knows exactly
when the bell cracked, it was repaired for the 1846 celebration of Washington's birthday. The
crack extended that day, rendering the bell irreparable. It now resides in a glass pavilion where it
may be viewed at any time. Information about the Liberty Bell is available in seventeen languages.

SECOND BANK OF THE UNITED STATES

Chestnut Street between Fourth and Fifth Streets, Philadelphia, PA 19106
PHONE: 215-597-8974
HOURS: Vary by season.
ADMISSION: A fee is charged.

The Second Bank of the United States
was built between 1819 and 1824 but
is of interest to Revolutionary War
historians for its portrait gallery,
which includes 185 paintings of colonial and federal leaders, military officers, explorers, and scientists. Many
of these paintings are by colonial artist
Charles Willson Peale. Self-guided or
guided tours are available.

Second Bank of the United States

CARPENTERS' HALL

320 Chestnut Street, Philadelphia, PA 19106
PHONE: 215-925-0167
HOURS: Open Tuesday to Sunday from
March to December and Wednesday to Sunday during January and February.
ADMISSION: Free.

Although Carpenters' Hall is on the grounds of the Independence National Historical Park, the building has always been privately owned by the Carpenters' Company. The hall was built in 1770 by the Carpenters' Company of the City and County of Philadelphia. The First Continental Congress met here in September of 1774. On December 18–28 in 1775, Benjamin Franklin met with the French emissary here. Together they hammered out a French-American alliance against England. During the Revolutionary War, the hall served as a hospital and an arsenal for American forces. Carpenters' Hall remains the property of the Carpenters' Company.

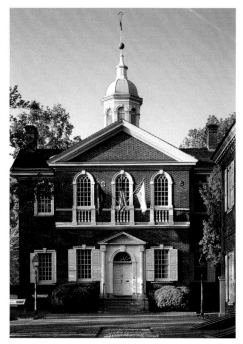

Carpenters' Hall

FRANKLIN COURT

Market Street between Third and Fourth Streets, Philadelphia, PA 19106
PHONE: 215-597-8974
HOURS: Vary by season.
ADMISSION: Free.

Franklin Court

This steel frame outlines the site of Benjamin Franklin's only house, which he built in 1763–1765. At the age of eighty, Franklin added a library to the house, remarking, "I hardly know how to justify building a library at an age that will so soon oblige me to quit it." The remains of the original foundations can be seen through viewing areas within the structure. Below the court is a museum with paintings and inventions associated with Franklin. A short film gives an overview of Franklin's family life.

Other properties on Market Street, some owned by Franklin, have been restored to their original exterior appearance. Number 314 is a bookstore, number 316 is a working United States post office and postal museum, and number 318 exhibits archeological finds from the area. The Printing Office, located at 320 Market Street, demonstrates eighteenth-century printing.

DECLARATION HOUSE

Corner of Seventh and Market Streets, Philadelphia, PA
PHONE: 215-597-8974
HOURS: Open daily.
ADMISSION: Free.

The Declaration House is a reconstruction of the house in which Thomas Jefferson rented rooms in the summer of 1776 while he served as a Virginia delegate to the Second Continental Congress. Jefferson lived here at the time he wrote the draft of the Declaration of Independence. A replica of his lap desk and swivel chair are on display at the house, along with other period pieces and exhibits. A movie about his life is also shown.

Declaration House

THE BENJAMIN FRANKLIN NATIONAL MEMORIAL

The Franklin Institute Science Museum, Philadelphia, PA
PHONE: 215-448-1280
HOURS: Open daily; closed major holidays.
ADMISSION: Free to the memorial. A fee is charged for admission to the institute.

The Benjamin Franklin National Memorial is located in the rotunda of The Franklin Institute Science Museum in Philadelphia. Dedicated by Congress in 1976, Memorial Hall features a 20-foot high marble statue of Franklin. Memorial Hall also houses many of Franklin's original possessions, including his original glass harmonica, his printing table, and several of his original publications. The glass static tube and electrostatic machine that he used to perform his scientific experiments are also on display. Two gifts that he received while he was in Paris, a tea set and a mystery clock, have been preserved. Even the odometer that Franklin used to measure the postal routes in Philadelphia is on display.

TOMB OF THE UNKNOWN SOLDIER

Washington Square, Sixth to Seventh and Walnut Streets, Philadelphia, PA
PHONE: Not available.
HOURS: Open daily.
ADMISSION: Free.

This is the only tomb in the United States erected in memory of the unknown Revolutionary War soldiers. A statue of General George Washington stands guard behind an eternal flame surrounded by the flags of the original thirteen colonies.

CHRIST CHURCH

Second Street above Market Street, Philadelphia, PA 19106
PHONE: 215-922-1695
HOURS: Open daily.
ADMISSION: Free.

Christ Church

This beautiful church was built between 1727 and 1744. Benjamin Franklin, George Washington, and Betsy Ross all worshiped here, as did John and Abigail Adams. Their pews are marked. James Wilson and Robert Morris, signers of the Declaration of Independence, are buried in the churchyard. Benjamin Franklin is buried in nearby Christ Church Burial Ground at Fifth and Arch streets. More Colonial and Revolutionary War leaders are buried at Christ Church Burial Ground than any other nonmilitary cemetery in the country. The burial ground is not open to the public; however, the grave of Benjamin Franklin is always visible from Arch Street. Guided tours are available.

BETSY ROSS HOUSE

239 Arch Street, Philadelphia, PA
PHONE: 215-627-5343
HOURS: Open Tuesday to Sunday and holiday Mondays.
ADMISSION: Free.

The Betsy Ross House features exhibits and furniture from the Revolutionary War period and provides a history of the American flag. Betsy Ross and her third husband are buried in the adjoining garden.

Children's room at the Betsy Ross House

Third, Scots, and Mariners Presbyterian Church (Old Pine Street Presbyterian Church)

412 Pine Street, Philadelphia, PA 19106
PHONE: 215-925-8051
HOURS: Open Monday to Saturday.
ADMISSION: Free.
www. libertynet.org/oldpine

Third, Scots, and Mariners Presbyterian Church was founded in 1768. Today, it is more likely to be recognized by its nickname of Old Pine Street Presbyterian Church. Its first pastor, George Duffield, served as chaplain to the First Continental Congress in 1774. Seventy-five Old Pine members joined General Washington at Valley Forge in the winter of 1776-77. During that winter of occupation, the British used Old Pine first as a hospital and later as a stable for their horses. They stripped the sanctuary of its plate and pews and the church of anything that could be sold or burned. They left behind the bodies of one hundred Hessian mercenaries who still lie under the east walk of the churchyard.

Interior of Old Pine Street Presbyterian Church

Old Saint Mary's Church

252 South Fourth Street, Philadelphia, PA
PHONE: 215-923-7930
HOURS: Open Monday to Saturday.
ADMISSION: Free.

Old Saint Mary's Church was established in 1763. At Sunday vespers in 1775, Old Saint Mary's hosted George Washington, John Adams, and other members of the First Continental Congress. The Continental Congress met here four times; and on July 4, 1779, the first public religious commemoration of the Declaration of Independence was here. In the church's burial ground lie members of the Continental Congress, George Washington's aide-de-camp; John Barry, the first to capture a British ship during the Revolutionary War; and other notable Revolutionary heroes. Self-directed tours are available any weekday; from May to October guided tours are offered the first Sunday of the month.

Pennsylvania Hospital
University of Pennsylvania Health System ——

800 Spruce Street, Philadelphia, PA 19107
Phone: 215-829-3971
Hours: Open Monday to Friday.
Admission: Free.

Pennsylvania Hospital, founded in 1751 by Benjamin Franklin and Dr. Thomas Bond, is literally the nation's first hospital. During the Revolutionary War, the hospital treated both British and Continental soldiers. A member of the hospital's medical staff at the time, Dr. Benjamin Rush, was one of the signers of the Declaration of Independence, as well as a pioneer in psychiatry. Unlike most of his peers, Dr. Rush

East Wing of the Pennsylvania Hospital at the time of the Revolutionary War

saw insanity as a disease rather than a manifestation of demons. His portrait, painted by Thomas Sully, hangs outside the hospital's historic library. The Pine Building has been in continuous use since 1755. Self-guided tours of the hospital's historic sites are available, and the hospital's walking-tour brochure is available at the welcome center inside the Eighth Street entrance.

Pine Building, Pennsylvania Hospital

St. Peter's Church

Third and Pine Streets, Philadelphia, PA 19106
Phone: 215-925-5968
Hours: Open daily. Interpretive guide available.
Admission: Free; donations welcome.

St. Peter's Church, built in 1761, is virtually unchanged with its wine-glass pulpit, ornate organ case, and original box pews, including number forty-one, the pew of the then-mayor, Samuel Powel. When George and Martha Washington were in the city, they often joined the Powels. The churchyard is the resting place of many national figures from the Revolutionary War days, including John Nixon, a lieutenant colonel in the Colonial army who gave the first public reading of the Declaration of Independence on July 8, 1776; Benjamin Chew, whose home, Cliveden, was the scene of the Battle of Germantown; Charles Willson Peale, portrait painter of many of the Revolutionary War heroes; and Dr. John Morgan, chief physician for the Continental army and founder of the University of Pennsylvania Medical School.

Interior of St. Peter's Church

Powel House

244 South Third Street, Philadelphia, PA 19106
Phone: 215-627-0364
Hours: Open Thursday to Sunday.
Admission: A fee is charged; reservations are recommended.

The Powel House, built by Samuel Powel, is notable as the residence of the last mayor of Philadelphia before the Revolution and the first mayor after the War. The house was built in 1765 and served as the setting for numerous gatherings that included guests such as George and Martha Washington, who were personal friends of the Powels.

CLIVEDEN OF THE NATIONAL TRUST

6401 Germantown Avenue, Philadelphia, PA 19144
PHONE: 215-848-1777
HOURS: Open Thursday to Sunday from April to December.
ADMISSION: A fee is charged.

Cliveden

On October 4, 1777, Cliveden was occupied by 120 red-coats under Lieutenant Colonel Thomas Musgrave, whose task was to slow down the Continentals and allow the British army to reach their home base. General Washington, on the way past Cliveden, gave the order to attack Cliveden with cannon fire and then send in the infantry. The cannonballs first bounced off the house's thick walls. Cannon were moved into place both at the front and the rear of the house, causing some casualties of Americans. After several hours, the Americans withdrew and left the British intact.

Cliveden stands as an example of one of America's finest Colonial homes. The house was built between 1763 and 1767 from local stone and is furnished with Philadelphia pieces from the eighteenth and nineteenth centuries. Visitors can walk the grounds where American soldiers fought and died and tour the home of the family that kept the memory of that battle alive. The outside of the house still bears the marks of Continental bombardment during the Battle of Germantown.

DESHLER-MORRIS HOUSE: THE GERMANTOWN WHITE HOUSE

5442 Germantown Avenue, Philadelphia, PA 19144
PHONE: 215-596-1748
HOURS: Open Wednesday to Sunday from April to mid-December.
ADMISSION: A fee is charged.

Quaker merchant David Deshler built this stone house in 1772. The Morrises were the last to live here and donated the property to the National Park Service. The Deshler-Morris House served as the headquarters of British commander Lieutenant General Sir William Howe during the Battle of Germantown in October of 1777. Ironically, Howe's great adversary during the Revolutionary War, George Washington, also used the house as a temporary residence during the yellow fever epidemic of 1793–94. During the time President Washington used the house, four cabinet meetings were held there.

Deshler-Morris House

GLORIA DEI CHURCH (OLD SWEDES')
NATIONAL HISTORIC SITE

Columbus Boulevard and Christian Street, Philadelphia, PA 19147
PHONE: 215-389-1513
HOURS: Open daily; tours by reservation only.
ADMISSION: Free.

Gloria Dei (Old Swedes') Church was built between 1699 and 1700. Today, it is an active Episcopal church. The church contains important historic relics and artifacts; and in the churchyard cemetery lie five of General Washington's officers, along with the gravestones of others. Also on the grounds is a memorial that honors John Hansen, first president of the Continental Congress, and John Morton, a signer of the Declaration of Independence.

UPSALA

6430 Germantown Avenue, Philadelphia, PA 19144
PHONE: 215-842-1798
HOURS: Open Thursday and Saturday for guided tours only.
ADMISSION: A fee is charged.

The mansion of Upsala was built in 1798 by John Johnson, Jr. and served as the site of the American headquarters for the Battle of Germantown on October 4, 1777. The front lawn of Upsala was the site of General Washington's army for the Battle of Germantown, the battle that led to Valley Forge. Upsala was home to the Johnson family for 175 years and today is a

National Historic Landmark. Set in 3½ acres of mature ornamental trees and landscaped lawns in the historic Germantown neighborhood of Philadelphia, Upsala is one of America's great federal houses. The interior of Upsala has been restored to its eighteenth-century grandeur with authentic period furniture, including original Johnson family antiques.

Upsala

Gen. William Howe

BRITISH

COMMANDERS:
Gen. William Howe,
Adm. Richard Howe

STRENGTH: 240 naval
war and supply ships,
27,000 troops on land

CASUALTIES: 12

THE SIEGE OF FORT MIFFLIN

November 10-15, 1777

Once the British captured Philadelphia in September of 1777, it quickly became apparent that, in order to hold the city, they must open the Delaware River to shipping and bring up much needed supplies. Obstructions called cheavaux de frise had been sunk into the river mud and were defended by Fort Mercer and Fort Mifflin, both located south of the city.

On October 21, 1777, the British began operations to secure the Delaware River by attacking Fort Mercer in New Jersey. Two thousand Hessians attacked the fort, which held 400 defenders. The colonials fought with such ferocity that the enemy finally withdrew, leaving 371 dead, including twenty-two officers. Within the fort, fourteen Americans were dead and twenty-three wounded.

It was during this battle that the sixty-four-gun ship *Augusta* became caught on a sandbar and was exploded by shot from both forts. Additionally, the *Roebuck* also became snagged and was abandoned and burned by the British sailors.

The British then turned their attention to Fort Mifflin, located on Mud Island, five hundred yards from the shores of Pennsylvania. Though constructed by the British in 1771, the fort was ill-prepared for the upcoming battle. Its east walls constructed of stone were sturdy enough, but the rest of the fort was composed of mud and wood, with the interior boasting buildings of wood and only four blockhouses. The garrison consisted of about three hundred men and a few cannon. Washington had relieved the fort of several of the big guns in September in anticipation of fighting a losing battle.

To the west and north of the fort lay Carpenter's Island and Province Island. It was here that the British erected gun batteries supplied with ten large cannon for bombarding the fort. The British also moved a floating battery within forty yards of the south end of the fort. On November 10 at 8:00 A.M., a signal sounded in the river from the British ships. This began what has come to be known as the greatest bombardment of the American Revolution. With all land guns and the ships, as well as the floating battery, firing simultaneously at Fort Mifflin, it is estimated that one thousand cannon balls every thirty minutes rained into the poorly constructed and weakly defended fort.

Cannon at Fort Mifflin

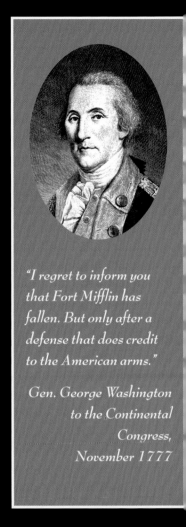

"I regret to inform you that Fort Mifflin has fallen. But only after a defense that does credit to the American arms."

Gen. George Washington to the Continental Congress, November 1777

The siege continued for five days, totally obliterating the fort buildings and most of the wooden walls. In the early morning hours of November 15, the British began sailing smaller ships, the *Vigilant* and the *Fury,* up the back channel. British marines were able to fire with handguns or muskets right into the fort at its valiant defenders. Additional floating batteries were moved into place and the siege continued. Fort Mifflin was down to two guns and approximately eighty defenders.

With nightfall, Major Simeon Thayer began the process of gathering the dead and wounded and removing them to Fort Mercer across the river. Of the fifty able-bodied men remaining, he chose several to stay behind and set fire to what remained of Fort Mifflin. Then they too sailed for New Jersey. Fort Mifflin had fought this battle alone with no assistance from the American navy. Commodore Hazelwood had failed to respond to calls for assistance. When Fort Mifflin was abandoned, Thayer left the colors flying. Fort Mifflin never surrendered.

With the fall of Fort Mifflin, the British were able to clear the Delaware of the obstructions and sail supplies into Philadelphia. But this was to prove a hollow victory. Winter had set in by the time the ships reached port on December 10. Howe was ill-disposed to march in cold, frigid temperatures. Washington and the Continental army found safety in the hills of Valley Forge without pursuit and spent the winter of 1778 preparing for the eventual victory.

AMERICAN

COMMANDERS:
Gen. George Washington, Lt. Col. Samuel Smith, Maj. Simeon Thayer

STRENGTH:
Approximately 300

CASUALTIES:
Approximately 250

FORT MIFFLIN ON THE DELAWARE

Fort Mifflin Road, Philadelphia, PA 19153

PHONE: 215-492-1881

HOURS: Open Wednesday to Sunday from April 1 to November 30.

ADMISSION: A fee is charged; group rates available.

Dungeons at Fort Mifflin

Located at the southernmost tip of Philadelphia on Mud Island, it was called Mud Fort for the obvious reason that it was constructed of mud. This defense has been called the "Alamo of the Revolution" for holding off a British siege for five days. The fort was rebuilt after the Revolution and named for Pennsylvania governor Thomas Mifflin. Daily tours, uniform and weapons demonstrations, and cannon firings are available. Weekend events include living-history programs and military reenactments.

VALLEY FORGE NATIONAL HISTORICAL PARK

Route 23 and North Gulph Road, Valley Forge, PA 19482

PHONE: 610-783-1077

HOURS: Open daily; closed Christmas Day.

ADMISSION: Free to the park. A fee is charged for admission to the historic buildings.

Valley Forge, above all other places, epitomizes the courage and grit of the patriots of the American Revolution. The story of Valley Forge is the story of the six month encampment of the Continental army of the newly-formed United States of America under the command of General George Washington. Although no battle was fought here, from December 19, 1777 to June 19, 1778, the army struggled against the elements and low morale. A light snow fell as 12,000 weary men made their way up Gulph Road to the area selected only days before as winter quarters.

The Valley Forge Visitor's Center offers an eighteen-minute film, shown every half hour, that introduces visitors to the winter encampment of 1777–78. The visitor's center offers maps featuring a self-guided tour past extensive remains and replicas of major forts and earthworks, the Artillery Park, Washington's Headquarters, and the Grand Parade, where General von Steuben trained the Continental army.

A living-history program with interpreters at Washington's Headquarters shows life at Valley Forge, with reconstructed huts nearby. Huts have been reconstructed to show the life of a soldier during the Revolution. From July through Labor Day, the Soldier Life programs and other ranger-led walks and talks are presented. In December, a reenactment of the march into Valley Forge is held; in May is the French Alliance Day reenactment; and in June, visitors may reenact the march out of Valley Forge. A road loops through the park where visitors may see the perimeter of the Grand Parade drill ground where von Steuben trained the militia into an army. Overlooking the Grand Parade is General James Varnum's Quarters. This house is open to the public, but other houses that quartered members of Washington's staff are private. The road also passes the Outer Line Defenses and the Inner Line Defenses. Mount Joy and Redoubt 4 have been reconstructed for viewing. The National Memorial Arch bears George Washington's words, "Naked and starving as they are, we cannot enough admire the incomparable patience and fidelity of the soldiery," spoken on February 16, 1778 in Valley Forge. Washington Memorial Chapel and Museum of the Valley Forge Historical Society are open to the public but are on private land within the park. A fee is charged for admittance.

General George Washington's headquarters during the Valley Forge winter encampment, Valley Forge National Historical Park

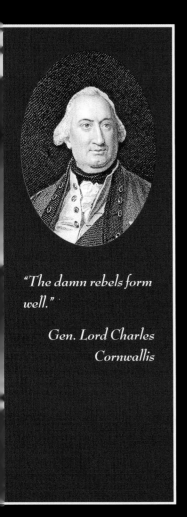

"The damn rebels form well."

Gen. Lord Charles
Cornwallis

BRITISH

COMMANDERS:
Maj. Gen. William Howe,
Gen. Lord Charles Cornwallis

STRENGTH:
Approximately 12,500

CASUALTIES:
Approximately 577

BATTLE OF BRANDYWINE

September 11, 1777

On September 8, General William Howe was moving toward Philadelphia. To counter this threat, General George Washington set up defensive positions at Chads Ford, located on one of the main roads to Philadelphia. On September 9, both armies were preparing to fight. One of Washington's commanders expressed concern to Washington about the vulnerability of the army's right flank. He asked whether any fords existed above those under his watch and was told that there were none within twelve miles.

Unfortunately, Washington's lack of reconnaissance was not duplicated by Howe, who knew of the other crossings and also knew how Washington had established his position. Howe planned one attack along Chads Ford where Washington waited, but a second British force would cross at two fords further north and hit Washington's right flank.

During the night of September 10, a light rain was falling over the Brandywine valley, and at dawn on September 11, a dense fog covered the countryside. Washington had two reports of Howe's movements, both indicating that Howe was dividing his forces with the main striking force under General Cornwallis's command. Washington devised a brilliant plan for attack, but then received messages to the effect that the sight-

Building at Brandywine Battlefield

ings of the British must have been mistaken. Washington canceled his attack orders and pulled back his advance elements from across the creek.

Later that afternoon, a farmer who had done some scouting on his own rode into Washington's headquarters and managed to see the general. He reported that he had suddenly confronted an advancing British column and had been fired upon but had escaped unhurt. The British were across the Brandywine and on their way south on Washington's right. Washington and his army would soon be surrounded, but the general and his staff did not believe him. The farmer became enraged and said, "You're mistaken, General. My life for it you're mistaken." The farmer even drew a map in the dust, pointing out where he had seen the British. The farmer couldn't convince Washington, but at that moment a missive came from General Sullivan reporting that the enemy was to his right and rear. Howe had managed to pull off a diversionary action identical to that which had defeated Washington at Long Island less than a year before.

Washington swung around part of his forces into a defensive stance and pulled all but two brigades off Chads Ford to meet the main force. These troops were still positioning themselves when the British attacked. At 3:30 P.M., British formations marched across the valley which lay between the American position and Osborne's Hill. They marched in parade-ground order, no hurry, with bayonets glinting in the sun, the scarlet of the British and the blue of the Hessians, with the arrogant assurance that marked the disciplined troops of that period, and with the bands playing "The British Grenadiers."

A captain of the Delawares wrote of the battle: "Cannon balls flew thick and many and small arms roared like the rolling of a drum. The Americans were driven back five times. Five times they surged back again. But the odds against them were too great. When darkness overtook them, Washington ordered his army to retreat."

The Americans took their defeat only as a setback. The American Captain Anderson wrote of the defeat: "I saw not a despairing look, nor did I hear a despairing word. We had our solacing words already for each other—'Come, boys, we shall do better another time'—sounded throughout our little army."

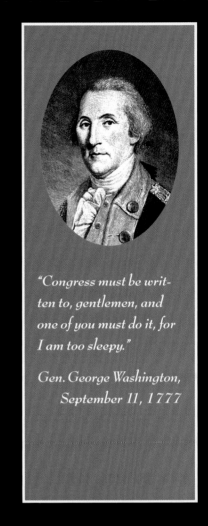

"Congress must be written to, gentlemen, and one of you must do it, for I am too sleepy."

Gen. George Washington, September 11, 1777

AMERICAN

COMMANDER:
Gen. George Washington

STRENGTH:
Approximately 11,000

CASUALTIES: Approximately 1,200–1,300

BRANDYWINE BATTLEFIELD PARK ———

Route 1, Chadds Ford, PA 19317

PHONE: 610-459-3342

HOURS: Open Tuesday to Sunday.

ADMISSION: Free; a fee is charged for admittance to the houses.

www.ushistory.org/brandywine/

The Brandywine Battlefield Park brings to life the largest battle of the Revolutionary War. The park includes a visitor's center with a museum and gift shop. The museum contains artifacts from the battle and various exhibits explaining the battle. Washington's Headquarters and Lafayette's Quarters are also on the grounds of the park. Washington's Headquarters was an early Quaker stone house where Washington lodged and met with his generals to plan his battle strategy. The original house was damaged by fire in the early twentieth century. Today, visitors are able to tour the historically-accurate reconstructed house. Lafayette's Quarters is the original farmhouse where the Marquis de Lafayette stayed on the eve of the battle, which was his first military action in America. The houses are accessible during guided tours only. The park also offers student-oriented educational programs, and visitors can retrace the steps of the Americans and British in the battle through driving tours.

Anthony Wayne Parlor at Historic Waynesborough

Historic Waynesborough

2049 Waynesborough Road, Paoli, PA 19301

PHONE: 610-647-1779

HOURS: Open Tuesday to Thursday from mid-March to December; closed major holidays. Special tours by prior arrangement.

ADMISSION: A fee is charged.

Historic Waynesborough

This was the home of seven generations of Waynes, the most famous of whom was Major General Anthony Wayne, who led troops during the Battles of Brandywine and Germantown. Starting with Anthony Wayne's grandfather, Captain Anthony Wayne, the Wayne family raised troops and/or fought in every war from the French and Indian War through the Civil War. Theodore Roosevelt is said to have called General Anthony Wayne "the greatest fighting general in American history." The house is furnished with period pieces, many original to the house, reflecting all seven generations of ownership by this distinguished family.

RHODE ISLAND

*R*hode Island was founded in 1644 by Roger Williams, Anne Hutchinson, and Samuel Gorton, all three of whom had been banished from Massachusetts Bay as troublemakers. The colony was founded upon the principle of religious liberty.

This colony was the birthplace and home of General Nathanael Greene, second in command to George Washington. Here also is the home of Gilbert Stuart, who painted just about every patriot of the time. Without Stuart's paintings, we would not know what many of these leaders looked like.

Newport, site of a battle in 1778 and final resting place of several Patriots, still has many churches, homes, and buildings that relate to the Revolutionary War.

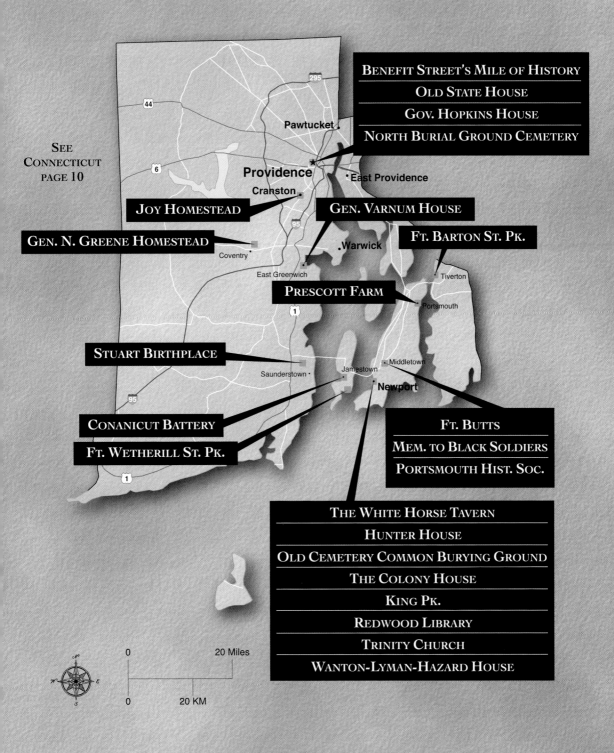

BENEFIT STREET'S MILE OF HISTORY

OLD STATE HOUSE

GOV. HOPKINS HOUSE

NORTH BURIAL GROUND CEMETERY

SEE CONNECTICUT PAGE 10

Pawtucket

Providence

Cranston

East Providence

JOY HOMESTEAD

GEN. VARNUM HOUSE

GEN. N. GREENE HOMESTEAD

FT. BARTON ST. PK.

Coventry

Warwick

Tiverton

East Greenwich

PRESCOTT FARM

Portsmouth

STUART BIRTHPLACE

Middletown

Saunderstown

Jamestown

Newport

CONANICUT BATTERY

FT. WETHERILL ST. PK.

FT. BUTTS

MEM. TO BLACK SOLDIERS

PORTSMOUTH HIST. SOC.

THE WHITE HORSE TAVERN

HUNTER HOUSE

OLD CEMETERY COMMON BURYING GROUND

THE COLONY HOUSE

KING PK.

REDWOOD LIBRARY

TRINITY CHURCH

WANTON-LYMAN-HAZARD HOUSE

0   20 Miles

0   20 KM

BENEFIT STREET'S MILE OF HISTORY

Benefit Street, Providence, RI

PHONE: 401-831-7440 (Providence Preservation Society)

HOURS: Tours available Monday to Friday.

ADMISSION: Walking tour is free; a fee is charged for the bus tour.

Benefit Street's "Mile of History" is a street of restored colonial homes and buildings, including churches and museums, that overlook the Providence waterfront. Several houses from the Revolutionary War era are on the street, including Joseph Jenckes House circa 1774, Samuel Staples House circa 1760, the Brick School House, which was occupied by French troops during the Revolution, and the John Carter House circa 1772. The first Baptist Church in America, founded in 1775, is also on the street. Both walking and bus tours are available during the week.

Benefit Street homes in College Hill

OLD STATE HOUSE

150 Benefit Street, Providence, RI

PHONE: 401-222-2678

HOURS: Open Monday to Friday.

ADMISSION: Free.

The Old State House was built in 1762 and was the primary seat of state government from 1776 to 1901. On May 4, 1776, Rhode Island renounced allegiance to George III at this site. The building hosted Patriots George Washington, Thomas Jefferson, and the Marquis de Lafayette. Today, the building is the home of the Rhode Island Historical Preservation and Heritage Commission.

Old State House

Governor Stephen Hopkins House

15 Hopkins Street, Providence, RI
PHONE: 401-421-0694
HOURS: Open Wednesday and Saturday from April to December by appointment only.
ADMISSION: A fee is charged.

The Hopkins House was built circa 1707 as the home of Stephen Hopkins, a member of the Continental Congress, a signer of the Declaration of Independence, and the governor of Rhode Island for ten terms. The house was moved from its original site and restored to its present condition.

North Burial Ground Cemetery

5 Branch Avenue, Providence, RI
PHONE: 401-331-0177
HOURS: Open daily.
ADMISSION: Free.

In the North Burial Ground Cemetery are the remains of William Barton, major general and hero of the Revolution, and of Stephen Hopkins, a signer of the Declaration of Independence.

North Burial Ground Cemetery

JOY HOMESTEAD

156 Scituate Avenue, Cranston, RI
PHONE: 401-463-6168
HOURS: Open by appointment only.
ADMISSION: A fee is charged.

The Joy Homestead was built in 1778 by Job Joy, a cobbler and farmer. This two-story, red gambrel-roofed house features ten rooms and a cellar. A central chimney provides three fireplaces on the first floor. The second floor has two master chambers, one with a fireplace. The house is furnished with antiques from the colonial period. The Joy Homestead has recently undergone repairs and renovations.

GENERAL NATHANAEL GREENE HOMESTEAD

50 Taft Street, Coventry, RI 02816
PHONE: 401-821-8630
HOURS: Open Wednesday, Saturday, and Sunday from April to October.
ADMISSION: A fee is charged.

The Greene Homestead was built in 1770. During the Revolutionary War, Nathanael Greene became George Washington's second in command. The house remained in the Greene family for five generations, and today the homestead features a mixture of fine furnishings from 1770 to the 1890s, some of which were original to the general. A Revolutionary War cannon forged by the Greene foundry stands on the site. Outside the house is a family cemetery and a formal garden.

GENERAL JAMES MITCHELL VARNUM HOUSE

57 Pierce Street, East Greenwich, RI 02818
PHONE: 401-884-1776
HOURS: Open Memorial Day to Labor Day.
ADMISSION: A fee is charged.

General James Mitchell Varnum built this mansion in 1773. Varnum graduated with honors from Rhode Island College (now Brown University) in its first class of 1769. He was a successful lawyer and became Colonel of the Kentish Guards in October 1774. Before dawn on the day of the Lexington and Concord battle, Varnum was awakened at 2:00 A.M. by the alarm at Tewksbury, where Paul Revere's message had been received. Varnum became one of George Washington's generals and was later elected to the Continental Congress. The house features a colonial garden, as well as furnishings from the colonial period.

STUART BIRTHPLACE

815 Gilbert Stuart Road, Saunderstown, RI 02874-2911
PHONE: 401-294-3001
HOURS: Open Thursday to Monday.
ADMISSION: A fee is charged.

The Stuart house was built in 1750, and five years later painter Gilbert Stuart was born. Stuart studied in Newport and painted portraits of George Washington, John Adams, Thomas Jefferson, James Madison, James Monroe, John Quincy Adams, and Generals Henry Knox and Horatio Gates, among others. On the site is the working snuff mill owned and operated by the elder Stuart and a grist mill that was built in 1662. The Gilbert Stuart House became a National Historic Landmark in 1966. It has been restored as the home of a colonial working man.

Stuart Birthplace

CONANICUT BATTERY

Prospect Hill, off Beavertail Road, Jamestown, RI
PHONE: 401-423-7200 (Town of Jamestown)
HOURS: Open daily from dawn to dusk.
ADMISSION: Free.

The Conanicut Battery dates from the eighteenth century and was in use during the Revolutionary War. The battery is on the second highest point on the island and affords a spectacular view of the water.

Fort Wetherill State Park

Fort Wetherill Road, Jamestown, RI 02835
Phone: 401-423-1771
Hours: Open daily.
Admission: Free.

Fort Wetherill, built by the Patriots during the summer of 1776 and later abandoned to the British, once stood on this site. After the Revolution, a stone tower with eight guns was erected in its place, and the site became Fort Dumplings. The fort that stands today was built in the late nineteenth century.

Hunter House

54 Washington Street, Newport, RI 02840
Phone: 401-847-1000 (The Preservation Society of Newport County)
Hours: Open daily from late May to early October.
Admission: A fee is charged.
www.newportmansions.org

The Hunter House was built between 1748 and 1754 by Jonathan Nichols, Jr., a Newport merchant. After his death, Colonel Joseph Wanton bought the house. Although Wanton was a deputy governor of Rhode Island, his sympathies lay with the British. Once war broke out, Wanton fled the state and French Admiral de Ternay, commander of the French fleet, appropriated the house for use as his headquarters. After the war, William Hunter, a Rhode Island U.S. senator, purchased the house and lent it his name. The Hunter House is considered one of the ten best colonial homes existing in America today and boasts a priceless collection of Townsend-Goddard furniture, silver, and portraits, one of which is by Gilbert Stuart.

Hunter House

COMMON BURYING GROUND

Farewell Street, Newport, RI 02840
PHONE: 401-846-0813 (Newport Historical Society)
HOURS: Open daily from dawn to dusk.
ADMISSION: Free.

Among the patriots buried in the Common Burying Ground is William B. Eller, who was a signer of the Declaration of Independence, a graduate of Harvard, a lawyer, and a representative from Rhode Island to the Continental Congress.

Common Burying Ground

COLONY HOUSE

Washington Square, Newport, RI 02840
PHONE: 401-846-0813 (Newport Historical Society)
HOURS: Open for guided tours depending on the season.
ADMISSION: A fee is charged.

The Colony House was built in 1739 and served as the state house of Rhode Island until 1901. The Declaration of Independence was read from the steps of the Colony House on July 20, 1776. During the British occupation of Newport from 1776 to 1779, British soldiers were housed in the Colony House. After the French liberation of Newport, the building was used as a hospital; and in 1782, General Rochambeau hosted a banquet in the great hall in honor of George Washington. A painting of George Washington by Gilbert Stuart hangs in the building.

Colony House

KING PARK

North Wellington Avenue, Newport, RI 02840
HOURS: Open daily from dawn to dusk.
ADMISSION: Free.

In King Park stands a monument that marks the place where French General Rochambeau and his troops landed on July 12, 1780, to begin their liberation of Newport from the British.

French General Rochambeau on monument at King Park

King Park

REDWOOD LIBRARY AND ATHENAEUM

50 Belleville Avenue, Newport, RI 02840
PHONE: 401-847-0292
HOURS: Open Sunday to Friday.
ADMISSION: Free.

The Redwood Library was chartered in 1747 and opened to the public in 1750. The library, designed by Peter Harrison, was built to house a collection of books purchased from London through the generosity of Abraham Redwood. During the Revolution, the library was occupied by the British and may have been used as their officer's club. After looting by some British troops, British Major General William Prescott posted a guard at its door. Today, the library contains a valuable collection of books, as well as early American paintings, including five each by Gilbert Stuart and Robert Feke. This is the oldest circulating library in America.

Redwood Library

TRINITY CHURCH

Queen Anne Square, Spring and Church
Streets, Newport, RI 02840
PHONE: 401-846-0660
HOURS: Open Monday to Friday
from May to June and from
September to October; open daily
from Independence Day to Labor
Day, or by appointment.
ADMISSION: Donation appreciated.

Trinity Church was completed in 1726.
George Washington worshiped here,
and George Frederick Handel tested the
church's pipe organ before it was sent
from England. The church contains two
Tiffany stained-glass windows and the
only center-aisle, three-tiered, wine-
glass pulpit in America. Admiral Charles
de Ternay, commander of the fleet that
escorted the French expeditionary force
of Rochambeau to America, is buried in
the adjacent cemetery.

Trinity Church

THE WHITE HORSE TAVERN

26 Marlborough Street, Newport, RI 02840
PHONE: 401-849-3600
HOURS: Open daily.

The White Horse Tavern was built in 1673 as a two-room, two-story residence of Frances Brin-
ley. For awhile the tavern became the meeting place of the colony's general assembly, criminal
court, and town council. No building is believed more typical of colonial Newport than this ven-
erable structure with its clapboard walls, gambrel roof, and plain pedimented doors bordering
the sidewalk. Inside, its giant "summer" beams, small stairway hard against the chimney, tiny
front hall, and cavernous fireplaces are the very essence of seventeenth-century American architecture. Today, the White Horse Tavern is a restaurant.

WANTON-LYMAN-HAZARD HOUSE

17 Broadway, Newport, RI 02840
PHONE: 401-846-0813
HOURS: Hours vary seasonally.
ADMISSION: A fee is charged.

The Wanton-Lyman-Hazard House was built around 1675. The house was purchased in 1757 by British Loyalist Martin Howard. In 1765, he, along with other Tories, wrote and published a pamphlet criticizing the opponents of the Crown. During the Stamp Act riots, Howard and two other Tories were hanged in effigy on Washington Square and their houses

Wanton-Lyman-Hazard House

vandalized. Howard fled under the protection of the British. The house has been home to colonial governors, justices, and patriots. It has been somewhat restored and contains furniture from the colonial period. Recent and ongoing archeological investigations have revealed previously unknown information about the house, the site, and the Stamp Act Riots.

FORT BUTTS

Sprague Street, Portsmouth, RI 02871
PHONE: 401-683-3255
HOURS: Open daily.
ADMISSION: Free.

Fort Butts is an earthwork redoubt erected during the Revolutionary War. Its location atop Butts Hill provides a panoramic view of Mt. Hope Bay and the central reaches of Narragansett Bay. It anchored the final American position during the Battle of Rhode Island in August of 1778, which was the first military campaign jointly undertaken by the Americans and their French allies.

MEMORIAL TO BLACK SOLDIERS

Routes 114 and 24, Portsmouth, RI 02871
PHONE: 401-683-3255
HOURS: Open daily.
ADMISSION: A fee is charged.

The Memorial to Black Soldiers commemorates the First Rhode Island Regiment, which was made up of mostly African Americans. This regiment prevented British troops from flanking the main American line during the Battle of Rhode Island in 1778.

Portsmouth Historical Society

P.O. Box 834, East Main Road and Union Street, Portsmouth, RI 02871
PHONE: 401-683-9178
HOURS: Open Sunday from Memorial Day to Columbus Day.
ADMISSION: Free.

The Portsmouth Historical Society Museum features collections of colonial farm and household tools. On the museum grounds stands a monument marking the site of the initial skirmish of the Battle of Rhode Island in 1778. Also on the grounds is the oldest one-room schoolhouse in Rhode Island.

Prescott Farm

2009 West Main Road, Middletown, RI 02840
PHONE: 401-847-6230
HOURS: Open Monday to Friday from April to November.
ADMISSION: Free.

The Prescott Farm is a restored colonial farm that served as the guardhouse of British General Richard Prescott. In 1775, Prescott was captured, but was later released in exchange for an American general. In 1776, Prescott became a colonel and was third in command of the British forces that occupied Newport. He remained at Newport as commander of the garrison and became known as arrogant, haughty, and ill-tempered. He was universally despised by the Patriots. In July 1777, Major William Barton learned that Prescott was quartered in the Overing House. Barton and several other raiders surprised Prescott at the home, captured him, and once again exchanged him for an imprisoned American general. The British press lampooned Prescott for his humiliating capture, but the episode gave the Patriots a much needed morale booster. The Overing House became the Prescott House. The restored farm contains a number of colonial buildings.

Fort Barton State Park

Highland Road, Tiverton, RI 02878
PHONE: 401-625-6700
HOURS: Open daily.
ADMISSION: Free.

Fort Barton was completed in 1777 as Tiverton Heights Fort with Lieutenant Colonel William Barton as commander. It was from this fort that Barton and forty men set out on the raid that would result in the capture of British General Richard Prescott. Following this event, the fort was renamed in honor of Barton, a soldier with outstanding patriotism and bravery. The site has three miles of trails and a thirty-foot high observation tower from which Sakonnet River, Mount Hope Bay, and the Portsmouth and Bristol shorelines are visible.

SOUTH CAROLINA

The war came to South Carolina in May 1780 when the British attacked Charleston and captured what was then America's fourth largest city and the capital of the South. Thereafter followed battles at Camden, Kings Mountain, and Cowpens. In early 1781, the British were pushed north following the decisive American victory at Cowpens.

Today, the battlefields of Camden and Kings Mountain are National Battlefields, and Ninety Six is a National Historic Site. There are several beautiful mansions that were built by the patriots and today are preserved in their original splendor.

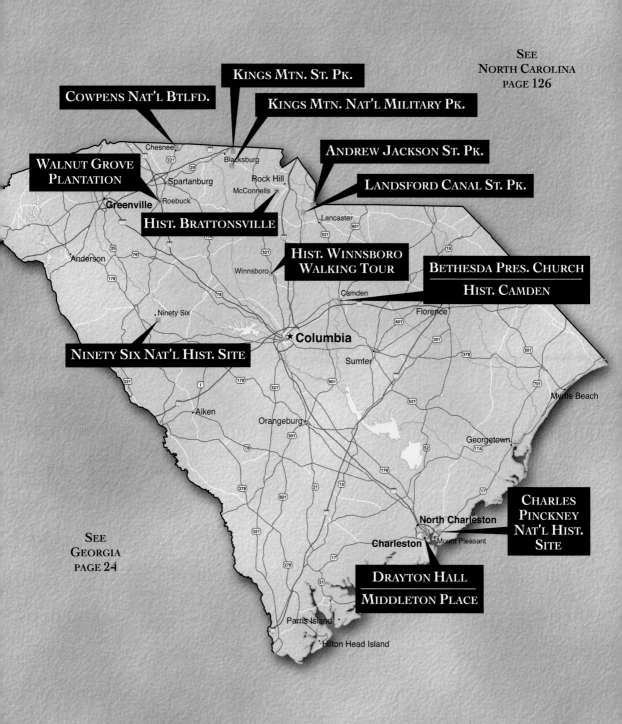

SEE
NORTH CAROLINA
PAGE 126

KINGS MTN. ST. PK.

COWPENS NAT'L BTLFD.

KINGS MTN. NAT'L MILITARY PK.

ANDREW JACKSON ST. PK.

WALNUT GROVE
PLANTATION

LANDSFORD CANAL ST. PK.

HIST. BRATTONSVILLE

HIST. WINNSBORO
WALKING TOUR

BETHESDA PRES. CHURCH

HIST. CAMDEN

NINETY SIX NAT'L HIST. SITE

CHARLES
PINCKNEY
NAT'L HIST.
SITE

DRAYTON HALL

MIDDLETON PLACE

Chesnee

Blacksburg

221 29

Spartanburg

Rock Hill

Roebuck

McConnells

Greenville

385

Lancaster

601

Anderson

25 76

170

521

178

321

15

Winnsboro

76

Camden

Ninety Six

401

Florence

★ Columbia

301

378

Sumter

501

221

1

178

321

601

701

20

Myrtle Beach

Aiken

78

521

Orangeburg

301

Georgetown

17A

52

176

278

601

21

15

17

North Charleston

321

Charleston

Mount Pleasant

278

17

Parris Island

21

Hilton Head Island

SEE
GEORGIA
PAGE 24

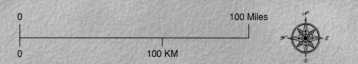

0   100 Miles

0   100 KM

N
W   E
S

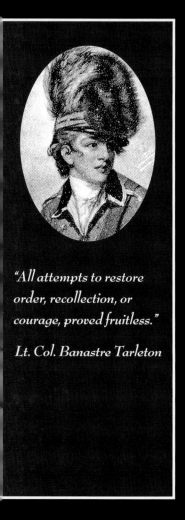

BRITISH

COMMANDERS:
Gen. Lord Charles Cornwallis, Lt. Col. Banastre Tarleton

STRENGTH: 1,530

CASUALTIES: 110 killed; 800 captured

BATTLE OF COWPENS

January 17, 1781

After the disaster at Camden, South Carolina, Washington replaced General Horatio Gates with General Nathanael Greene. Greene decided to split his army in half, with General Daniel Morgan proceeding to western South Carolina with 600 troops in the middle of December. His force grew to 1,000 with militia units, and they made guerrilla raids on the British in the area for the next two weeks.

British General Cornwallis learned of the unorthodox split of the Patriots and sent Tarleton to "destroy Morgan's corps or push it over the Broad River toward Kings Mountain." Morgan learned where Tarleton was heading and proceeded to an area between Thicketty Creek and a bend in Broad River called Cowpens. A rise in the ground was an excellent place to entrench.

Most of Morgan's men were short-term militia as opposed to trained Continentals, and he knew that they would not stand and fight once the British attacked. Therefore, the night before the battle, Morgan went around the camp asking that the riflement fire only two times. These shots, however, were to be accurate; and he told the militiamen to aim for the "epaulettes," in other words, to shoot the officers. Morgan then told the men to retreat into the next line after those two shots.

In the morning, Morgan lined up his crack marksmen on the front line. Behind them were more dependable militia, with a third of this line composed of veterans who would hold longer. The rear consisted of Continentals, reliable veterans. His mounted reserve were near the militia's horses in the rear.

When the British assaulted the first line, the marksmen fired, picking off fifteen British officers. Tarleton persisted in his frontal attack. The second line of Patriots delivered their two shots also before they melted into the next line. Morgan was in the rear regrouping the riflement as they made for their horses. The mounted militia came up from the rear around the American right flank and drove off the British mounted dragoons while the third line of veteran Continentals continued a steady rate of fire.

Tarleton misinterpreted the riflemen's withdrawal as a retreat and pursued the Patriots. Morgan stopped his militia, ordered them about face, fire, fix their bayonets, and charge. This so surprised the British that they turned and ran, just as Morgan's mounted militia hit them on their right and the militia charged their left. Tarleton ordered his reserve dragoons to charge, but they, having witnessed the battle up to that point, refused. After a short saber duel between the two commanders, Tarleton retreated what was left of his army.

The Battle of Cowpens is known for the genius of General Morgan in that he was able to harness the weakness of his army (the militia's propensity to run when charged) and design a battle plan that made use of this weakness.

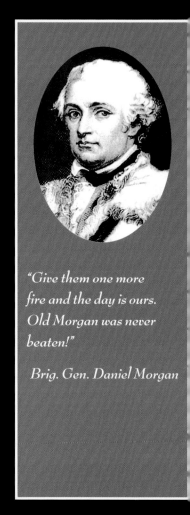

"Give them one more fire and the day is ours. Old Morgan was never beaten!"

Brig. Gen. Daniel Morgan

AMERICAN:

COMMANDERS:
Gen. Nathanael Greene, Brig. Gen. Daniel Morgan

STRENGTH: 1,100

CASUALTIES:
12 killed (estimated); 60 injured

The Battle of Cowpens

COWPENS NATIONAL BATTLEFIELD ⸻

4001 Chesnee Highway, Chesnee, SC 29323

PHONE: 864-461-2828

HOURS: Open daily.

ADMISSION: Free.

Cowpens National Battlefield covers 845 acres and retains the same terrain and landscape as seen by the forces that fought here in 1781. The battlefield is preserved in its 1781 appearance, with the meadow rising to seventy feet above the surrounding forest. A self-guided auto or foot tour with markers enables visitors to see Daniel Morgan's strategic use of this terrain. The visitor's center includes a lighted map of the battlefield and a slide show which depicts the course of the battle.

Cowpens National Battlefield

WALNUT GROVE PLANTATION

1200 Otts Shoals Road, Roebuck, SC 29376

PHONE: 864-576-6546

HOURS: Open Tuesday to Sunday from April to October and Saturday and Sunday from November to March.

ADMISSION: A fee is charged.

www.spartanarts.org/history/Walnut Grove

Walnut Grove Plantation

Walnut Grove Plantation sits on land King George III granted to Charles Moore in 1763. Buried on the grounds in the Moore family cemetery are Margaret Katherine Barry, a local Revolutionary War heroine, as well as other family members, slaves, and Revolutionary War soldiers. The house has double shouldered chimneys, clapboard-over-log construction, and Queen Anne mantles and includes a collection of antique furnishings and accessories. Other buildings on the grounds include a separate kitchen, a blacksmith's forge, a wheat house, a smoke house, a well house, and a barn.

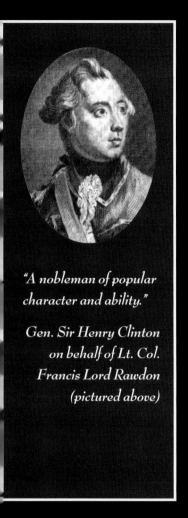

BRITISH

COMMANDERS
Lt. Col. Francis Lord Rawdon, Lt. Col. John Cruger

STRENGTH:
550

CASUALTIES:
27 killed; 58 wounded

SIEGE OF NINETY SIX

May 22–June 19, 1781

The siege of this frontier post grew out of the second attempt by the British to conquer the South. The first attempt in the campaign of 1775-76 had failed. The second began in late 1778 with an assault on Savannah, Georgia. On May 12, 1780, loyalists captured Charleston, South Carolina, America's fourth-largest city and commercial capital of the South. By September 1780, loyalists held Georgia and most of South Carolina. A powerful British army, led by General Lord Cornwallis, was poised to carry the war northward. British forces seemed unstoppable.

American patriots turned the tide of the war against Cornwallis through victories at Kings Mountain, South Carolina in the fall of 1780 and Cowpens, South Carolina in January of 1781. Cornwallis departed for Virginia and Lieutenant Colonel Francis Lord Rawdon assumed command of the British forces in the Carolinas. By early 1781 the British faced a strong Continental army under the command of General Nathanael Greene. Greene set out to reduce the chain of backcountry posts held by the British. One of these was the post at the hamlet named Ninety Six.

Ninety Six in 1781 was a vital political and economic center in the backcountry of the state. Lieutenant Colonel John Cruger commanded the fort with 550 American loyalists. Soldiers and slaves from nearby farms reinforced the walls of the stockades and built the star fort.

Greene and his 1,000 regular troops, along with a few militia, arrived on May 21, 1781. Because of the formidable defenses of Ninety Six, Greene knew he could bring down the fort by only a siege.

Greene focused on the star fort. His aide, Colonel Thaddeus Kosciuszko, a military engineer, directed sappers (trench diggers) to dig a system of parallels and approach trenches through the hard clay—an exhausting labor made worse by intense heat, mosquitoes, and cannon fire from the fort. They completed the first parallel on June 1, the second on June 3, and the third on June 10. They were now within musket range of the loyalists.

Reenactors at the Ninety Six National Historic Site

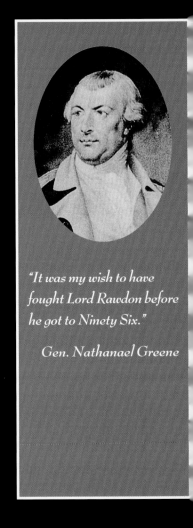

"It was my wish to have fought Lord Rawdon before he got to Ninety Six."

Gen. Nathanael Greene

During the night of June 13, Greene's men built a 30-foot tower of logs close to the fort, hoping to suppress loyalist cannon and musket fire from its top. Then, Greene learned that a relief column of 2,000 British troops led by Rawdon was marching to Cruger's aid. He resolved to storm the post before he was trapped between two forces.

The attack began at noon on June 18. Colonel Henry "Light-Horse Harry" Lee's legion captured the stockade fort to the west of the village. Greene launched his attack on the star fort from the third parallel. But the cannon fire was not powerful enough to breach the ten- to twelve-foot-thick earthen wall. Greene ordered fifty soldiers forward to prepare the way for the main army. Men with axes cut through the sharpened stakes that protruded from the fort's walls, and those with hooks sliced the sandbags piled on the parapet. Cruger, seeing the fort under direct assault, ordered troops out into the ditch that surrounded the fort. Fighting hand-to-hand, loyalists drove the patriots off, with much bloodshed on both sides.

This repulse decided the contest. The rescue column was too near for Greene to organize a general attack. Americans spotted cannon fire on the eastern hilltops, a warning that British relief was near. Gathering his wearied army, Greene slipped away before dawn on June 20, moving north up the Island Ford Road and across the Saluda River before the loyalists could give chase. By July, the loyalists abandoned Ninety Six and moved to a post nearer the coast.

AMERICAN

COMMANDER:
Gen. Nathanael Greene

STRENGTH: 1,000

CASUALTIES:
58 killed; 70 wounded; 20 missing

Ninety Six National Historic Site ━━━

1103 State Highway 248, Ninety Six, SC 29666

Phone: 864-543-4068

Hours: Open daily; closed Thanksgiving Day, Christmas Day, and New Year's Day.

Admission: Free.

www.nps.gov/nisi

Ninety Six National Historic Site's visitor's center features a short video, museum, and bookstore; maps of a one-mile walking tour are also available. Featured on the walking tour are the star fort, earthwork embankments of the 1781 star-shaped earthen fortification, a reconstructed stockade fort, British fortifications, siege trenches, and the underground remains of the town of Ninety Six. The visitor's center contains a ten-minute video and exhibits. There is a one-mile trail that loops around the embankments and two primitive trails.

Star Fort at Ninety Six National Historic Site

LANDSFORD CANAL STATE PARK ─────────────

2051 Park Drive, Catawba, SC 29704
PHONE: 803-789-5800
HOURS: Open Thursday to Monday.
ADMISSION: A fee is charged; children and seniors free.

The Landsford Canal State Park area was crossed by Lord Cornwallis in his march to Winnsboro after the Battle of Kings Mountain. General Thomas Sumter also used the area of Lands Ford as a meeting place and campsite. The state park features the remains of an early eighteenth-century log cabin and early nineteenth-century canal.

HISTORIC WINNSBORO WALKING TOUR ─────────────

Town Clock Building, South Congress Street, Winnsboro, SC 29180
PHONE: 803-635-4242 (Chamber of Commerce)
www.fairfieldchamber.org

The town of Winnsboro features a walking tour of fifty-one historic places. Only three of these are associated with the Revolutionary War. Tour brochures are available at the Fairfield Chamber of Commerce located in the Town Clock. The story is that Lord Cornwallis gave the county its name in 1780 when Cornwallis looked over the countryside and remarked, "What fair fields."

CORNWALLIS HOUSE

When Lord Cornwallis was defeated at Kings Mountain, he moved what was left of his troops to the town of Winnsboro and used the Cornwallis House as his headquarters from October 1780 to January 1781. The original part of the house, which still stands, contains massive masonry walls. The house was owned and occupied at one time by Captain John Buchanan, a Revolutionary soldier and friend of General Lafayette.

BRITISH HEADQUARTERS

A marker on the Mount Zion campus marks the area where British troops encamped from October 1780 to January 1781. During this time, the troops were further reduced by an outbreak of smallpox. A plot was formed by Colonels John and Minor Winn to shoot Cornwallis during one of his daily rides down Camden Road. After they were arrested and sentenced to hang, their brother, General Richard Winn, sent Cornwallis a message advising that he would kill the first one hundred British officers he captured should the sentence of death be carried out. The brothers were pardoned. From Winnsboro, Cornwallis moved his troops to Charlotte, North Carolina, and later to Yorktown to surrender.

BRATTON HOUSE

The Bratton House is also known as Wynn Dee after Richard Winn, the man for whom the town of Winnsboro was named. Winn acquired the house in 1777 and gave it to his daughter as a wedding gift when she married Colonel William Bratton, who served in the Revolutionary War.

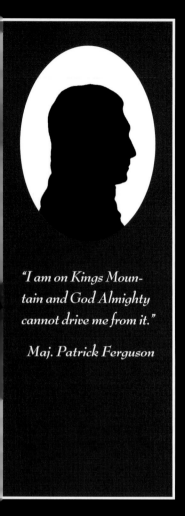

"I am on Kings Mountain and God Almighty cannot drive me from it."

Maj. Patrick Ferguson

BRITISH

COMMANDER:
Maj. Patrick Ferguson

STRENGTH: 1,100

CASUALTIES:
225 killed; 163 wounded; 698 captured

BATTLE OF KINGS MOUNTAIN

October 7, 1780

Lord Cornwallis took command of the southern campaign on June 8, 1780. After the American defeat at Camden, the British were confident that the entire south would soon be in their hands. In September 1780, Cornwallis dispatched Major Ferguson with 1,000 Provincial Regulars and Loyalist Militia sympathizers to clear away his left flank. Ferguson (who had mercilessly plundered and destroyed homes in the western Carolinas) sent a warning to the "overmountain" men in Watauga settlements (see Sycamore Shoals, Tennessee) to declare for the Crown or face invasion, destruction of their settlements, and hangings. Not known for their submissive nature, the overmountain men, led by Isaac Shelby from Virginia and John Sevier, joined forces with Colonel William Campbell from Virginia and Colonels Benjamin Cleveland and Charles McDowell, both of North Carolina, and set out over the mountains to meet Ferguson in South Carolina.

Ferguson positioned himself at the northeast summit of Kings Mountain with his men lined up on the 500-yard-long flat summit. Ferguson was the only British soldier; all others were Americans. The Patriot frontiersmen reached the mountain at about 3:00 P.M., tied up their horses, and positioned themselves around the broader end of the summit. They had no bayonets, so each rifleman positioned himself behind a tree for cover. There were enough frontiersmen to almost encircle the Tories. The Patriots fought with an uncommon fury, but Ferguson would not give up. Twice, when white flags were raised by the Tories, Ferguson cut them down. Finally, with his men surrounded and beyond hope, he tried to cut his way through the riflemen and was killed.

The Patriots kept firing as the Loyalists tried to surrender. Campbell implored his men to cease fire, and he told the Tories to throw down their arms. The carnage continued until finally the riflemen encircled the few remaining Tories and called out the names of those who had committed atrocities upon their neighbors. Of the 1,100 Tories in the fight, 225 were killed, 163 wounded so badly they were left on the field, and 698 were taken prisoners. The Patriots lost 28 men (62 were wounded), and they gained 1,500 muskets and rifles, as well as a large

Monument at Kings Mountain National Military Park

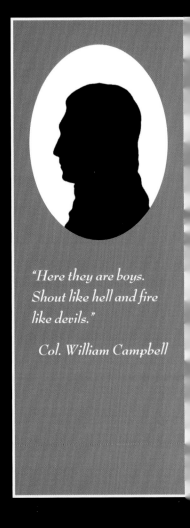

AMERICAN

COMMANDER:
Col. William Campbell

STRENGTH: 910

CASUALTIES:
28 killed; 62 wounded

store of ammunition. The prisoners were marched to Gilbertown, North Carolina, where nine were hanged in revenge for the looting and burning of Patriot homes.

The effect of the victory at Kings Mountain was immediate and great, providing a much-needed victory to the Americans after the losses at Charleston and Camden. Rumor increased the size of the Patriots and forced Cornwallis to retreat and delay his invasion of North Carolina. More importantly, few Americans were willing to come out and support the British after this battle. The battle was one of the most decisive of the era, and the only major engagement fought entirely between Americans.

KINGS MOUNTAIN NATIONAL MILITARY PARK ——

Off I-85, 2625 Park Road, Blacksburg, SC 29702

PHONE: 864-936-7921

HOURS: Open daily; closed Thanksgiving Day, Christmas Day, and New Year's Day.

ADMISSION: Free.

www.nps.gov/kimo

The 3,945-acre park commemorates the significant victory of the American Patriots over the American Loyalists that destroyed the British theory of conquering America with Americans. The visitor's center features an 18-minute film, exhibit area, and bookstore. A one-and-a-half mile self-guided trail includes Ferguson's Cairn, the burial site of Major Ferguson; the U.S. Monument; and interpretive markers and exhibits. Kings Mountain National Military Park is the end of the Overmountain Victory National Historic Trail commemorating the route of the Patriot army from the mountains to the battle. The Overmountain Victory National Historic Trail follows the Revolutionary War route of militia from Virginia, Tennessee, North Carolina, South Carolina, and Georgia to the Battle of Kings Mountain. The primary access is by car.

KINGS MOUNTAIN STATE PARK ——

1277 Park Road, Blacksburg, SC 29702

PHONE: 803-222-3209

HOURS: Open daily.

ADMISSION: A fee is charged.

The Kings Mountain State Park covers 6,884 acres adjacent to Kings Mountain National Military Park. The state park contains a living-history farm demonstrating life during the nineteenth century. Original structures from 1850 have been relocated here for self-guided tours.

Log dwelling at Kings Mountain State Park

Kings Mountain State Park

HISTORIC BRATTONSVILLE

1444 Brattonsville Road, McConnells, SC 29726
PHONE: 803-684-2327
HOURS: Open Monday to Sunday from March to November.
ADMISSION: A fee is charged; students and seniors discounted.

British soldiers led by Captain Christian Huck arrived at Brattonsville Plantation, the home of Colonel William Bratton, on July 11, 1780. Mrs. Bratton refused to tell them where her husband was hiding and sent her servant, Watt, to warn the colonel and his troops. The Patriots were able to ambush the British the following day, and Captain Huck was

The Col. Bratton Revolutionary War house, Historic Brattonsville

killed in the battle that has come to be known as the Battle of Huck's defeat. A marker has been erected on the grounds in honor of Watt and his wife Polly. In addition, there are restored eighteenth- and nineteenth-century buildings on the site of the Bratton family complex.

ANDREW JACKSON STATE PARK

196 Andrew Jackson Park Road, Lancaster, SC 29720
PHONE: 803-285-3344
HOURS: Open daily.
ADMISSION: Free.

The Andrew Jackson State Park is located at the boyhood home of President Andrew Jackson. During the time of the Revolution, this settlement was repeatedly raided by the British because of the fierce and widespread support the inhabitants held for the Patriots. The park features a museum and an eighteenth-century schoolhouse replica.

BETHESDA PRESBYTERIAN CHURCH

502 DeKalb Street, Camden, SC 29020
PHONE: 803-432-4593
HOURS: Open Monday to Friday.
ADMISSION: Free.

The Bethesda Presbyterian Church was built in 1820, but in its burial ground is the grave of the Baron deKalb. DeKalb died as a result of wounds received at the Battle of Camden, and his remains were reinterred here in 1825. The Marquis de Lafayette officiated at the final burial ceremony. There is a monument that marks the grave of the baron, and the church is on the national historic register.

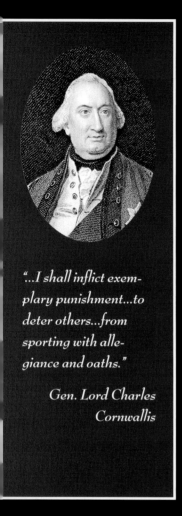

BRITISH

COMMANDER:
Gen. Lord Charles Cornwallis

STRENGTH: 2,239

CASUALTIES:
68 killed, 256 wounded

BATTLE OF CAMDEN

August 16, 1780

General Gates was given orders to destroy British forces under Lord Francis Rawdon and to occupy Camden, South Carolina. By doing so, British supplies of clothing, ammunition, and other military stores on their way from Charleston to Camden would fall into the hands of the Americans.

Gates decided on an overnight march to a point about seven miles north of Camden. Before the march, the men were given fresh beef, quick-baked bread, and mush mixed with molasses, a meal that resulted in dysentery for most of the men. With sick and exhausted troops, Gates began his march at 10:00 P.M. on the hot and sultry night of August 15 through swamps and sandy ground.

Meanwhile, British Lord Cornwallis had hastened from Charleston to join Rawdon. He too had begun a night march to meet Gates and, unexpectedly, the two armies met in the dark. Suddenly the woods were alive with musket and cannon fire. British soldiers were fresh and well-trained, unlike the untried, weary American troops.

In the first few minutes, the British charged, throwing the American troops into general confusion. Then, Lieutenant Colonel Charles Porterfield moved to support Colonel Charles Armand's legion, and they poured such heavy fire onto the British that they gave way. After about fifteen minutes, both sides ceased firing in the dark, but Porterfield had been killed.

The American officers met to assess the situation, which seemed to call for a retreat, but they determined to fight at daybreak instead. Both armies deployed for a frontal attack, but Gates ordered General Edward Stevens and his seven hundred Virginians to attack the British right flank before the British had completed their deployment. The men, who were sick and frightened in their first battle, faced the Welch Fusiliers and the West Riding Regiment charging in scarlet and glittering bayonets. The Virginians turned and ran for their lives.

When the Virginians fled, 1,800 North Carolina militiamen under General Richard Caswell also broke and ran. Only the Maryland and Delaware Continental troops under General Mordecai Gist and Major General Baron Johannes de Kalb and a Maryland unit under General William Smallwood were left to face 2,000 British. The Americans held off Rawdon's Volunteers of Ireland, the Bristol Legion infantry, the Royal North Carolina Regiment, and Colonel Morgan Bryan's North Carolina Volunteers, more than 1,000 men against possibly 600. DeKalb ordered fix bayonets, and, to the astonishment of the British, began one of the fiercest hand-to-hand fights of the war. Gist and De Kalb, not aware that they were the only troops left, continued fighting for almost an hour. Even when DeKalb was wounded by a saber to the head, he kept fighting. Only after being wounded in eleven places did DeKalb succumb and the battle end. Meanwhile, General Gates was in full flight and slept that night in Charlotte, North Carolina, sixty miles away from the battlefield. What was left of his army was scattered over the area with no orders or leadership. Eventually the Continentals staggered into Hillsboro, North Carolina, where Gates was waiting. The militiamen headed for home. The Battle of Camden has been called by some historians "the most disastrous defeat ever inflicted upon an American army."

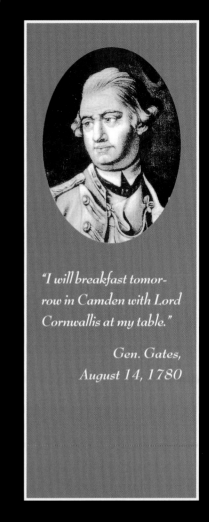

"I will breakfast tomorrow in Camden with Lord Cornwallis at my table."

Gen. Gates,
August 14, 1780

AMERICAN

COMMANDER:
Gen. Horatio Gates

STRENGTH: 3,052

CASUALTIES:
250 killed;
800 wounded;
1,000 captured

The Battle of Camden

HISTORIC CAMDEN REVOLUTIONARY WAR SITE —

Highway 521 South, P.O. Box 710, Camden, SC 29020

PHONE: 803-432-9841

HOURS: Open daily; closed Mondays and major holidays.

ADMISSION: A fee is charged for guided tours.

The Historic Camden Revolutionary War Site stands on the site of the early town of Camden, where Lord Charles Cornwallis, after his success in Charleston, came to set up his supply head-quarters. Fourteen battles of the Revolution were fought in the nearby area. This 98-acre park features restorations of the British fortifications, earthen breastworks, and palisade walls. The museum complex includes the eighteenth-century townsite, the furnished 1789 Craven House, the reconstructed and furnished Kershaw-Cornwallis House, reconstructed military fortifications, the partially-restored McCaa House circa 1800, and two log cabins with exhibits.

KERSHAW-CORNWALLIS HOUSE

The Kershaw-Cornwallis House is a reconstruction of the home of Camden's founder, Joseph Kershaw, and was the headquarters for General Lord Charles Cornwallis during the occupation of Camden in 1780-81. Kershaw was exiled to Bermuda until after the war. After the Treaty of Paris ended the Revolutionary War, Kershaw returned home. He died in the house in 1791. The original house was burned to the ground in 1865 during the Union occupation of the Civil War. The house was reconstructed based upon archeological evidence and two oil paintings of the

original house. The first floor of the interior contains period furniture. The house features research and library facilities on the second floor that include books, pamphlets, maps, and documents pertaining to the town, state, and country during the American Revolutionary period.

Kershaw-Cornwallis House

DRAYTON HALL

3380 Ashley River Road, Charleston, SC 29414
PHONE: 843-769-2600
HOURS: Open daily for guided tours.
ADMISSION: A fee is charged.

Drayton Hall

Drayton Hall was the birthplace of patriot William Henry Drayton, whose father built the mansion from 1738 to 1742. Drayton Hall is the only house on the Ashley River today that has survived both the Revolutionary and Civil Wars. It was spared by Union troops during the Civil War when many other houses were burned. The main house remains close to its original condition, unmarred by the addition of plumbing and electricity.

Grounds of Drayton Hall

MIDDLETON PLACE

4300 Ashley River Road, Charleston, SC 29414
PHONE: 843-556-6020
HOURS: Open daily for guided tours.
ADMISSION: A fee is charged.

Middleton Place is a carefully preserved eighteenth-century plantation and a National Historic Landmark. The site includes the house museum, America's oldest landscaped gardens, and the plantation stableyards. The main house is in ruins and dates to the late 1730s. This house, along with 200 acres of land, formed part of the dowry brought by Mary Williams to her marriage to Henry Middleton in 1741.

Benjamin West painting of Arthur Middleton, his wife Mary Izard, and their son Henry on display at Middleton Place

Middleton Place House

Henry Middleton served as a delegate to the Continental Congress from South Carolina and as president of the Continental Congress in 1774. His son, Arthur Middleton, who grew up in Middleton Place, was also a delegate to the Continental Congress and a signer of the Declaration of Independence. When Charleston fell in 1780, Arthur Middleton was sent to the British stronghold of St. Augustine, Florida, as a prisoner of war. The following year, he was released in Philadelphia with other Carolinians in a general exchange of prisoners. He remained in that city attending Congress until October 1782, when he returned to Middleton Place and his family. The gardens have been restored to their former splendor, with reflection pools, terraces, and butterfly lakes, and may be visited along with the house and stableyards, where craftsmen demonstrate blacksmithing, woodworking, and weaving. The house museum features portraits by Benjamin West and Thomas Sully, as well as the Middleton family furniture, silver, and books dating to the eighteenth century.

CHARLES PINCKNEY NATIONAL HISTORIC SITE ———

1254 Long Point Road, Mount Pleasant, SC 29464
PHONE: 843-881-5516
HOURS: Open daily; closed Christmas Day.
ADMISSION: Free.

The Charles Pinckney National Historic Site features an interpretation of Pinckney's role in the writing of the United States Constitution and life at Snee Farm, a low-country plantation. The twenty-eight acre site is only a remnant of the 715-acre Snee Farm, a rice plantation and one of Pinckney's seven plantations. Pinckney is known for his contributions as a framer and signer at the Constitutional Convention, as well as his life of public service. Pinckney fought in the American Revolution, served four terms as the governor of South Carolina, and held many other offices at the state and national level. After Charleston fell to the British in May 1781, Generals William Moultrie and Charles Cotesworth Pinckney both served parole, or house arrest, at Snee Farm. Charles Pinckney was held by the British aboard a ship and later sent to Philadelphia in prisoner exchange. As governor of South Carolina, Pinckney hosted George Washington to a breakfast at Snee Farm during the president's 1791 tour of the south. Today, an 1828 cottage contains exhibits on low-country life, the role of African Americans in the development of Snee Farm, archeology, and the shaping of the Constitution. Two twenty-minute videos and a nature walk enhance the visitor's experience at this national park service site.

TENNESSEE

*D*uring the Revolutionary War, the area of Tennessee belonged to North Carolina; and many of its inhabitants came from North Carolina, seeking wider spaces and less governmental interference from the Crown.

Notable in Tennessee is the Sycamore Shoals State Historic Area, located in the eastern part of the state. This park commemorates the Watauga Settlement, which was the first free and independent community on the continent in that it had the first majority-rule system of democracy. The settlement was attacked by Indian war parties that were goaded on by the British. Men from this settlement fought in several battles and were instrumental in the Battle of Kings Mountain. Because the British and Indian parties they had armed had been particularly vicious to the settlers in Watauga by killing families and burning homes, the men of Watauga showed little mercy at Kings Mountain.

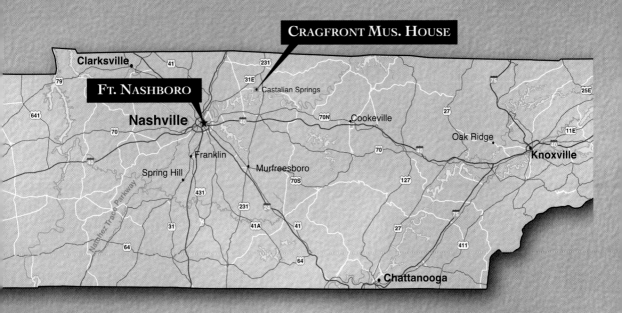

SEE KENTUCKY
PAGE 32

CRAGFRONT MUS. HOUSE

Clarksville

FT. NASHBORO

Nashville

231

31E

Castalian Springs

41

79

641

70

70N

Cookeville

Oak Ridge

Franklin

Spring Hill

40

75

25E

27

Knoxville

11E

70

431

31

231

41A

24

41

70S

Murfreesboro

127

27

75

64

64

411

Chattanooga

SEE GEORGIA PAGE 24

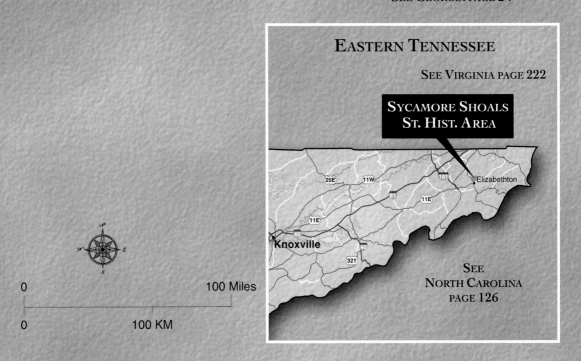

EASTERN TENNESSEE

SEE VIRGINIA PAGE 222

SYCAMORE SHOALS
ST. HIST. AREA

25E

11W

181

Elizabethton

81

11E

11E

Knoxville

40

321

SEE
NORTH CAROLINA
PAGE 126

0   100 Miles

0   100 KM

FORT NASHBORO

First Avenue North, Nashville, TN 37201
PHONE: Not available.
HOURS: Open daily.
ADMISSION: Free.

Fort Nashboro was constructed in 1779 on a bluff overlooking the Cumberland River and was named for General Francis Nash, who was killed in the Battle of Germantown, Pennsylvania. Nash was the commander of the North Carolina brigade under George Washington. Francis Nash's brother Abner Nash was the governor of North Carolina, and some historians say Fort Nashboro was named for him. Today's Fort Nashboro is a replica of the original fort and sits a few blocks south of the original site. It is smaller than the original, which covered two acres.

The fort was built at French Lick, so named because of a trading post run by a Frenchman on the site of the salt and sulphur spring. The fort proved a defense against the Indians and was in use until 1794.

Fort Nashboro

CRAGFONT MUSEUM HOUSE

200 Cragfont Road, Castalian Springs, TN 37031
PHONE: 615-452-7070
HOURS: Open Tuesday to Sunday from mid-April to October.
ADMISSION: A fee is charged.

Cragfont House was built by General James Winchester, a Revolutionary War soldier who was present at the surrender of Yorktown. He is buried on the site. After Tennessee was admitted into the Union, Winchester served as the first speaker of the state senate. The house is not of typical Tennessee architecture but is built in the style of the best of the late Georgian-period homes; it contains the first second-floor ballroom in Tennessee. Much of the original architecture has survived, and many of the original furnishings have been recovered. The family cemetery may also be seen at the rear of the house.

SYCAMORE SHOALS STATE HISTORIC AREA ————

1651 West Elk Avenue, Elizabethton, TN 37643
PHONE: 423-543-5808
HOURS: Open daily.
ADMISSION: Free.

Sycamore Shoals State Historic Area commemorates several significant events in Tennessee and American history. The historic Sycamore Shoals crossing on the Watauga River was the hub of the earliest permanent settlement in what is now Tennessee. The Watauga Settlement began in 1769 when its first settlers crossed the Appalachian Mountains and built cabins, hunted, and planted crops.

Patriots from the Watauga Settlement fought in several battles early in the American Revolution. During the summer and fall of 1780, the British took Charleston, South Carolina, and Lord Cornwallis marched toward Charlotte, North Carolina. He sent Major Patrick Ferguson to operate along the mountains with his Loyalist militia. Ferguson sent a warning to the settlements west of the mountains to lay down their arms or he would "march over the mountains, hang the leaders, and lay waste their country with fire and sword." Eleven hundred of the militia over the mountains, known as the Overmountain Men, met at Sycamore Shoals on September 25, 1780. From there they marched in search of Ferguson. They found him on October 7, 1780, and defeated his army at the Battle of Kings Mountain. In 1980 the U.S. Congress designated the trail from Sycamore Shoals to Kings Mountain National Military Park as the Overmountain Victory National Historic Trail.

The visitor's center at Sycamore Shoals contains a theater, museum with interpretive displays, gift shop, and bookstore. This day-use park also has a picnic area and two-mile walking trail. Each July the park sponsors a two-act outdoor drama *The Wataugans*, which dramatizes the early settlement of northeast Tennessee during the American Revolution. The presentation takes place in the 450-seat Fort Watauga Amphitheater.

Sycamore Shoals State Historic Area

VERMONT

*V*ermont was not a colony and was not represented in the Continental Congress, but it played a part in the Revolution as a de facto independent state. In May 1775, Ethan Allen and the Green Mountain Boys of Vermont stormed Fort Ticonderoga, taking it "in the name of the great Jehovah and the Continental Congress."

The Battle of Hubbardton was the only battle fought entirely on Vermont soil, and although it was not an American victory, historians credit Americans with a measure of success in that they delayed the British, who were in pursuit of the main column of American troops.

Today, in addition to the Hubbardton Battlefield State Historic Site, the Lake Champlain Maritime Museum displays a replica of Benedict Arnold's gunboat, the Greenmount Cemetery features a monument to Ethan Allen, and the Bennington Battle Monument can be seen as a tribute to the Green Mountain Boys.

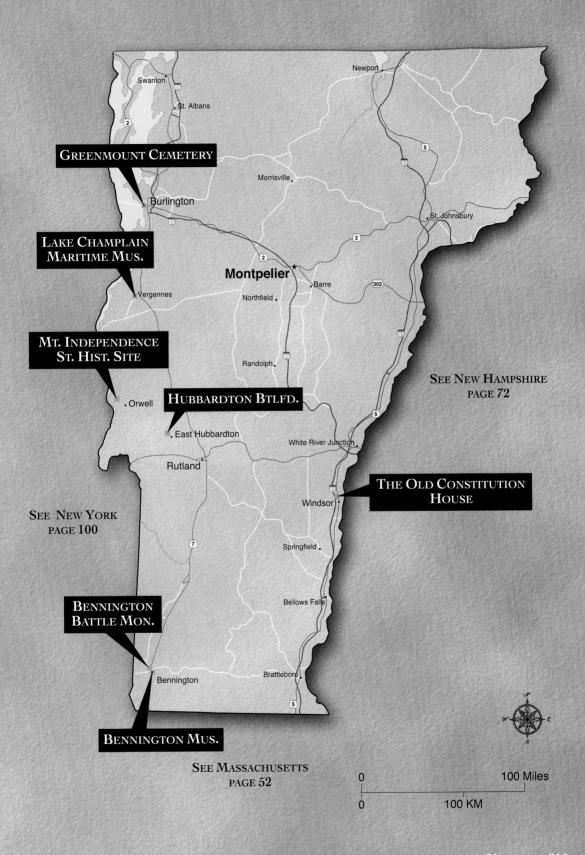

Swanton

St. Albans

2

89

GREENMOUNT CEMETERY

Morrisville

Newport

5

91

St. Johnsbury

Burlington

89

LAKE CHAMPLAIN
MARITIME MUS.

Montpelier

2

Barre

302

Vergennes

Northfield

MT. INDEPENDENCE
ST. HIST. SITE

Randolph

89

91

SEE NEW HAMPSHIRE
PAGE 72

Orwell

HUBBARDTON BTLFD.

East Hubbardton

5

White River Junction

Rutland

THE OLD CONSTITUTION
HOUSE

91

SEE NEW YORK
PAGE 100

Windsor

7

Springfield

BENNINGTON
BATTLE MON.

Bellows Falls

Bennington

Brattleboro

BENNINGTON MUS.

5

SEE MASSACHUSETTS
PAGE 52

0   100 Miles

0   100 KM

GREENMOUNT CEMETERY

South Side of Colchester Avenue, Burlington, VT 05401
PHONE: Not available.
HOURS: Open daily from dawn to dusk.
ADMISSION: Free.

Greenmount Cemetery is the final resting place of Vermont's Revolutionary War hero Ethan Allen. A forty-two-foot tall column with a statue of Ethan Allen in his moment of triumph at the surrender of Fort Ticonderoga marks the gravesite.

LAKE CHAMPLAIN MARITIME MUSEUM

4472 Basin Harbor Road, Vergennes, VT 05491
PHONE: 802-475-2022
HOURS: Open daily from May 1 to October 15.
ADMISSION: A fee is charged.

Lake Champlain Maritime Museum is dedicated to preserving the maritime history of Lake Champlain. On display is a fifty-four-foot replica of Benedict Arnold's gunboat *Philadelphia II,* which is rigged, armed, and afloat in the museum's North Harbor. A special exhibit, "The Revolutionary War in the Champlain Valley," depicts the naval defense of Lake Champlain.

Replica of 1776 gunboat Philadelphia II *at Lake Champlain Maritime Museum*

MOUNT INDEPENDENCE STATE HISTORIC SITE ———

5 miles west of State Route 22A, Orwell, VT 05760
PHONE: 802-759-2412
HOURS: Open daily from late May to mid-October.
ADMISSION: A fee is charged.

American Revolutionary troops built Mount Independence as a fort to guard against a British attack from Canada, and they named it in honor of the Declaration of Independence. This fort stood across the lake from Fort Ticonderoga—a floating bridge across Lake Champlain connected Fort Ticonderoga and Mount Independence. When the British recaptured Fort Ticonderoga, the bridge became the Americans' way of retreat. Today, the site is designated a National Historic Landmark and is considered the most important Revolutionary War site in Vermont. Mount Independence has several miles of hiking trails that wind past the batteries, blockhouses, hospital, barracks, and other archeological remains of this once-bustling fort complex. Still visible are the remnants of foundations and gun batteries erected after the Americans decided to fortify this rugged promontory. Self-guided trails of the ruins span from a quarter mile to three miles of easy walking. A museum on the premises retells the story of Mount Independence through artifacts from the lake and archeological excavations, parts of the floating bridge, exhibits, and a video. The site also features living-history programs, encampments, and lectures throughout the season.

Mount Independence on Lake Champlain

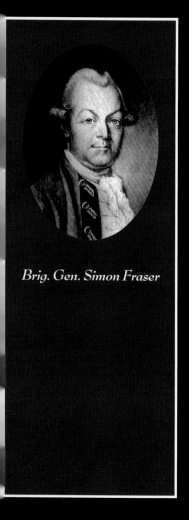

Brig. Gen. Simon Fraser

BATTLE OF HUBBARDTON

July 7, 1777

The Hubbardton Battle, the only battle fought entirely on Vermont soil, occurred during the early morning hours of July 7, 1777. American forces, numbering about 2,500 and led by Major General Arthur St. Clair, were fleeing Fort Ticonderoga and Mount Independence. Eight hundred British troops, led by General Simon Fraser, joined by 250 Hessians under the command of General Baron Friedrich von Riedesel, were close behind them. St. Clair camped at Castleton for the night, leaving Seth Warner behind to wait for rear guard regiments. Warner was to join the main body at Castleton. Instead, he remained at Hubbardton for the night. In addition to his own men, Warner was joined by Colonel Francis's Massachusetts Regiment and Colonel Nathan Hale's New Hampshire Regiment. They all numbered only about 1,000.

Fraser bivouacked for the night about three miles from Warner's camp at what is now Hubbardton. During the night, when his Indian scouts happened upon Warner's camp, Fraser made hasty plans to attack at dawn. Fraser's forces first caught Hale's New Hampshire troops at breakfast, then went on to attack the regiments of Warner and Francis. The British were not accustomed to fighting in a heavily wooded area, which gave the advantage to the Americans, who were winning the battle. Then von Riedesel and his troops rushed in to save the British. The Americans heard fifes, trumpets, and drums playing a German hymn and hundreds of voices singing in German. The singing not only surprised the Americans but also bolstered the morale of the Germans. The voices and music also served to exaggerate the number of attacking Germans to the Americans.

The ground was covered with forest and underbrush. For the Americans, this was good cover, but for the British and Germans, it was a quagmire in which there could be no orderly fighting. St. Clair heard the fighting and ordered two of his regiments, who had dropped away from his marching men the night before and had encamped only two miles from Hubbardton, to go to the aid of Warner and Francis. In a show of the lack of discipline evidenced by the American army of the time, the regiments refused and hurried on to Castleton.

BRITISH

COMMANDERS:
Brig. Gen. Simon Fraser,
Maj. Gen. Baron von Riedesel

STRENGTH: 1,050

CASUALTIES: 35 killed;
148 wounded

Hubbardton Battlefield

Colonel Francis was killed in the battle, and Warner's last order was "Scatter and meet me at Manchester." The two-hour battle was "as bloody as Waterloo," according to one historian.

Casualty figures vary, but estimates run as high as forty dead in addition to Francis, with 320 taken prisoner. British and German casualties are listed at thirty-five killed and 148 wounded.

Although the patriots suffered heavy losses, some historians believe that by delaying the British pursuit of the main American column, they achieved a measure of success.

"Scatter and meet me at Manchester."

Col. Seth Warner

AMERICAN

COMMANDERS:
Col. Seth Warner,
Col. Ebenezer Francis,
Col. Nathan Hale

STRENGTH: 1,000–1,200

CASUALTIES: 40 killed; 320 captured

HUBBARDTON BATTLEFIELD STATE HISTORIC SITE

Seven miles north of Route 4, East Hubbardton, VT 05749
PHONE: 802-273-2282 or 802-759-2412 during the off-season
HOURS: Open Wednesday to Sunday from late May to mid-October.
ADMISSION: A fee is charged.

The visitor's center houses a museum which features period artifacts, a fiber-optic map that details the various phases of the battle, and a diorama of the battle. Just outside the entrance to the battlefield is a large marble monument that marks the place where Colonel Ebenezer Francis was supposedly buried by British troops. Tradition holds that Hessian General von Riedesel had so admired his youthful American officer adversaries, that upon finding the body of Francis, he personally saw to it that the young colonel received a Christian burial with full military honors.

OLD CONSTITUTION HOUSE

Main Street, Windsor, VT 05089
PHONE: 802-672-3773
HOURS: Open Wednesday to Sunday from late May to mid-October.
ADMISSION: A fee is charged.

The Old Constitution House was originally a tavern owned by Elijah West and was used as a meeting place for the local men. On July 2, 1777, delegates from the length and breadth of the newly Free and Independent State of Vermont met here to write a state constitution. Before this task could be completed, British troops under General Burgoyne captured Fort Ticonderoga and Mount Independence. Eager to get home, the delegates were nevertheless delayed by a timely and violent thunderstorm, which gave them enough time to vote on and adopt the constitution. Vermont's new constitution was the first in America to prohibit slavery, establish universal voting rights for all males, and authorize a public school system. Vermont became a republic and remained so until 1791 when it was admitted to the Union as the fourteenth state.

Old Constitution House

BENNINGTON BATTLE MONUMENT

15 Monument Circle, Old Bennington, VT 05201
PHONE: 802-447-0550
HOURS: Open daily from April 1 to November 1.
ADMISSION: A fee is charged.

This 306-foot obelisk monument marks the site where a large number of military supplies were stored. These supplies were the object of the Battle of Bennington, which was fought two miles away in what is now New York. An elevator takes visitors to the observation level. At the monument's entrance is a diorama of the Battle of Bennington; and on the grounds are a number of additional monuments, including statues of the two heroes of the battle: John Stark of New Hampshire and Seth Warner, commander of the Green Mountain Boys. One of the more unique monuments is a large boulder commemorating the 1,400 New Hampshire men who were involved in the Battle of Bennington.

Bennington Battle Monument

BENNINGTON MUSEUM

West Main Street, Bennington, VT 05201
PHONE: 802-447-1571
HOURS: Open daily.
ADMISSION: A fee is charged.
www.benningtonmuseum.com

The Bennington Museum was created in 1875 for the purpose of memorializing the 1777 Bennington Battle. The museum contains items of local history and military artifacts, including the Bennington Flag, one of America's oldest flags, dating to the early 1800s. The flag commemorates the spirit of the American Revolution and is unique in that it contains the number "76" surrounded by an arch of seven pointed stars. The stripes start and end with white rather than the customary red. This is believed to be the oldest surviving Stars and Stripes.

Bennington Museum

VIRGINIA

Virginia was indispensible to the American Revolution, giving it orators, writers, and military heroes. Sites in this state still pay tribute to the following men who called it home: Patrick Henry, who spoke the famous words "Give me liberty, or give me death," Thomas Jefferson, who wrote the Declaration of Independence that severed ties with Britain, James Madison, who has been called the "Father of the Constitution," George Washington, without whom America could not have won the fight for independence, and without whom she would not have seen democracy flower in the government, and General Henry "Light-Horse Harry" Lee, who was not only the hero of battlefields but who said of his commander in chief General Washington, "first in war, first in peace, and first in the hearts of his countrymen."

Today, homes of all of these men are extant, as is the National Historical Park of Yorktown, where the surrender of the British army took place. Virginia is a must-see for any Revolutionary War enthusiast.

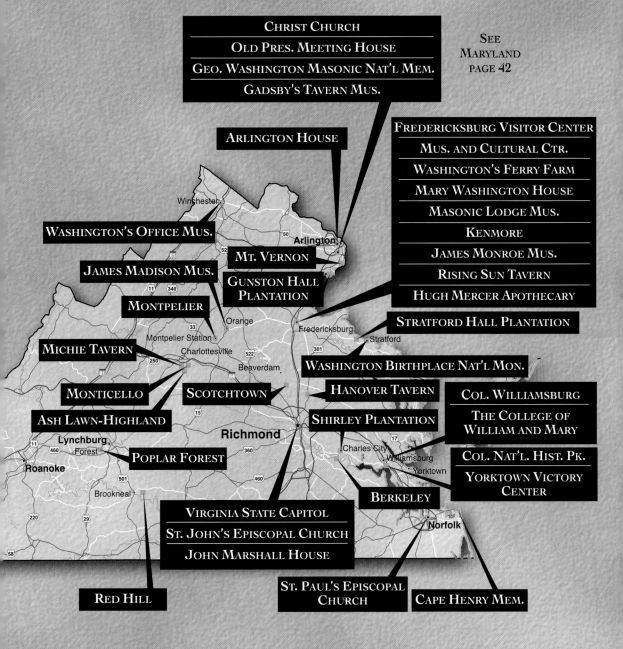

SEE
MARYLAND
PAGE 42

CHRIST CHURCH

OLD PRES. MEETING HOUSE

GEO. WASHINGTON MASONIC NAT'L MEM.

GADSBY'S TAVERN MUS.

ARLINGTON HOUSE

FREDERICKSBURG VISITOR CENTER

MUS. AND CULTURAL CTR.

WASHINGTON'S FERRY FARM

MARY WASHINGTON HOUSE

MASONIC LODGE MUS.

KENMORE

JAMES MONROE MUS.

RISING SUN TAVERN

HUGH MERCER APOTHECARY

WASHINGTON'S OFFICE MUS.

JAMES MADISON MUS.

MT. VERNON

GUNSTON HALL
PLANTATION

MONTPELIER

STRATFORD HALL PLANTATION

MICHIE TAVERN

WASHINGTON BIRTHPLACE NAT'L MON.

MONTICELLO

SCOTCHTOWN

HANOVER TAVERN

COL. WILLIAMSBURG

THE COLLEGE OF
WILLIAM AND MARY

ASH LAWN-HIGHLAND

SHIRLEY PLANTATION

POPLAR FOREST

COL. NAT'L. HIST. PK.

YORKTOWN VICTORY
CENTER

BERKELEY

VIRGINIA STATE CAPITOL

ST. JOHN'S EPISCOPAL CHURCH

JOHN MARSHALL HOUSE

RED HILL

ST. PAUL'S EPISCOPAL
CHURCH

CAPE HENRY MEM.

Winchester
Arlington
Orange
Montpelier Station
Charlottesville
Fredericksburg
Stratford
Beaverdam
Richmond
Charles City
Williamsburg
Yorktown
Lynchburg
Forest
Roanoke
Brookneal
Norfolk

SEE NORTH CAROLINA PAGE 126

0   100 Miles

0   100 KM

GEORGE WASHINGTON'S OFFICE MUSEUM ——————

32 West Cork Street, Winchester, VA 22601
PHONE: 540-662-6550
HOURS: Open daily.
ADMISSION: A fee is charged.

George Washington used this office from September 1755 until December 1756 during the French and Indian Wars. The museum displays a reproduction of the fort that Washington built to protect Winchester from the French.

GADSBY'S TAVERN MUSEUM ——————

134 North Royal Street, Alexandria, VA 22314
PHONE: 703-838-4242
HOURS: Open Tuesday to Sunday; closed major holidays.
ADMISSION: A fee is charged; students discounted.
ci.alexandria.va.us/oha

Gadsby's Tavern remains one of the few eighteenth-century taverns still in existence. Here, colonial figures ate and spent the night. General and Mrs. Washington attended the annual Birthnight Ball held in his honor in 1798 and 1799. The general spent his last birthday here and danced with his wife in the tavern's ballroom. The tavern boasts restored bedrooms and a replica of the original ballroom, which is in the American Wing of the Metropolitan Museum of Art in New York.

Gadsby's Tavern Museum

ARLINGTON HOUSE, THE ROBERT E. LEE MEMORIAL —

Arlington National Cemetery, Arlington, VA 22211
PHONE: 703-557-0613
HOURS: Open daily; closed Christmas Day and New Year's Day.
ADMISSION: Free.

Few places in the country reflect the history of the nation with as much poignancy as Arlington House, the Robert E. Lee Memorial. The house, sometimes called the Custis-Lee Mansion, was originally the home of George Washington Parke Custis, the grandson of Martha Washington. After his father died, Custis went to live with his grandmother, who, with her second husband, George Washington, raised the boy at Mount Vernon. Custis was interested in perpetuating the memory of George Washington and used part of his home at Arlington (which he began building in 1802) as a treasury of Washington artifacts. In June 1831, his daughter Mary married Lieutenant Robert E. Lee. Mary inherited Arlington upon her father's death in 1857. Robert E. Lee took a leave of absence from the U.S. army to renovate the house and improve the farming on the estate. He was home at Arlington in April of 1861 when the Civil War broke out. Lee, who opposed slavery and secession, nevertheless remained loyal to his native state of Virginia, and it was at Arlington where he resigned from the U.S. army. Within a few days of his resignation, he traveled to Richmond to accept the command of Virginia's military force. He never returned to Arlington. Mary Custis Lee evacuated the house and it became a Union headquarters. During the Civil War, the United States government created a national cemetery on the grounds. Today, the house is restored and refurbished to reflect its original owner's love of his adoptive father and includes a huge canvas depicting Washington at the Battle of Monmouth.

THE OLD PRESBYTERIAN MEETING HOUSE ————

321 South Fairfax Street, Alexandria, VA 22314
PHONE: 703-549-6670
HOURS: Open Monday to Friday.
ADMISSION: Free.

The Old Presbyterian Meeting House was established in 1772 and is still an active church. Four funeral services for George Washington were held at the Meeting House. When Washington died on December 18, 1799, few people knew or heard about the funeral before it was held at Mount Vernon four days later. Several funeral services were held around the country, including the four at Old Presbyterian. The first two were held on December 29, the third in January, and a fourth on Washington's birthday, February 22. There are several reasons why these funeral services were held at Old Presbyterian Meeting House. First, although Washington was actually a member of Christ Church in Alexandria, that church was considered far out of town and difficult to get to, whereas Old Presbyterian was more accessible, especially by river boat. In addi-

tion, Dr. James Muir, pastor of Old Presbyterian and personal friend of Washington, and Dr. James Craik, Washington's personal physician, attended Old Presbyterian. Craik is buried in the graveyard adjacent to the church, which also contains the Tomb of the Unknown Soldier of the Revolutionary War. The church features two pipe organs: a 151-year-old organ that is still in use, and a large, new one. To the west of the Old Presbyterian Meeting House is a manse (parsonage), which was built in 1787 and now serves as the church office.

Old Presbyterian Meeting House

CHRIST CHURCH

118 North Washington Street, Alexandria, VA 22314
PHONE: 703-549-1450
HOURS: Open daily; closed major holidays.
ADMISSION: Free.

The historic Christ Church dates from about 1773. George Washington purchased a pew here for 36 pounds, 10 shillings. Although many churches in the area were converted to hospitals and soldiers' barracks during the Civil War, Christ Church was spared. Most believe that Washington's affiliation with the church was the reason that the building was not burned or used by troops. Today, the church retains most of its original woodwork, and a silver plaque marks Washington's pew.

GEORGE WASHINGTON MASONIC NATIONAL MEMORIAL

101 Callahan Drive, Alexandria, VA 22301
PHONE: 703-683-2007
HOURS: Open daily; closed Thanksgiving Day, Christmas Day, and New Year's Day.
ADMISSION: Free.
www.gwmemorial.org

The George Washington Masonic National Memorial was dedicated in 1932, having been built by the contributions of Masons throughout the U.S. as a tribute to their fellow Mason, George Washington. The first view upon entering the 333-foot memorial is a massive bronze statue of George Washington depicted as Master of Alexandria Masonic Lodge, of which he was the Charter Master. Also in the hall are two huge murals. One depicts Washington laying the cornerstone of the United States Capitol in 1793, and the other shows General Washington and his staff at Christ Church in Philadelphia in 1778. The museum collection includes Washington's family Bible, his penknife, the trowel used by Washington to lay the cornerstone of the Capitol, The Washington Bodyguard Flag, and the field trunk used by Washington during the Revolutionary War. The collection also includes the clock from Washington's bedroom at Mount Vernon, which was stopped by the doctor at the moment of his death.

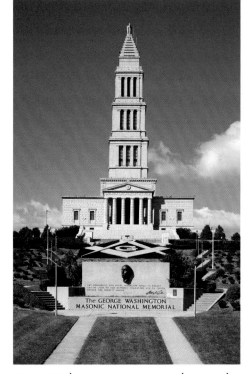

George Washington Masonic National Memorial

MOUNT VERNON

George Washington Memorial Parkway, Mount Vernon, VA 22121

PHONE: 703-780-2000
HOURS: Open daily.
ADMISSION: A fee is charged.
www.mountvernon.org

Mount Vernon Mansion

George Washington lived at his estate of Mount Vernon until his death in 1799. His father built a cottage on 2,300 acres, and George inherited the property from his older half-brother. He enlarged his brother's cottage and acquired land until the house resembled an English Palladian Mansion and the estate contained 8,000 acres. Mount Vernon features a working colonial farm, a new museum containing many of Washington's personal effects, and collections of manuscripts, original books, prints, historical photographs, postcards, early newspapers, and microfilm of the Library of Congress' papers of George Washington. The house boasts a beautiful interior that is simple but elegant in design. Guides throughout the home interpret the mansion and answer questions during the self-guided tour. The Mount Vernon Ladies' Association, which owns the home, has been able to acquire many of the original furnishings. The first president and first lady are buried on the grounds.

GUNSTON HALL PLANTATION

10709 Gunston Road, Mason Neck, VA 22079

PHONE: 703-550-9220 or 1-800-811-6966
HOURS: Open daily; closed Thanksgiving Day, Christmas Day, and New Year's Day.
ADMISSION: A fee is charged.

Gunston Hall is the eighteenth-century home of George Mason. Mason drafted the Fairfax Resolves and the Virginia Declaration of Rights, which stated that "all men are by nature equally free and independent and have certain inherent rights. . ." This document became the basis of the Declaration of Independence. Mason was also a framer of the Constitution, but he refused to

Gunston Hall

sign it because it did not contain a Bill of Rights and it allowed the continuation of slavery and tariffs. He was on the committee that authorized the western operations of George Rogers Clark, thereby becoming responsible for the expansion of the fledgling United States. Mason began construction of Gunston Hall in 1755, utilizing the services of indentured servant William Buckland to design and create the elaborately carved woodwork inside and out. Mason designed and planted his formal garden, which included a long boxwood-lined allée to a Potomac River outlook.

FREDERICKSBURG VISITOR CENTER

706 Caroline Street, Fredericksburg, VA 22401

PHONE: 800-678-4748
HOURS: Open daily; closed Thanksgiving Day, Christmas Day, and New Year's Day.
ADMISSION: Free.

The Fredericksburg Visitor Center offers a thirteen-minute audio-visual orientation of the area's history and attractions. Maps, brochures, parking passes, discount touring tickets, and special events tickets are available. Trolley tours and self-guided tours depart from the visitor center. A city walking tour begins across the street, and carriage rides begin nearby.

Fredericksburg Visitor Center

FREDERICKSBURG AREA MUSEUM AND CULTURAL CENTER

907 Princess Anne Street, Fredericksburg, VA 22401

PHONE: 540-371-3037
HOURS: Open daily; closed major holidays.
ADMISSION: A fee is charged.

Fredericksburg Area Museum and Cultural Center

The Fredericksburg Area Museum has displays that feature the iron and gun making industries that were so important to the war effort, as well as displays on everyday colonial life. Two extremely rare muskets made in Fredericksburg at the local gun manufactories are the highlights of the exhibits.

GEORGE WASHINGTON'S FERRY FARM

268 Kings Highway, Fredericksburg, VA 22405
PHONE: 540-370-0732
HOURS: Open daily from March to December and Saturday and Sunday from January to February; closed Thanksgiving Day, Christmas Eve and Day, and New Year's Eve and Day.
ADMISSION: A fee is charged. Group discounts are available.

Located across the Rappahannock River from the old town of Fredericksburg, Ferry Farm was George Washington's home from the age of six until he reached young adulthood. There, in fable, he cut down his father's cherry tree and threw a stone across the river. Visitors may watch archeology in progress and learn about young Washington.

Ferry Farm, Surveyor's Cottage

MARY WASHINGTON HOUSE

1200 Charles Street, Fredericksburg, VA 22401
PHONE: 540-373-1569
HOURS: Open daily; closed major holidays.
ADMISSION: A fee is charged.

Washington bought this house in 1772 for his mother, Mary Washington. The elder Mrs. Washington resided in this home for the last seventeen years of her life. The general visited his mother here. Some of Mrs. Washington's personal possessions are on display and can be seen during the guided tour. The house hosts a birthday party each year on February 22. Each Mother's Day, the house re-creates Washington's sentimental farewell to his mother upon leaving for his 1789 inauguration.

Mary Washington House

MASONIC LODGE MUSEUM

803 Princess Anne Street, Fredericksburg, VA 22401
PHONE: 540-373-5885
HOURS: Open daily; closed Thanksgiving Day and Christmas Day.
ADMISSION: A fee is charged; children discounted.

It was in this local lodge that George Washington became a Mason in 1752. The lodge's museum contains memorabilia relating to his membership. It also features an original Gilbert Stuart portrait of Washington.

KENMORE

1201 Washington Avenue, Fredericksburg, VA 22401
PHONE: 540-373-3381
HOURS: Open daily; closed major holidays.
ADMISSION: A fee is charged; children are discounted.
www.kenmore.org

Kenmore was built by Lewis Fielding and his wife Betty, George Washington's only sister. Lewis was an ardent patriot who helped bankroll the Revolution. The mansion has been called one of the most elegant Colonial mansions in America, and its dining room is one of the 100 most beautiful rooms in America. Guided tours are available with spiced tea and ginger cookies served in the kitchen. "A Christmas with the Washington Family" is celebrated annually in December with colonial entertainment, refreshments, and children's activities.

Kenmore Mansion

RISING SUN TAVERN

1304 Caroline Street, Fredericksburg, VA 22401
PHONE: 540-371-1494
HOURS: Open daily; closed major holidays.
ADMISSION: A fee is charged; children discounted.
www.apva.org/apva/rising.html

The Rising Sun Tavern is in a building originally constructed in 1760 by Charles Washington, George's younger brother. The structure became a tavern in 1792, operating in the bustling port town of Fredericksburg.

Rising Sun Tavern

HUGH MERCER APOTHECARY

1020 Caroline Street, Fredericksburg, VA 22401
PHONE: 540-373-3362
HOURS: Open daily.
ADMISSION: A fee is charged; children discounted.

Hugh Mercer, a Scottish doctor who fled to America after the defeat at the Battle of Culloden, fought in the French and Indian War and became a friend of George Washington. After the war, Mercer settled in Fredericksburg and opened this apothecary. During the Revolutionary War, Mercer held a command at the Battle of Trenton and at Princeton, where he was mortally wounded. A monument to him stands in Fredericksburg at

Hugh Mercer Apothecary Shop

Washington Avenue and Faquier Streets. His apothecary has been restored with period furnishings and is open for guided tours, which tell of Mercer's life and eighteenth-century medicine.

JAMES MONROE MUSEUM

908 Charles Street, Fredericksburg, VA 22401-5810
PHONE: 540-654-1043
HOURS: Open daily; closed major holidays.
ADMISSION: A fee is charged; seniors and children discounted.

James Monroe was not only the fifth president of the United States, he was also a member of the Continental army and served in the 3rd Virginia as a Second Lieutenant under Colonel Hugh Mercer. Monroe fought at Trenton, where he was wounded, but he continued to fight at Brandywine, Germantown, and Monmouth before resigning. His wife, Elizabeth Kortright, was a daughter of a New York merchant who was a Loyalist officer. Monroe began his law career in Fredericksburg. The James Monroe Museum contains a large collection of his personal possessions, furnishings, and papers. Many of the furnishings were purchased while Monroe served as emissary to France and were later used in the Monroe White House.

GEORGE WASHINGTON BIRTHPLACE NATIONAL MONUMENT

1732 Popes Creek Road, Washington's Birthplace, VA 22443
PHONE: 804-224-1732
HOURS: Open daily; closed Christmas Day and New Year's Day.
ADMISSION: A fee is charged.

George Washington was born at Popes Creek Plantation in Westmoreland County, Virginia, on February 22, 1732. His father began the plantation with 150 acres in 1718; by the time of George's birth, the plantation had grown to 1,300 acres. George lived here until he was three, at which time his family moved, first to Mount Vernon, then to Ferry Farm in Fredericksburg. The original structure at Popes Creek burned in 1779. A memorial house was built near the spot in 1930. The style is a typical plantation house of the period, but is not intended to be a reconstruction of the original. Little if any clues are known as to the style or size of the original house. More than thirty Washingtons are buried in the family cemetery, including George Washington's father, grandfather, great-grandfather, and great-grandmother. Today, the National Park Service operates a colonial plantation, recreating eighteenth-century plantation life.

George Washington Birthplace

STRATFORD HALL PLANTATION

Virginia Route 214, Stratford, VA 22558
PHONE: 804-493-8038
HOURS: Open daily; closed Thanksgiving Day, Christmas Day, and New Year's Day.
ADMISSION: A fee is charged.

Stratford was built by Thomas Lee in the late 1730s. Five of Lee's sons served in various capacities during the Revolutionary period. Thomas Ludwell was a member of Virginia's Committee of Safety, Francis Lightfoot was elected to the Continental Congress, and Richard Henry introduced the resolution that called for independence. Richard Henry and Francis Lightfoot signed the Declaration of Independence. General Henry "Light-Horse Harry" Lee lived at Stratford from 1782 to 1811. He was a cavalry commander during the Revolutionary War, and later he was elected governor of Virginia. He was also elected as a member of Congress. It was "Light-Horse Harry Lee" who said of George Washington, "first in war, first in peace, and first in the hearts of his countrymen."

HANOVER TAVERN

13181 Hanover Courthouse Road, Hanover, VA 23069
PHONE: 804-537-5050
HOURS: Open Wednesday or by appointment.
ADMISSION: A fee is charged.

The Hanover Tavern is located on the old stage road between Washington and Williamsburg. The site has entertained travelers since 1733. The earliest part of the current building is believed to date from the mid- to late-eighteenth century. Patrick Henry's in-laws owned the tavern, and Henry lived here for several years while he studied law and argued the famous Parson's Cause case.

Hanover Tavern

SCOTCHTOWN

16120 Chiswell Lane, Beaverdam, VA 23015
PHONE: 804-227-3500
HOURS: Open daily from April to October.
ADMISSION: A fee is charged.

Scotchtown: Home of Patrick Henry

Scotchtown was the home of Patrick Henry, who uttered the unforgettable vow, "as for me, give me liberty or give me death!" He lived here with his wife Sarah Shelton Henry and their six children from 1771 until 1778, his most active political years. During this time he attended the First Continental Congress in Philadelphia, Second Virginia Congress in Richmond, and the Fifth Virginia Convention in Williamsburg. Later, Henry became the first elected governor of Virginia. The 1719 house has been restored with period furnishings, including several Henry pieces.

JAMES MADISON MUSEUM

129 Caroline Street, Orange, VA 22960
PHONE: 540-672-1776
HOURS: Open daily; closed weekends from December to February.
ADMISSION: A fee is charged; children and seniors discounted.
www.jamesmadisonmuseum.org

The James Madison Museum features exhibits relating to the fourth president's life and political career, as well as his agricultural interests. Madison was a member of the Continental Congress and House of Representatives, a U.S. Secretary of State, a U.S. President, and rector of the University of Virginia. Known as the "Father of the Constitution," he also sponsored the Bill of Rights. Other exhibits at the museum represent cultural life in rural Orange County.

MONTPELIER

11407 Constitution Highway, Montpelier Station, VA 22057
PHONE: 540-672-2728
HOURS: Open daily.
ADMISSION: A fee is charged.
www.montpelier.org

Montpelier was the home of the "Father of the Constitution," fourth President, and delegate to the Continental Congress, James Madison. His grandfather, Ambrose Madison, first settled Montpelier (originally named Mount Pleasant) in 1723. Although his career of public service often took him away from Virginia, Montpelier was Madison's lifelong home. James and Dolley Madison made two major additions to the home and structural changes to the interior. Changing exhibits inside Montpelier and around the 2,700-acre estate tell of Madison's life. He and his wife are buried on the property.

Montpelier Mansion

MICHIE TAVERN

683 Thomas Jefferson Parkway, Charlottesville, VA 22902
PHONE: 804-977-1234
HOURS: Open daily.
ADMISSION: A fee is charged.
www.michietavern.com

William Michie served as a corporal in George Washington's Continental army. When the soldiers reached Valley Forge, young Michie received an urgent message to return home. By the time he reached his family's homestead, his ailing father had passed away. William inherited a large tract of land, where he established a tavern. Today, the tavern offers living-history tours, and meals are served daily.

Michie Tavern

MONTICELLO

Virginia Route 53, Charlottesville, VA 22902
PHONE: 804-984-9822
HOURS: Open daily, closed Christmas Day.
ADMISSION: A fee is charged.
www.monticello.org

Monticello is the home designed and built by Thomas Jefferson, our third president, who was also an architect and innovator. Monticello means "little mountain," and the home sits atop a high vista. The interior is restored to the style of the period of 1809 to 1826, and the first floor is open to the public for guided tours. It includes the entrance hall which was Jefferson's private museum, as well as his bedroom where he died on July 4, 1826, the fiftieth anniversary of the signing of the Declaration of Independence. A short distance from the house is the family burial ground, which is still in use. Jefferson is buried here with an obelisk marking his grave. The inscription reads as he wished, listing those three accomplishments of which he was most proud: "Here was buried Thomas Jefferson/ Author of the Declaration of American Independence/ of the Statute of Virginia for Religious Freedom/ And Father of the University of Virginia."

Monticello

ASH LAWN-HIGHLAND

1000 James Monroe Parkway, Charlottesville, VA 22902
PHONE: 804-293-9539
HOURS: Open daily; closed Thanksgiving Day, Christmas Day, and New Year's Day.
ADMISSION: A fee is charged.

Ash Lawn-Highland was the home of fifth president James Monroe, who bought this 3,500-acre farm, "Highland," to be near his friend Thomas Jefferson at Monticello. Jefferson, in fact, selected the house site and sent his gardeners to establish the estate's orchards. The Monroes moved into Highland on November 23, 1799. Frequent guests included Jefferson and James and Dolley *Ash Lawn-Highland* Madison. The home is furnished with Monroe family pieces. Monroe's "cabin-castle" and the gardens have been restored by his alma mater, the College of William and Mary.

POPLAR FOREST

Virginia Route 661, Forest, VA 24551
PHONE: 804-525-1806
HOURS: Open daily from April to November; closed Thanksgiving Day.
ADMISSION: A fee is charged.

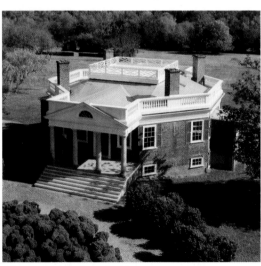

Thomas Jefferson's Poplar Forest

Thomas Jefferson designed and built Poplar Forest on his Bedford County plantation near Lynchburg to escape the crowds at Monticello. Poplar Forest is the first octagonal home in America and one of Jefferson's architectural masterpieces. He began building the villa in 1806, at age sixty-three, and traveled from the White House to Poplar Forest several times a year, staying from two weeks to two months. The exterior restoration of the home earned the coveted Honor Award from the National Trust for Historic Preservation. Visitors can still watch craftsmen and archeologists as restoration and research continue. During the summer, a hands-on history tent is open midday for visitors of all ages to experience Jefferson's era by doing activities related to his time. Special events are held during the season, including an annual Fourth of July celebration highlighted by the reading of the Declaration of Independence.

RED HILL—
THE PATRICK HENRY NATIONAL MEMORIAL

1250 Red Hill Road, Brookneal, VA 24528
PHONE: 804-376-2044
HOURS: Open daily; closed major holidays.
ADMISSION: A fee is charged.
www.redhill.org

Red Hill is the last home and burial place of Patrick Henry, who retired here in 1793 and died in 1799. Patrick Henry was a self-taught lawyer and fiery orator. He led the campaign against the Stamp Act in the House of Burgesses, in which he ended his speech by saying, "If this be treason, make the most of it." He served in the Continental Congress and is best remembered for his stunning speech in which he proclaimed, "Give me liberty, or give me death." Henry served as governor of Virginia and a member of the Virginia constitutional ratification convention of 1788. He refused to ratify the Constitution until the Bill of Rights was added. The visitor's center features

a fifteen-minute video on Henry's career and his life at Red Hill. The reconstructed plantation encompasses Henry's house, kitchen, cook's house, carriage house, law office, and museum displaying items owned by Henry. In addition to his grave are those of other members of the Henry family. His tombstone contains a simple inscription, "His fame his best epitaph."

Red Hill—Patrick Henry House

VIRGINIA STATE CAPITOL

910 Capitol Street, Richmond, VA 23219
PHONE: 804-698-1788
HOURS: Open daily; closed major holidays.
ADMISSION: Free.

A marble statue of George Washington by French sculptor Jean Antoine Houdon stands in the rotunda of the Virginia State Capitol. It is the only statue in existence for which Washington actually posed and is considered the most valuable statue in America. In one of the meeting rooms of the Virginia legislature is a mural entitled "Siege of Redoubt 10," a depiction of Alexander Hamilton's critical assault on an outpost at Yorktown. In addition to these sights, there is a bust of the Marquis de Lafayette inside the capitol.

Saint John's Episcopal Church

2401 East Broad Street, Richmond, VA 23223
PHONE: 804-648-5015
HOURS: Open daily; closed major holidays.
ADMISSION: A fee is charged; children and seniors discounted.

At Saint John's Episcopal Church on March 23, 1775, Patrick Henry stirred Virginians, and the country, to action with his speech that ended with the words, "Give me liberty or give me death." Built in 1741, St. John's is the oldest church in Richmond and has been active for over 250 years. In the church's graveyard lies George Wythe, signer of the Declaration of Independence and legal mentor of Thomas Jefferson and Patrick Henry.

Saint John's Episcopal Church

John Marshall House

816 East Marshall Street, Richmond, VA 23219
PHONE: 804-648-7998
HOURS: Open Tuesday–Saturday.
ADMISSION: A fee is charged; children and seniors discounted.

John Marshall, known as the "Great Chief Justice" of the U. S. Supreme Court, built and lived in this circa 1790 Federal-style house for forty-five years. Marshall, a first lieutenant during the Revolutionary War, fought in the battles of Brandywine, Germantown, Monmouth, and Stony Point. After the war, he was a member of the Virginia Assembly, a delegate to the state convention that ratified the Constitution, a Federalist congressman, and Secretary of State under President John Adams. Adams nominated Marshall as chief justice, and he held that position from 1801 until his death in 1835. While chief justice, Marshall wrote a five-volume biography of George Washington. The John Marshall House, a national landmark museum, contains the largest collection of Marshall family furnishings and memorabilia in America.

BERKELEY

12602 Harrison Landing Road, Charles City, VA 23030
PHONE: 804-829-6018
HOURS: Open daily.
ADMISSION: A fee is charged.

Berkeley was built in 1726 by Benjamin Harrison IV and his wife, Anne, on a hilltop overlooking the James River. The house has an amazing history spanning its 250-plus years. Benjamin Harrison V, son of the builder, was a signer of the Declaration of Independence and Governor of Virginia three times. George Washington and the succeeding nine presidents visited the plantation. The Adam woodwork

Berkeley Plantation

and double arches of the great rooms were installed in 1790 at the direction of Thomas Jefferson by Benjamin Harrison VI. His brother William Henry Harrison and his grandson became presidents of the United States. The home is furnished with an exquisite collection of eighteenth-century antiques, and the gardens surrounding the home are magnificent.

SHIRLEY PLANTATION

Virginia State Route 5, 501 Shirley Plantation Road, Charles City, VA 23030-2907
PHONE: 800-232-1613
HOURS: Open daily; closed Thanksgiving Day and Christmas Day.
ADMISSION: A fee is charged; children and seniors discounted.

Shirley Plantation was founded six years after settlers arrived at Jamestown. The present mansion was begun in 1723 and is largely in its original state. During the Revolution, the house became a supply center for the Continental army; and both sides used it as a listening post since it

was located between the British at City Point and Lafayette's army at Malvern Hill. Guided house tours feature eighteenth-century family portraits, silver, furniture, and a free standing square flying stairway. The tenth and eleventh generations of the Hill-Carter family still reside on the eight-hundred-acre James River Plantation.

Shirley Plantation

Colonial Williamsburg

P.O. Box 1776, Williamsburg, VA 23187-1776
PHONE: 800-447-8679
HOURS: Open daily.
ADMISSION: A fee is charged.

In 1699, a decision was made to move the colonial capitol of Virginia from Jamestown to the newly-named city of Williamsburg. Today, visitors to colonial Williamsburg may explore 173 acres of authentic taverns, shops, and homes still inhabited by costumed eighteenth-century residents including men and women, slaves and freemen. The historic area includes five hundred original and reconstructed buildings and sixty colorful gardens. A broad array of interpretive programs, historic trades and crafts, evening programs, and character interpreters allow visitors to experience colonial life on the eve of the American Revolution. The most notable of the original and reconstructed buildings are as follows:

BRUTON PARISH CHURCH

Before the College of William and Mary was built, Bruton Parish Church was the most important public building in Williamsburg, then known as Middle Plantation. The church was established in 1674 after several smaller parishes joined together. By 1712, a larger church was needed, and construction began. Presidents George Washington, Thomas Jefferson, and James Monroe all attended this church. The church is owned by, and still serves, the three-hundred-year-old parish.

Bruton Parish Church

THE CAPITOL

The Capitol building of eighteenth-century Virginia is a visible reminder of the political importance of Williamsburg three hundred years ago. Within the original building were the governor's council chambers, the House of Burgesses, and the general court. The original building was destroyed by fire in 1832 and reconstructed in 1934.

The Capitol

THE MAGAZINE

The Magazine is one of the original buildings built in 1715 to store the city's arms and ammunition. During the early days of the Revolution, Governor Dunmore had the gunpowder removed in the night. Patrick Henry publically demanded that the powder be restored. The governor backed down and reimbursed the province, explaining that he took the powder because of fear of a slave uprising. In actuality, the governor was threatening to instigate such a revolt.

THE GEORGE WYTHE HOUSE

The George Wythe House was built in 1750 by architect Richard Taliaferro as a conservative brick home. Wythe was a close friend to Royal Governors Fauquier and Bolefourt, and was one of the first signers of the Declaration of Independence. He was also a teacher of law and an advisor. Wythe's students included Thomas Jefferson, James Monroe, Henry Clay, and John Marshall.

THE PASTEUR AND GALT APOTHECARY SHOP

Built in 1760, the apothecary shop features eighteenth-century medicines, druggists' equipment, and surgical instruments.

RALEIGH TAVERN

The Raleigh Tavern became a place of official state business in 1769 when the Loyalist governor dissolved the House of Burgesses gathered at Raleigh Tavern and proceeded to vote a boycott of

British goods. In 1774, they convened again in Raleigh Tavern to successfully pass Henry Lee's resolution to "consider means of stopping exports and of securing the constitutional rights of America." The Raleigh Tavern was a place of daily news and gossip over dinner, cards, or billiards. A billiard table from 1738 is on display in the Billiard Room.

PEYTON RANDOLPH HOUSE

The Peyton Randolph House was probably the most elegant private residence in Williamsburg. Randolph was the cousin of Thomas Jefferson, served as speaker of the House of Burgesses, and was elected president of the First Continental Congress. Both Washington and Lafayette lived in this house during the Yorktown Campaign.

GOVERNOR'S PALACE

The Governor's Palace was built between 1708 and 1720 for the governors for the crown. George Washington, at the age of twenty-two, presented himself to Governor Dinwiddie as a volunteer for a mission to investigate French incursions in the Ohio country. Later, the palace was the residence of the governor of the Commonwealth of Virginia. Both Thomas Jefferson and Patrick Henry resided here during their respective terms. Today, the Governor's Palace has been restored to its 1768–70 appearance.

Governor's Palace

THE WREN BUILDING AT THE COLLEGE OF WILLIAM AND MARY

Junction of Jamestown Road and Richmond, Williamsburg, VA
PHONE: 757-221-1540
HOURS: Open daily; closed New Year's Day, Thanksgiving Day, and Christmas Day.
ADMISSION: Free.

The Wren Building, designed by noted British architect Sir Christopher Wren, is the oldest academic building in continuous use in the United States. Construction took place between 1695 and 1699, but a fire destroyed it in 1705. Reconstruction was completed in 1732. Several colonial officials are buried in the crypt under the chapel in the south wing. The two cannon flanking the east door to the building were taken from the British after the Battle of Yorktown in 1781.

BRITISH

COMMANDER:
Gen. Lord Charles Cornwallis

STRENGTH: 8,300

CASUALTIES: 482;
8,091 taken prisoner

THE SIEGE OF YORKTOWN

September 28–October 19, 1781

In the autumn of 1781, General Washington had been gathering American and French forces under Rochambeau to attack the British under Clinton in New York. He counted on the French fleet, under the command of Admiral de Grasse, to guard the Chesapeake coastline against the British. The French fleet came in September, but it was under orders to be off the coast of the West Indies by the middle of October. Washington persuaded de Grasse to stay until the end of November and changed his plans to make use of the French's thirty-five naval vessels. He used his maneuvers around New York as a feint and left a small contingent in West Point to guard the Hudson River forts while the rest of the Continental army headed to Virginia. On September 28, the allied armies marched from Williamsburg to Yorktown. The next day, the siege artillery was brought in from the James River. The next morning, Washington learned that Cornwallis had moved his British units from the redoubts that commanded the approaches to Yorktown. The British had just given up positions that could have held the approach for weeks. Cornwallis, however, was relying upon relief troops from General Clinton, and therefore withdrew his outposts inside the perimeter of his defense.

On October 6, the soldiers began digging trenches and constructing redoubts and battery positions. On October 9, the bombardment began with the French being given the honor of firing the first shot. Washington himself fired the first American round. On October 14, Washington and the French attacked and took British Redoubts No. 9 and No. 10, which cut off the last British escape route and allowed the allied guns to move to point-blank range of the British lines. Cornwallis wrote General Clinton, "The safety of the place is so precarious that I cannot recommend that the fleet and army should run great risk in endeavoring to save us."

The siege continued until October 17, when the British had exhausted their options for escape. A small scarlet-coated drummer boy appeared and began to beat a parley. The guns were silenced and a British officer came out holding a white

Surrender of Cornwallis at Yorktown, Virginia, by John Trumbull

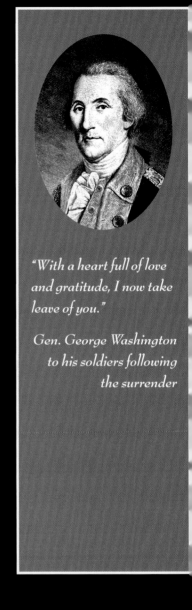

handkerchief. Blindfolded, he was led to Washington's headquarters. The officer presented Cornwallis's request for a cease-fire and surrender.

At 2:00 on the afternoon of October 19, American and French units lined up to face each other, the French wearing white uniforms, the Americans erect and in line, but more shabbily dressed. British troops, led not by Cornwallis, but by Brigadier General Charles O'Hara, marched with their colors cased and a slow drumbeat. General O'Hara rode up to Count Rochambeau, who stood at the head of the French troops, to surrender his men. But Rochambeau shook his head and directed O'Hara to General Washington, who accepted the surrender. The prisoners were marched away to prisons in Virginia and Maryland.

The British still held New York, Charleston, Wilmington in North Carolina, and Savannah. But when the news of the Yorktown surrender reached the prime minister in London, his reaction was, "O God! It is all over!" It would be another two years before the British government finally accepted the defeat. American independence was formally acknowledged at the Treaty of Paris dated September 1783.

AMERICAN

COMMANDERS:
Gen. George Washington, Comte de Rochambeau

STRENGTH: 17,000
(9,000 American, 8,000 French)

CASUALTIES:
70 Americans; 186 French

COLONIAL NATIONAL HISTORICAL PARK
YORKTOWN BATTLEFIELD

P.O. Box 210, Yorktown, VA 23690
PHONE: 757-898-2410
HOURS: Open daily; closed Christmas Day.
ADMISSION: A fee is charged; children free.
www.nps.gov/colo

Yorktown Battlefield is dedicated to preserving the English colonial history of the United States. The Yorktown Visitor Center features a fifteen-minute film entitled *Siege at Yorktown*. Museum exhibits focus on the 1781 Siege of Yorktown, the Battle of the Capes, and the equipment used by the armies during the campaign, including a campaign table used by British General Cornwallis during the siege. There is an observation deck on the roof of the visitor center that overlooks the battlefield, and the panoramic view aids in the understanding of the battle. A self-guided tour (for which a narrated cassette tape is available) includes the fortifications and siege lines of the opposing armies; the Moore House, where the terms of the British surrender were negotiated; and Surrender Field, where the ceremonial surrender of the British army took place. Park rangers conduct tours of the siege lines and the eighteenth-century town on a daily basis.

NELSON HOUSE

HOURS: Open daily during spring and fall.
Nelson House was the home of Thomas Nelson, Jr., a signer of the Declaration of Independence and commander of the Virginia militia during the Siege of Yorktown. During the siege, Nelson feared that his home was being used by the British as a headquarters and requested that allied artillery shell the house to drive out the foe. Today, the house features displays about the history of the house and the Nelson family. During the summer months, a twenty-minute presentation dramatizes Nelson's life and his role in the Revolution. Nearby is the Yorktown Victory Monument, authorized by the Continental Congress on October 29, 1781, and dedicated to the French alliance that helped ensure the victory.

THE YORKTOWN VICTORY CENTER

Old Route 238 and Colonial Parkway, Yorktown, VA
PHONE: Toll-free: 888-593-4682 or 757-253-4838
HOURS: Open daily; closed Christmas and New Year's Day.
ADMISSION: A fee is charged; children discounted.

Yorktown Victory Center museum is maintained by the Commonwealth of Virginia to impart an understanding of the events that led to America's war for independence and the impact that war had upon ordinary men and women. An outdoor walkway that leads to the museum features exhibits that describe the twenty-five years that transformed the colonies from obedience to rebellion. Inside the museum are permanent exhibits that feature some of the individuals who were involved in the colonies' struggle for independence. Exhibits include the Declaration of

Independence; "Witnesses to Revolution," in which people have recorded their lives in letters and diaries; "Converging on Yorktown," in which the siege at Yorktown is described; and "A Soldier's Lot," which features the daily life of a Revolutionary War soldier. Outside the museum are an army encampment, in which costumed historical interpreters demonstrate activities of Continental soldiers, and a re-created 1780s farm.

COLONIAL NATIONAL HISTORICAL PARK
CAPE HENRY MEMORIAL

Fort Story, Virginia Beach, VA
PHONE: 757-898-2410
HOURS: Open daily; closed Christmas Day.
ADMISSION: A fee is charged; children free.
www.nps.gov/colo

Cape Henry Memorial, a part of Colonial National Historical Park, is administered by the National Park Service and marks the approximate site of the first landing of the Jamestown settlers in Virginia in April 1607. The site also overlooks the Chesapeake Bay site of the naval Battle of the Capes, fought on September 5, 1781. This engagement of the Revolutionary War occurred as the British navy attempted to break a French blockade of the York River in order to reinforce the British army in Yorktown. Neither side lost any ships during the two-and-a-half-hour battle; and the blockade successfully held, forcing the British to return to New York without providing reinforcements to their forces in Yorktown. Today, Cape Henry includes markers about the naval battle, a monument to the French victory, and a statue of Admiral Comte de Grasse, the French commander during the engagement.

SAINT PAUL'S EPISCOPAL CHURCH

201 St. Paul's Boulevard, Norfolk, VA 23510
PHONE: 757-627-4353
HOURS: Open daily.
ADMISSION: Free.

Saint Paul's Episcopal Church, known as the Borough Church prior to 1827, is the oldest church in Norfolk and one of the only links to the area's colonial past. The original church was constructed between 1640 and 1643 and was eventually replaced by the cur-

Saint Paul's Episcopal Church

rent structure, which was built in 1739. It was the only building to survive the January 1, 1776 bombardment of the city by Lord Fairfax's fleet. A cannonball fired by one of Lord Fairfax's ships is embedded in the wall of the church. In the graveyard, headstones date back to the seventeenth century, and several Revolutionary War veterans are buried here. A museum in the Parish Hall details some of the historic events that have occurred at the church.

WASHINGTON, D.C.

Although the District of Columbia didn't even exist at the time of the Revolution, there are some notable places in the city that remind us of the justness of the cause for which the Revolution was fought. In the Capitol building are scenes of the Revolutionary period, but the greater memorial may lie in the building itself. Without the Revolution, there would be no self-government, no representation at all.

At the National Archives' downtown location, the original Declaration of Independence is on display, as are the Bill of Rights and the Constitution. In the Smithsonian National Museum of American History are many exhibits from the Revolution. And, of course, the skyline of Washington itself is enhanced by the memorials to Revolutionaries Thomas Jefferson and George Washington.

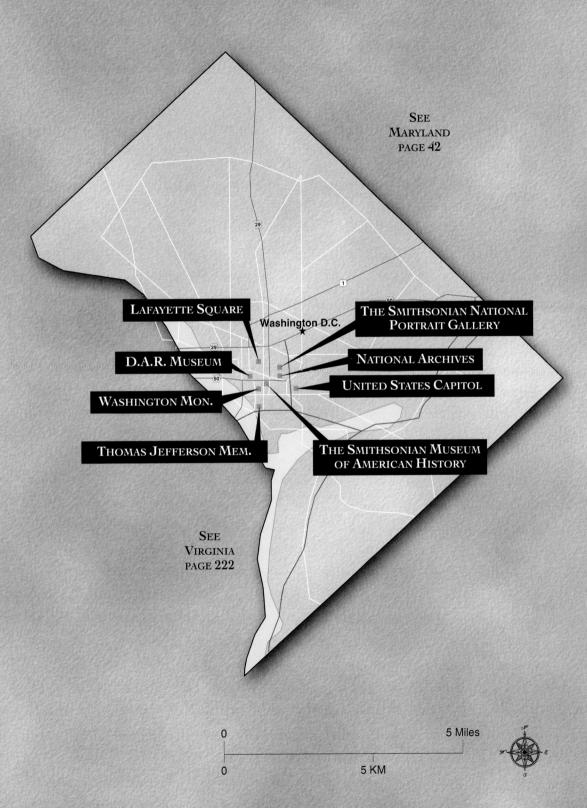

SEE
MARYLAND
PAGE 42

LAFAYETTE SQUARE

THE SMITHSONIAN NATIONAL
PORTRAIT GALLERY

Washington D.C.

D.A.R. MUSEUM

NATIONAL ARCHIVES

UNITED STATES CAPITOL

WASHINGTON MON.

THOMAS JEFFERSON MEM.

THE SMITHSONIAN MUSEUM
OF AMERICAN HISTORY

SEE
VIRGINIA
PAGE 222

0   5 Miles

0   5 KM

UNITED STATES CAPITOL

Capitol Hill, Washington, DC
PHONE: 202-225-6827
HOURS: Open daily; closed New Year's Day, Thanksgiving Day, Christmas Day, and Inauguration days.
ADMISSION: Free.

The cornerstone of the Capitol was placed by President George Washington in 1793, and the building first opened in 1800. It was burned by the British in the War of 1812, then rebuilt and completed in 1826 as originally planned. On the second floor are the Chambers of the House of Representatives (in the south wing) and the Senate (in the north wing), as well as the offices of the congressional leadership. This floor also contains three public areas, including the Rotunda, the large circular ceremonial space in the center of the building. The Rotunda contains a gallery of paintings and sculptures depicting significant people and events in the nation's history. Four of the eight large oil paintings are Revolutionary-period scenes commissioned by Congress in 1817 from Connecticut artist John Trumbull. Completed by 1824 and installed in 1826, they depict: *The Declaration of Independence in Congress at Philadelphia, July 4th, 1776; Surrender of General Burgoyne at Saratoga, 1777; Surrender of Lord Cornwallis at Yorktown, 1781; and General George Washington Resigning his Commission to Congress as Commander-in-Chief of the Army, 1783.* Since Trumbull himself had served in the Continental army, he personally knew many of the people he painted. References to the Revolution also appear in Constantino Brumidi's fresco painting in the canopy of the dome, *The Apotheosis of Washington,* as well as in the frescoed frieze under the windows depicting events in American history. A number of sculptures in the Rotunda depict Revolutionary heroes, including busts of Washington and Lafayette and a statue of Thomas Jefferson, all by P.J. David d'Angers, a statue of Washington by Antoine Houdon, and one of Alexander Hamilton by Horatio Stone.

United States Capitol

THOMAS JEFFERSON MEMORIAL

Ohio Drive on the Mall, Washington, DC
PHONE: 202-426-6841
HOURS: Open daily; closed December 25.
ADMISSION: Free.

The Thomas Jefferson Memorial was built in 1939. The memorial was designed by John Russell Pope, and its architecture is similar to Jefferson's home of Monticello. Inside the rotunda of the memorial stands a statue of Jefferson, sculpted by Rudolph Evans, and on the walls are inscribed his two most famous literary works: the Declaration of Independence and the Virginia Statute for Religious Freedom. A museum and bookstore are located in the basement of the memorial.

Thomas Jefferson Memorial

DAUGHTERS OF THE AMERICAN REVOLUTION MUSEUM

1776 D Street, NW, Washington, DC 20006
PHONE: 202-628-1776
HOURS: Open Monday to Friday and Sunday afternoon.
ADMISSION: Free.
www.dar.org

Daughters of the American Revolution Museum

The Daughters of the American Revolution Headquarters houses the Americana Collection, which contains more than 5,000 historical documents and imprints primarily pertaining to Colonial America, the Revolutionary War era, and the Early Republic. The headquarters also houses the Genealogical Library, which contains an extensive array of historical resources including 150,000 books, 300,000 research files, and thousands of manuscripts.

LAFAYETTE SQUARE

Lafayette Square, Pennsylvania Avenue, Washington, DC

Lafayette Square is approximately two city blocks in size and is probably the most famous unimproved plot of ground in the United States. The square was laid out in the 1790s by Pierre Charles L'Enfant, the Parisian architect of the city, who worked with President George Washington to locate sites for the principal federal government buildings. The square was originally part of the White House grounds; it was not separated from the White House until the presidency of Thomas Jefferson. When Pennsylvania Avenue was opened directly in front of the President's mansion, the square was cut off from the White House by the street. After Lafayette's final visit to the United States in 1824, the square was officially named for him. At each of the four corners of the Square stands the statue of one of four foreigners who served as generals in the Revolutionary War: Lafayette, Rochambeau, von Steuben, and Kosciuszko.

NATIONAL ARCHIVES

700 Pennsylvania Avenue, NW, Washington, DC 20408
PHONE: 1-800-234-8861
HOURS: Rotunda open daily; closed Christmas Day. Research rooms open Monday to Saturday; closed Sunday and federal holidays.
ADMISSION: Free.
www.nara.gov

National Archives

The National Archives is the repository of the original Declaration of Independence, the Constitution, and the Bill of Rights, all of which are on display in the Rotunda. The Rotunda will temporarily close for renovation in July of 2001 and reopen in the summer of 2003. The research rooms will remain open during the renovation.

THE SMITHSONIAN NATIONAL PORTRAIT GALLERY

Eighth and F Streets, NW, Washington, DC 20560
PHONE: 202-357-2700
HOURS: Closed for renovation until fall 2004.
ADMISSION: Free.
www.npg.si.edu/

The Smithsonian National Portrait Gallery contains historical portraits including George and Martha Washington by Gilbert Stuart, John Adams by John Trumbull, Thomas Jefferson by Charles Bird King and Mather Brown, and James Madison by Chester Harding and John Vanderlyn.

THE SMITHSONIAN NATIONAL MUSEUM OF AMERICAN HISTORY

Fourteenth Street and Constitution Avenue, NW, Washington, DC 20560
PHONE: 202-357-2700
HOURS: Open daily; closed Christmas Day.
ADMISSION: Free.
www.americanhistory.si.edu/

The Smithsonian National Museum of American History contains many exhibits from America's history, including the Revolutionary War era. Included in the large collections are artifacts from George Washington: his general officer's uniform, his headquarters tent, his mess chest, and his battle sword. In addition, the museum has on display the wreck of the gunboat *Philadelphia* that was built in 1776 and is the oldest American fighting vessel still in existence. The *Philadelphia* sank on October 11, 1776, in Lake Champlain and was raised in 1935. Its newest exhibition, *Within These Walls*, opens May 16, 2001 and includes a rare Revolutionary War uniform.

Revolutionary War uniform

WASHINGTON MONUMENT

15th Street, SW, Washington, DC
PHONE: 202-426-6841
HOURS: Open daily.
ADMISSION: Free passes can be obtained on day of visit. A fee is charged for advance tickets.

The Washington Monument was begun in 1848 and officially opened to the public in 1888. The 555-foot high obelisk designed by Robert Mills honors the first president, George Washington, and is distinctive in the Washington, D.C. skyline. In fact, Washington, D.C. itself was named in honor of our first president. Washington has been remembered in works of art, but no monument has so captured the imagination of the people around the world like the Washington Monument.

Washington Monument

INDEX

PHOTO CREDITS